Writers in Training

A Guide to Developing a Composition Program
for Language Arts Teachers

Rebekah Caplan
Teacher consultant
Bay Area Writing Project

DALE SEYMOUR PUBLICATIONS

Grateful acknowledgment is made to the following publishers for permission to reprint excerpts from previously published material:

From *Practice in Exposition: Supplementary Exercises for the Practical Stylist*, 5th Edition, by Sheridan Baker and Dwight Stevenson. Copyright © 1981 by Harper & Row, Publishers, Inc. Reprinted by permission of the publisher.

"Speech by Senator Yakalot to His Constituents" from *Speaking of Words: A Language Reader* by James MacKillop and Donna Woolfolk Cross. Copyright © 1982 by CBS College Publishing. Reprinted by permission of Holt, Rinehart and Winston, CBS College Publishing.

Portions of this book originally appeared in a University of California research publication, *Showing-Writing: A Training Program to Help Students Be Specific* by Rebekah Caplan and Catharine Keech (Berkeley, Calif.: Bay Area Writing Project, 1980). We are grateful to the Bay Area Writing Project for allowing the author to use much of that original work in this new publication. *Writers in Training* represents the author's further expansion and development of her continuing work with BAWP.

Order number DS03403
ISBN 0-86651-203-9

DALE
SEYMOUR
PUBLICATIONS
P.O. BOX 10888
PALO ALTO, CA 94303

11 12 13 14 15-MA-00 99 98 97 96

Contents

1   Overview of the Training Program

CHAPTER ONE   The Training of Young Artists   1
CHAPTER TWO   The Four-Part Program   5

2   The Daily Workouts

CHAPTER THREE   Using the Daily Telling Sentence   17
CHAPTER FOUR   Evaluating the Showing Paragraphs   30
CHAPTER FIVE   Variations for the Daily Workouts   36

3   Preparing for Longer Compositions

CHAPTER SIX   Structuring through Comparison and Contrast   55
CHAPTER SEVEN   The Argumentative Essay: A Study in Concessions   78
CHAPTER EIGHT   Saturation Reporting: The I-Search Paper   102

4   Training in Revision Techniques

CHAPTER NINE   Using Response Groups for Effective Criticism   139
CHAPTER TEN   Seeing the Effects of Revision   144

Afterword: Making the Training Ideas Work for You   157

References   163

Appendix: Reproducible Teaching Aids   165

Acknowledgments

I am indebted to James Gray, founder and director of the Bay Area Writing Project and National Writing Project, for inspiring me to become a teacher in the first place and for showing me how to do it. Jim served as my supervisor in teacher education at the University of California, Berkeley, and later invited me to become a Bay Area Writing Project summer fellow. Through this summer program I was introduced to the successful teaching practices of outstanding Bay Area instructors and first received recognition for my own approaches to the teaching of composition; in this exhilarating setting, the seeds of this book were sown.

In addition, I am grateful to a number of colleagues and friends for their valuable criticism and support. Special thanks go to Stephanie Gray, who showed me how to turn theory into practice and who was for me a model of the teacher I wanted to become. The argumentative essay assignment in this book originated with Stephanie, who graciously shared it and allowed me to embellish it with my own "showing, not telling" strategies and exercises in spotting fallacious argumentation. I also owe thanks to Mary K. Healy, co-director of the Bay Area Writing Project, who manages at all times to be the perfect "response partner," asking just the right questions with just the right mix of support and guidance to keep a writer going; to Catharine Keech, who worked with me on the research study for *Showing-Writing*; to Keith Caldwell, who helped me learn about teacher attitude; to Mary Ann Smith, who showed me how to set up response groups; to Gerry Camp, editor of *Showing-Writing*, who taught me how to blend creativity and discipline; to Laury Fischer, who inspired me to try Ken Macrorie's I-Search paper; to Nancy Crosby and Larry Aladeen, who helped me find clichés to use for *telling* sentences; to Erik and Katin Storm, who forced me to learn to use a word processor and then kindly lent me their own; to Patricia Padgett, who listened to long chapters over the telephone; to Wayne Kemp, my seventh-grade English teacher, who made the classroom a joyous place to be; and to Jenelle Turner of the New Mexico State Writing Project, who told me I should write a book.

I would like to applaud the superhuman efforts of my editor, Beverly Cory, who had the patience to see me through this project and who taught me ways to strengthen my own writing.

Finally, I am indebted to my students at Foothill High School in Pleasanton, California. It is these young people who kindly permitted me to use their papers in this book as models of student work. They have always been enthusiastically willing to give every assignment their best and, in so doing, have helped me prove that high school students can indeed write competently and spiritedly.

This book is dedicated to my parents, who inspired and nurtured my love of the fine arts.

1 Overview of the Training Program

CHAPTER ONE
The Training of Young Artists

Year after year we make student writers cringe with the reminder to "be specific." We extend arrows over words, under words, circling around and through words, accompanying them with the captions "What do you mean? Needs more detail. Unclear." When composing essay questions for exams, we underline the "Why or why not?" at the end of the question *twice* so that our students might feel the importance of that part of the response. Recently I talked with one teacher who had designed a rubber stamp that bore the words "Give an example," so that he would not have to scribble the phrase again and again.

The assumption behind this guide to developing a writing program is that most students have not been trained to *show what they mean*. By training, I do not mean the occasional exercises taken from composition texts, nor do I mean the experience of writing several major essays over the course of a year. What I mean by training is a plan of ritualistic exercise, a plan that attempts to engrain craft through regular and disciplined practice. By treating a student writer the way, let's say, a trainer would treat a young musician, dancer, or athlete, we can require periods of warm-up, periods of rigorous practice, periods of instructional technique.

I realized the important connection between disciplined practice in the fine arts and the need for it in a writing program during my first year of teaching, working with eighth graders in a suburban middle school. As I learned from those students, knowing how to generate detail in both narrative and analytical writing is not a skill they acquire with several textbook exercises; it is a skill that they develop, one that becomes automatic, only with hours of practice. It was not difficult to discover that although immature writers *do* write with enthusiasm and energy—underlining fervent words, punctuating with scores of exclamation marks—not many of them write with extended description or specific examples. About a favorite movie, students write: "It was *fantastic* because it was so real!" About the substitute teacher: "She is really *weird!*" And if they mean something very strongly, they take the time to spell it out: "School is b-o-r-i-n-g!!"

When I became impatient, that first year, with the repetition of empty words like *fantastic, weird, really, neat, beautiful, wonderful,* and *b-o-r-i-n-g,* over and over in the same composition, I attacked their papers, inscribing in the margins those same suggestions that teachers have stamped out for years: "Give more detail. Describe more. Unclear." Then in class I passed out models of glorious description—character sketches, settings, feelings and emotions—all expertly detailed by talented and gifted writers. I advised students, as they scanned each model and glanced back to their own papers, that they needed to be *that* explicit, *that* good. *That* was what writing was all about. I said, "I *know* that you know what makes a thunderstorm frightening; I *know* you know the same things Mark Twain knows about a thunderstorm. Now, what details does he use?" And we would list "trees swaying" and "sky turning blue-black" until we had every last descriptive phrase classified on the board. "Now," I continued, "*you* try writing about a sunset, keeping in mind the techniques Twain used to describe a storm."

The compositions from such follow-up assignments were admittedly better, but without prepping, without fussing and reminding, I could not get students to remember to use specifics naturally, on their own; there seemed to be no carry-over in their ability, or more likely, their *desire,* to generate examples.

With growing frustration, I tried examining my own history as a student writer. I wanted to track down what it had been like for me to write in the eighth grade; I tried to remember whether I had received any form of instruction that trained me, at age 14, to write with detail and example. I wanted to uncover *when* it was that I reached a turning point or felt a sense of discovery about language and expression. When I tried to recall my own junior high experience, however, I could not remember one assignment, let alone any instruction in composing. I talked with old friends, also, and they corroborated my story; we all remembered daily exercises in grammar and diagraming sentences on the board, but had no recollection of being taught how to develop ideas. Oddly enough, there was one form of writing we all remembered very well, a form that brought back terrific moments and made us giggle and smile to recall them. We remembered, all too well, passing notes in class, signing autograph books, recording memories in diaries, and filling out "slam books"—a pastime in which students evaluated each other through brief character descriptions: "Roger Mead—great athlete; wonderful sense of humor; best looking redhead in the class!" Of course everyone hoped that he or she would not be "slammed" or ridiculed, but instead glowingly praised. This was the sort of writing that mattered the most to us. We cared deeply about who was one's friend and who was one's enemy, who was loved and who was hated, who was worthy of secrets, who was not. And, as these issues came under our judgment, we based our verdicts on the degree of someone's *good personality*. In fact, the supreme compliment one paid a friend in an autograph book or slam book amounted to "fantastic personality." And it is still so today.

This discussion with my old friends seemed especially significant. Our recollection of the importance of "personalities" reminded me of the necessary developmental stage of the adolescent; the notion that each person has a personality separate from his or her visual appearance or economic background is a new and unique concept to the junior high student. It is safe to say that in the world of "who is popular and who is not," the idea of personality reigns high. Students are fascinated by people's differences, yet cannot say exactly what makes them like one personality and dislike another. Could it be, then, that the elaborate writing I was demanding was something my students were not ready to produce? It seemed crucial to respect their excitement over many of these clichéd discoveries. I had to allow room for their naive, exploratory generalizations, but at the same time, challenge them to move beyond simple abstractions and discover what concepts like *personality* were based on—how they derived their meanings from concrete perceptions.

Then I examined myself as an adult writer. What did I strive for as I composed? What methods or strategies had I learned to make my own? I surely strove for specificity. I had kept a journal for years, commenting on cycles of personal change. I usually began in a stream-of-consciousness style, listing sensations, noting the details that would explain perceptions to myself. I wrote often, even if I had little to say, in the hope I would discover something to write about. I believe this ritual of writing regularly developed from my training as a dancer and a pianist. As a young ballerina, I was required to do leg-lifts at the bar for thirty minutes each lesson; only the remaining few minutes were devoted to dancing. How we wished for it to be the other way around! As a young piano student, I practiced daily finger exercises to increase my manual agility at the keyboard, to prepare myself for a Bach concerto. The same principle applies in other arts as well. In drama classes I attended in college, acting lessons consisted mainly of short improvisations that allowed us to experiment with emotions *before* we rehearsed major scenes for performance. And, I have noticed that beginning painters practice drawing the human figure again and again, from varying angles, using different materials—charcoals, oils, inks—working to capture their subject in sketches before they attempt more complex works.

After drawing these conclusions about the training of artists, I decided to build into my curriculum a training program for students learning the art of writing, a program that attempts to engrain certain skills and works to make the use of specific detail and examples in writing automatic, habitual, through regular and rigorous practice. I created a writing program that has four coordinating features:

1. Daily workouts (practice) in expanding a general statement into a paragraph, or what I call "showing, not telling."

2. Daily practice in evaluating writing; students learn how to articulate what makes writing effective or not effective.

3. Bringing a recognition of the difference between general writing and specific writing to the revision process; students use the skills they have learned in daily exercises as a tool for strengthening their rough drafts of major composition assignments.

4. Practicing specific ways to select and arrange concrete details in developing an idea or structuring an essay; students learn new techniques to expand their knowledge of effective elaboration.

What follows is a description of that four-part training program as I have used it in my classes in both junior and senior high schools. As I continue to use the ideas and to share them with other teachers, I keep gaining new insights and discovering new ways to refine or expand the practice exercises or the revision techniques. I hear from other teachers that they, too, keep generating new materials, applying the two basic concepts—daily practice and changing *general* to *specific*—in new ways. As I hope to show in this book, the program itself is an extremely workable framework that allows for much *teacher* creativity in designing composition units. Also, I strongly recommend that teachers outside of English consider adapting this framework in their own content areas. Teachers concerned with the need for increased writing across the curriculum will find the structure of this program useful for incorporating more composition work into their particular subject areas. The program offers such teachers an idea of the kinds of writing assignments they might demand in their courses, and at the same time shows them how to prepare the students for such writing.

Before I describe the program in detail, let me suggest an analogy between my writing program and a ballet class, an analogy that might help in understanding the larger scheme of things. Suppose we put the workings of a dance class on a continuum, outlining the various stages and experiences of the maturing dancer.

rehearsals   dance instructor

exercises at the bar;   recital   professional dancer
spins across the floor   in Swan Lake

At the beginning stages, young dancers work diligently at the bar to develop competence in executing difficult maneuvers on the dance floor. As they rehearse and rehearse the piece they will perform for the recital, students integrate the skills they acquired in the exercises into the dramatic workings of "the Dance." The recital serves as proof to parents and friends that the hours of training have paid off; we see the final performance of the year as a measure of the growth and maturation of the dancer. Each year the recital piece becomes more complicated and sophisticated as the maturing dancer executes more difficult and strenuous movements. If such a student were to continue in the world of dance, she would perhaps, at the peak of her profession, perform with the New York City Ballet in a production of *Swan Lake*; if her talent does not take her that far, she might enjoy teaching others how to dance.

Let's look at a similar continuum for a writing class.

rough drafts **English teacher**

← ——————————————————————————— →

| exercises in specificity; practice in evaluation | final drafts of major assignments | professional author of full-length novel |

Students begin with simple paragraph exercises that encourage the development of ideas. As they become more familiar with and adept at generating examples, they begin using this skill as they expand rough drafts into stronger final drafts. As the student writer moves up through the grade levels, the kinds of major assignments he will be required to write will increase in difficulty, and his performance on these major pieces will be a measure of his growth and sophistication. The competent instructor will design a program each year that will teach the student new and more difficult strategies for developing ideas. If the student finally chooses to enter the world of professional writers, he will have a rich and expansive repertoire upon which to call.

CHAPTER TWO
The Four-Part Program

The Program, Part 1:
Daily Practice in "Showing, Not Telling"

Since students need the discipline of a regular routine to reinforce the use of concrete details in place of, or in support of, their generalities, I assign a daily homework challenge: I give them what I call a *telling* sentence. They must expand the thought in that sentence into an entire paragraph that *shows* rather than tells. At the most, students may write two paragraphs, for I want to encourage brevity and exactness in the elaboration of ideas. They take home sentences like the following:

The room is vacant.

The jigsaw puzzle was difficult to assemble.

My mother bugs me.

They then bring back descriptive *showing* paragraphs, focused on demonstrating the thought expressed in the assigned *telling* sentence.

This approach is the backbone of the training program. This type of exercise is not revolutionary; textbooks on the teaching of writing often assign particular "topic sentences" and demand that students write paragraphs supporting them. However, I challenge students to *eliminate* the *telling* sentence in the body of the paragraph and to try to convince me that a room is vacant, or a puzzle is difficult to assemble, without once making that claim directly. The challenge is much like the game of charades: they have to get an idea across without giving the whole thing away. This approach does not mean I undervalue the topic sentence; we *need* topic sentences to introduce ideas. However, because students so often rely on generalities to do their explaining, for the purposes of this exercise I challenge them to avoid abstractions.

In order to establish the difference between *telling* and *showing*, I distribute copies of the following two paragraphs to my students. I ask them to discern why one paragraph has been categorized as *telling* while the other has been called *showing*. Both passages are descriptions of a bus stop. The first was written by a seventh grader, the second by a professional, E. L. Doctorow in *The Book of Daniel.*

A TELLING PARAGRAPH

Each morning I ride the bus to school. I wait along with the other people who ride my bus. Sometimes the bus is late and we get angry. Some guys start fights and stuff just to have something to do. I'm always glad when the bus finally comes.

A SHOWING PARAGRAPH

A bus arrived. It discharged its passengers, closed its doors with a hiss and disappeared over the crest of a hill. Not one of the people waiting at the bus stop had attempted to board. One woman wore a sweater that was too small, a long skirt, white sweater socks, and house slippers. One man was in his undershirt. Another man wore shoes with the toes cut out, a soiled blue serge jacket and brown pants. There was something wrong with these people. They made faces. A mouth smiled at nothing and unsmiled, smiled and unsmiled. A head shook in vehement denial. Most of them carried brown paper bags rolled tight against their stomachs.[1]

---

1. E. L. Doctorow, *The Book of Daniel* (New York: Random House, Signet Edition, 1971), p. 15.

When asked to distinguish the difference between the two paragraphs, most students respond by saying the second paragraph is better because they can "picture" the scene more easily. I follow that response with the question, "What are the people in the second paragraph like?" The students tell me that the people described are "weird, lonely, and poor." They, in effect, are reverting to *telling* in their responses. Nowhere in the paragraph is there mention of those words. Their interpretation comes from the "pictures" (their word) of people wearing torn clothing and carrying brown paper bags instead of lunch boxes *(poor)*, of people smiling, then unsmiling, and not talking to each other *(weird, lonely)*. Students can easily spot effective description. Getting them to write with such close detail themselves is not managed as smoothly.

Of course we all begin our conversations or our introductions with generalities; this is the way the mind organizes itself. We begin by giving our general impression about, or our reaction to, a specific experience. We say "Our vacation was great," or "The meal at The Ritz was a disappointment." With encouragement to continue our stories, we elaborate and embellish the original impression. It is not *incorrect* to generalize. However, when composing, we do not usually have a listener available to ask the questions that will help us refine our explanations; therefore we must ourselves imagine and present all the details that will be necessary to help the reader see the experience from our point of view.

I remind students that the storybooks they read as children are filled with colorful illustrations that *show* the events or scenes described on accompanying pages. The writer of *The King's Crown*[2] does not have to show us in words that a mischievous pig is wearing the golden crown, perched between his two pink ears, or that he is outrunning the frantic king who puffs along behind,

The pig ran and ran.

---

2. B. J. Cory, *The King's Crown*, ill. by Robert Larsen (San Francisco: Fanciful Publications, 1984), p. 15.

his royal robes flapping, his stone castle receding into the distance as he pounds down the country lane to retrieve his treasured crown. The illustrator, Robert Larsen, supplies these details in his full page picture, while the writer's caption, "The pig ran and ran," tells us only the most basic sense of what's going on. Pictures and words work in tandem to carry the story along.

However, in more mature literature, drawings disappear from the pages, and the writer assumes the role of illustrator. Language must be the writer's brush and palette. Following such a discussion, I initiate the daily training exercise, explaining to students they they will expand one sentence from *telling* to *showing* as a regular homework assignment throughout the school year. Examples of such assignments and the results I get are explored more fully in section 2 of this book, "The Daily Workouts."

The idea of daily writing is, of course, nothing new in itself. I know many teachers who have their students write for ten minutes the moment they arrive in class. My daily writing approach, however, is different in a number of ways. First, many teachers assign topics for elaboration, maybe "School," or "Family," or "Sports." Although such a topic is open-ended and allows much room for creativity, students often spend more time narrowing the topic down to a workable idea than they spend writing about it. The type of statement I use is similar to the thesis sentence, the controlling sentence of an essay. The generalization supplies the point; students are *given* the idea they must support. They are free then to concentrate on experimenting with various expressions of that idea. Further, since all students are working on the same idea, they are in a position to compare results—to learn from one another's crafting.

Another departure from other common daily writing warm-ups is that I have students do this daily writing at home. They must come to class with their pieces finished and ready to be evaluated. Although quick, timed, in-class writings are effective in getting students directed and on-task, I want students to come to class with a piece of writing they have given some thought to. I want to give them the time—if they will take it—to play with and think about what they're trying to do.

Finally, unlike private journals or some free-writing assignments, these exercises are written to be shared. I use the writings in much the same way a drama instructor might use improvisation as an instructional technique. The daily sentence expansion becomes a framework for practicing and discovering different ways of showing ideas. Just as drama students search for ways to express ambition or despair by imagining themselves in real-life situations that would evoke these feelings, and in so doing discover wide ranges of bodily and facial expression, my students arrive at ways of showing "empty rooms" or "difficult puzzles" by experimenting with language expression. For the first six weeks of a new course, I instruct the class very little, preferring that they find their own solutions. If they are to learn new or different ways of expressing the same idea, it will come from comparing the results of different interpretations written by fellow students. It is interesting *and* instructive to see, for example, how one student develops the statement "The jocks think they're cool" in comparison to another student's version.

This brings me to the idea of the daily "public performance." My students know in advance that I will read some papers aloud to the class for analysis and evaluation. However, they do not know which ones. The morning after a homework assignment, I select for oral reading those student papers I feel like reading. I say "feel like" because whim is important to my approach. In fact, the secret to getting students to give equal attention to all the exercises is to keep them guessing as to whose paper I'll read. Because I cannot read everyone's papers every day (no matter how dedicated a teacher is, he or she can't evaluate 150 papers every night or even every *other* night of a semester), I must choose only a limited number for evaluation. Usually I read as many papers aloud as I can manage in the first ten to fifteen minutes of a period. If a given student thinks that because I chose her paper on Monday, she is off the hook for Tuesday, she might find that her guess is completely wrong! I may purposely seek out her paper on Tuesday, on Wednesday, even every day for the rest of the week, keeping her unable to predict my pattern. The secret is to be unpredictable at all costs. When students think that someone may hear what they have to say the following morning, they are likely to be more prepared, to have put more effort into their work.

The Program, Part 2: Daily Practice in Evaluating Writing

The performance or the sharing of improvisational or experimental efforts is an important learning experience for the selected performers *and* their audience. This is where part 2 of the training program begins: the first ten minutes of the class session we devote to evaluations of the papers I read aloud. These evaluations are meant to come primarily from the student audience. Of course I, the teacher, could present a lovely analysis of each piece, telling the class why the composition was particularly effective or non-effective. But if I take the stage, I allow the students to remain uninvolved. Yes, I could give a fine lecture on what makes a good piece of writing. But if ever I want students to evaluate a piece of writing articulately, *now* is the time to hand over the responsibility for evaluation. If ever I would ask them to help *each other* improve a piece of writing, and I will, now is the time to train them how to do it—not by putting words into their mouths, but by letting them struggle to make specific criticisms.

At the start of the year, when asked to comment on the merits of a particular piece I have read aloud, students generally begin by saying, "It was really good."

I respond with, "What was good about it?"

"Well, he really *showed.*"

"What did he show?"

"He showed his mother really bugging him."

"How did he show that?"

"With all those great details."

"Give me an example of a specific detail you remember."

"When he says his mother wears curlers in the supermarket; that would bug me, too!"

At last I get from someone a rock-bottom detail that is evidence of effective *showing*. At this juncture I point out to them the difference between saying "it's good" and citing "curlers in the supermarket" as a vivid and effective detail. Then I ask for additional details that bring to mind pictures of the event. As more and more students give back *specific* responses, I teach them that this kind of pinning-down is what we mean by effective criticism.

In addition to eliciting favorable responses, I usually ask whether or not the writer could make one improvement. In the drama class, the instructor might ask her students to evaluate a scene performed by a few fellow students; she might ask the rest of the class to identify the moments that were real, that were believable. Next, she might ask everyone to consider which moments were not as effective, not as believable; and she might ask the class to suggest remedies. In my class, beginning critics usually respond, "Well, he could have written a little more," or "He didn't really need that *telling* sentence at the end." With these usually accurate responses, I push them to explain *why* they feel this way. You'll see more examples of how I elicit specific evaluations in chapter 4, "Evaluating the Showing Paragraphs."

If a certain paper warrants a closer look—that is, if I see merits that the class is failing to react to—I will, of course, state my own evaluation. Sometimes a student may use a particularly interesting approach to an assignment; let's say he relies on the use of metaphor or simile to explain a certain concept. I may, at that point, go to the board and demonstrate what constitutes a metaphor; I might even spend the rest of the class doing a lesson on imagery as an outgrowth of someone's expert use of metaphor. Usually, though, I move right into reading the next paper, knowing that after ten to fifteen minutes I must stop; we have a world of other things to accomplish in our remaining 45 minutes.

There is one final note to this oral reading and evaluating procedure: I do *not*, at this time, give attention to mechanical perfection. This is one of the few times I will not comb their papers for proper spelling, grammar, and usage. Knowing this, students can give full attention to being specific without the pressure of worrying about correctness. An analogy: When learning to perform the backstroke in swimming, we might learn how to move our arms at one point, our legs a little later on; only much later will we try putting the whole act together. Similarly, our attention here is on only one aspect of writing. For these daily exercises, we respond exclusively to the content of each piece, commenting on the success of the elaboration. For students who have poor usage skills, or for students who are new to our language, I can help the sense of their writings by editing a bit as I read them aloud, making the weakest pieces sound respectable. If a student neglects to put an *-ed* on a verb, I will add it for him as I read his piece aloud. If another student has a series of run-ons or fragments, I will add the correct pauses so that the class will get the essence of the piece without stumbling over awkward phraseology. This practice gives insecure students more confidence in letting me share their papers aloud. Because I can make the weakest writer sound adequate—by reading aloud with enthusiasm and respect—that writer is likely to take more interest in improving his or her own quality.

Grading Procedures

I grade each paper as the discussion of it concludes. When students isolate particularly good phrases that *show* rather than *tell*, I immediately underline these and write "good showing" in the margin next to them. If students suggest an idea for improvement, I jot down the suggestion at the bottom of the page. Finally, I assign a letter grade—an A, B, or C—as long as the student has turned in some reasonable response to the challenge. This grade is private, however; it is not meant to be shared with the rest of the class. In a classroom situation where individualized instruction is imperative because of the varying abilities represented, this individual assigning of grades is a marvelous way to encourage individual success and growth.

Papers that are not selected for oral evaluation on a given day receive a check mark and my initials at the top of the page, indicating to the student full credit for fulfilling the assignment. If students do not turn in their writings, they receive in my gradebook an NC, indicating "no credit." I try to have all papers recorded and handed back to the students by the end of the period (or the following day at the latest), giving them immediate feedback and recognition for their work.

At the end of the semester, I average the letter grades the student has earned in the entire series of assignments. An excerpt from my gradebook for one student might look like this:

DAILY WRITINGS

Kathy	B	✓	A	A	✓	DNR	B+	✓	C	NC		

I average all the letter grades into one, cancelling the checks out as simply "credit." This letter grade becomes one-third of the student's total grade for the course, the rest of the grade coming from major essay assignments, grammar and vocabulary quizzes, panel discussions, and so forth. If a student has only one or two no-credits (NC marks) for the entire semester, I probably will not lower the final grade as a result; however, I don't tell the student this in advance. To secure against numerous no-credits, I also give students a chance to turn in weak papers with the special request that they *not* be read and evaluated orally. I tell them that if they had trouble developing one of the assigned sentences—had trouble maybe because the sentence was difficult, or because they had a lot of other homework the same night, or even because they simply weren't in the mood—they may write "DO NOT READ" at the top of the paper. I promise not to select any such paper for oral reading that day, yet the student still earns credit for having completed the assignment. Students are allowed only *four* DNR's a semester, though, so they have to choose very

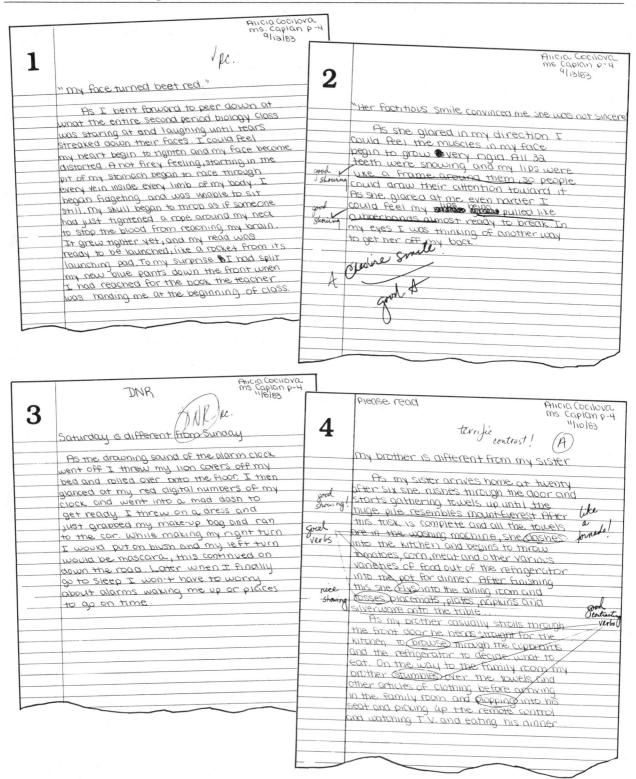

Here are four papers from the same student, each showing one of the daily *telling* sentences. They illustrate (1) a paper not selected for oral evaluation, which received a check mark; (2) a paper I chose to read orally, which received an A grade; (3) a "Do not read" or DNR; and (4) a "Please read" that I selected for oral evaluation in response to the writer's request.

carefully how to use their allotment. (As a corollary, when a student especially *wants* me to read a particular paper aloud, he or she can write "PLEASE READ" at the top of the paper, and I will make every effort to honor the request.)

I am not so unpredictable in my paper selection that one student might be read 25 times for oral evaluation while a classmate gets his or her papers read only 15 times. That would be unfair. So, I consult my gradebook regularly, checking to see whether I am neglecting anyone. If I find that I have ignored someone, I simply ask that student to bring me a series of the previously ungraded (checkmarked) papers. These I can evaluate privately at home in order to figure a more realistic grade.

It is important to note that occasionally I will have a student who feels very strongly about my reading his or her work aloud. I had one such student who begged me privately *never* to read her work orally. Hearing such insistent pleading, I certainly respected her wishes; instead of reading and evaluating her work in front of the class, I took her papers home with me and wrote comments privately. On the whole, though, I encourage students to trust me, to let themselves relax with the exercises and give the whole program a fair chance. As a responding group, the students are here to tell each other what makes their writing effective, what works; they do not emphasize what someone does wrong. When (if ever) that emphasis is needed, we will conference privately—just the student and the teacher.

Teachers often ask me how many papers I manage to evaluate a day, and of course there is no absolute answer. Some days I spend only five minutes and read only two papers; other days we might be so intrigued by a topic that we spend 35 minutes and read ten or more samples. Each teacher knows how to gauge class time, and I am certainly not so regimented that I always follow the suggested fifteen-minute time frame. One way to get more writing read and evaluated is to have each student take someone else's paper and write a constructive comment immediately. When everyone's paper has been evaluated, I might say, "Is there a good one out there begging to be read? Whose paper should we hear?" Usually someone has a terrific example, and after the student reads his friend's paper aloud, I say, "Good. Give her an A."

The Benefits of Daily Practice

I have found five major advantages to using this daily training exercise with its follow-up sharing and discussion:

1. *Students write regularly.* I keep them writing as often as possible, although I do not assign sentences on the eve of exams, final-draft due dates, holidays, or special school events.

2. *I am freed from having to grade an entire set of papers each night, yet I provide daily evaluation.* This time spent on in-class, peer-group evaluation is instrumental in the development of the writer's ability to explain effective writing.

3. *Students selected for evaluation hear useful comments immediately.* They do not have to wait a week to receive response and criticism. At the same

time, the other students learn from the process of specifying writing strengths as well as weaknesses.

4. *Students learn developmental techniques, even linguistic patterns from one another.* They assimilate new ideas for specificity by regularly hearing other students' writing. In addition, they often internalize the linguistic patterns of other students, either consciously or unconsciously. This process is similar to the way we assimilate the speech patterns of a person with a different accent. After close association with such an individual, we may tune our own speech to the inflections of that person's attractive or entertaining accent. When we learn a new language, as well, we seem to internalize it more effectively when we spend time in the country of its origin. Hearing the language all the time, we are more likely to use it ourselves with better vocabulary and increased fluency. I believe it is easier for students to learn from each other, hearing regularly the effective writing of peers, rather than from professional writers whose solutions might be beyond the students' capabilities.

5. *Students write for a specific audience.* They write with the expectation that classmates might hear their compositions the following day. So, they usually put more effort into their pieces than if they were writing for their private journals or for only the teacher-as-evaluator.

The Program, Part 3: Using "Showing, Not Telling" in Revision

The third part of this training program consists of using the basic technique of sentence specificity and elaboration to help students revise their first drafts of major compositions. Whenever students are working on major writing assignments—an essay related to the reading of a novel, a character sketch for a short story, an argument for a persuasive essay—I have them take their rough drafts to small response groups. This is the chance for the student to "rehearse his piece" in front of an audience, eliciting responses and suggestions for improvement. In addition to helping another writer correct spelling, grammar, or usage errors, a student editor is instructed to scan the paper for underdeveloped ideas. If a student writer fails to develop adequately an important section of her composition, the editor underlines the sentence or sentences that generalize rather than specify and writes *Show* in the margin. The writer must then take the *telling* sentence and expand it for homework.

Instead of the usual daily routine in which everyone has the same sentence to develop, students now use sentences from their own writing. Just as the drama instructor stops the rehearsal of a scene midway and asks the actor to approach the scene from a different perspective through exercises in improvisation, so I halt my writers midstream in their discourse, urging them to consider important elements that may need focusing and elaboration. Students put aside their rough-draft compositions for the time being and zero in on generalities that need more development. With practice, students become more effective self-editors, too; their training both as writers and as evaluators of description pushes them to spot underdeveloped ideas and nonspecific language. When a writer has elaborated her own generalization—and on a given night she might have three or four to develop—she takes the new versions to her response group the following day for further criticism and suggestion. Usually a writer finds that the attention to more *showing* will improve the quality of her whole composition, and she can insert the changes easily.

A sample revision below illustrates the process. A seventh grader, when recounting her favorite childhood experience, describes the fun of playing hide-and-seek with her brother. As she attempts to create excitement and suspense around the moment of being found, she writes:

> **Leonardo was approaching her. He was getting closer and closer. She thought for sure she was going to be caught.**

Editors in her group suggested that she *show* "He was getting closer and closer," because this sentence signals an approaching climax. Her revision:

> **Leonardo was approaching her. She could hear him near the barn, his footsteps crunching the gravel. Next he was on the lawn, and the sounds of the wet grass scraping against his boots made a loud, squeaky noise. Next she could near him breathing. She thought for sure she was going to be caught.**

The writer is now *re-creating* her experience. By carefully remembering each sensation as her brother drew nearer—footsteps crunching gravel, the squeaky noise of boots in wet grass, the soft sound of breathing—she leads her reader through the experience. And because she has been training regularly to change *telling* to *showing,* she is much better prepared to make these additions. The *showing* sentences she has developed can be inserted smoothly into her original version in place of the *telling* sentence—a simple but effective revision.

Additional models of revision that grew out of response-group suggestions are discussed in section 4 of this book, "Training in Revision Techniques."

The Program, Part 4: Learning Specific Techniques

In the fourth part of the training program, students tackle more sophisticated "showing, not telling" exercises. After six weeks during which students experiment with *showing,* I begin deliberate units of instruction in developing certain kinds of ideas. I begin exposing my students to methods of generating details that they might not have discovered or practiced during the initial six weeks. This is the time for them to study literary devices for revealing ideas, a time to try different stylistic techniques. To alter the procedure in this way, I make two specific changes in the daily sentence practice:

1. I assign *telling* sentences derived from a particular mode of writing (for example, persuasive argument, comparison-contrast essays, saturation reporting).

2. I require students to expand these sentences in what might be new or unfamiliar ways. This requirement might be called *directed elaboration* as opposed to the undirected responses of earlier daily writings.

Three units I use regularly are described in section 3 of this book, "Preparing for Longer Compositions." The first unit prepares students to write a major essay structured through comparison and contrast, in conjunction with the study of literature. The second unit introduces special techniques students will need in writing a successful argumentative essay, using controversies that arise in their own daily lives—usually arguments with families. The third unit helps students develop techniques of personal journalism, including ways to evoke character, setting, and mood, as they prepare to write a major research essay—the I-Search paper.

For instance, if we're currently studying the unit on persuasive argument, I structure all the daily sentences as controversies:

Lunch period is too short at this high school.

Teenagers should have their own telephones.

P.E. should not be required.

Each day we practice different strategies for developing good arguments—dealing with the opposition first, saving our best argument until the last—and we try them out in the assigned daily sentence. At the same time, we examine published essays that deal with effective persuasion. Students study alternative ways to argue and try out the various strategies in their daily sentence homework.

A final major composition assignment, in this case an argumentative essay, culminates the unit of study. Students write better compositions because the directed elaboration of the daily practices has given them a variety of techniques to draw on. Like the drama instructor who teaches his students the conventions of Shakespearean acting—proper gesturing, curtseying, entering and exiting on stage—so must we provide students with conventional techniques for organizing compositions. The drama instructor, trying to get his actors to be more spontaneous and original in their deliveries, must shape the creative environment in order to encourage individual expression. That is, if an actor exaggerates Hamlet's lament, looking earnestly into the spotlight above center stage, never moving his gaze, the instructor might suggest he try delivering the soliloquy with his back turned, seated in a chair. Certainly he does not expect the student to deliver the speech with his back turned for the final performance; he simply wants the student to experience a new way of expressing despair, an *experience* he can apply to his final delivery. In the same way, I want my students to experiment with challenging and unfamiliar ways of expressing ideas. At the same time, I do not expect them to follow some *exact* pattern or structure in designing arguments or creating characters; the goal instead is simply to stretch their limits and help them discover options. Section 3 of this book, "Preparing for Longer Compositions," describes some of the ways I do this.

When my students write their final compositions, when they sit down to deliver their finest performances, I want them to feel that their hours of training have paid off. I want them to gain some notion of what being a writer is all about. And if they freeze up midway in the process, if they encounter the blank that all writers sometimes face, I hope they will learn to use the art itself as a tool of release.

2 *The Daily Workouts*

CHAPTER THREE
Using the Daily Telling Sentence

Before I initiate the daily workouts with the first *telling* sentence assignment, I have students perform an experiment that offers visual "proof" of the importance of detailed, effective description. I ask them to describe, in a paragraph or two, the scariest monster or figure in their imaginations. This beast might be a disfigured animal or an alien from outer space; it could be a face at the window or a dark-cloaked figure in an alley. The idea is to describe the figure as accurately as possible. Next, on a separate sheet of paper, they draw the monster according to the way they have described it. I have crayons and colored pencils available so they can make their sketches as colorful as possible. In fact, they know in advance they will be drawing their own descriptions; I tell them to use vivid color words if they want their pictures lively.

It is important that students draw their descriptions privately, allowing no other students to see their final portrait. Students will later be paired to draw each other's creatures, so it is crucial that they not see their partner's drawing in advance. I usually have students do the initial sketching at home, then let them add the final touches of color in my classroom. I always remind students that they need not be van Goghs or Picassos; our purpose is not to evaluate art, but rather *imagery.* I'm curious to see how closely their partner's sketch *resembles* their own version. If both drawings carry similar images, then most likely the written description has been effective. After both partners have drawn their classmate's monster according to its description, they unveil the drawings to each other and to the class. As a group, we judge whether or not the images correspond.

Obviously, if the drawings of two beings are rather dissimilar, I can emphasize the importance of specific language in description—that is the point of the exercise. Students really enjoy this activity, especially high school students, for many have not picked up a crayon since grade school. They also enjoy having their monsters displayed, so we usually wallpaper the room with the matching sets of pictures and the paragraph descriptions. Students get to see which pairs of creatures are closest in resemblance and, reading the descriptions, may discover *why.* The pictures and paragraphs on the following pages illustrate some very successful creature descriptions with their accompanying sets of drawings.

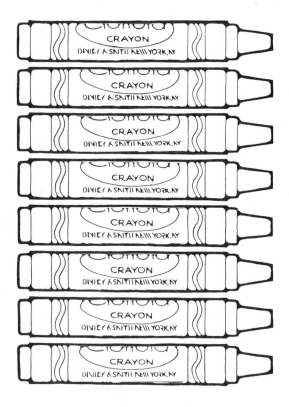

Writer's concept of monster
—Daniela Privari

Partner's drawing from description
—Dina Tavares

My creature has the body of a balloon. Its arms are long, thin, and gangly and his hands are thin with bony fingers. He also has thin, bony feet and sharp toenails. His orange hair is about shoulder length but stringy and flies all over. His head is oval in shape and sits close on his rounded shoulders. He has big almond eyes that hold an evil red glare. He always has an evil grin on his face, which reveals his shark-like teeth. He is a slimy green color and wears a shredded black scarf around his neck.

—Daniela Privari

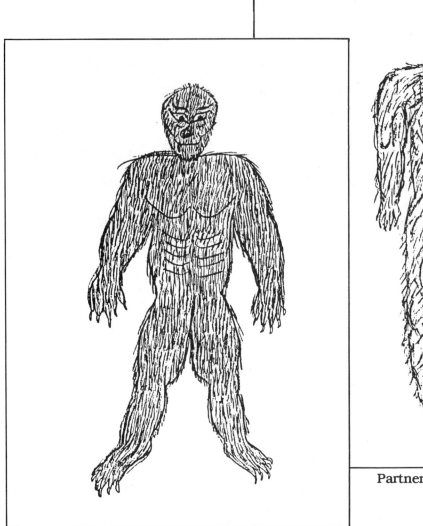

Partner's drawing from description
—Stephanie Picard

Writer's concept of monster
—Dina Tavares

The scariest figure I can imagine is dark black and stands about six feet tall. It has a very evil looking face with yellow fangs that have blood dripping off of them. This beast has the basic build of a human, but it has hair all over its body. Its hands have five fingers with razor-sharp claws on each. The eyes of this creature are extremely evil and devilish looking. They are slanted upward from each side of its nose. He has very defined cheekbones and his eyebrows arch up like Spock's on "Star Trek."

—Dina Tavares

Writer's concept of monster
—Jacque Lee

Partner's drawing from description
—Tegan McLane

I sat there just staring at the weird thing. It is purple, dark dark purple. It has *long* legs and huge feet. It has on white high-tops and green and orange knee socks. At the top of the legs, there's a funny ball head, no body. Its red eyes are barely visible through all the fur. It has a huge black nose but no mouth is visible. It has short, stubby arms with three-fingered hands coming straight out from the sides of the head. There's a *long* red and white striped tongue coming from where the mouth should be. It's so long it touches the floor.

I looked at it and felt creepy so I pushed the remote-control button and turned off the TV.

—Jacque Lee

Once students have seen firsthand that the use of specific details in their writing can create effective pictures in the reader's mind, they are ready to begin the daily workouts—turning general *telling* sentences into specific *showing* paragraphs. Now I begin to assign the daily sentence, a practice I will continue through the first six weeks of the course. For these assignments, I choose generalizations familiar to students to increase the likelihood of getting effective elaboration. I assign the sentences in no particular order, and I make no special effort to link them by recurring themes.

Below is a list of fifty *telling* sentences I have used for the daily workouts in the training program.

The room was vacant.

She has a fantastic personality.

The party was great.

I was very embarrassed.

My room is a mess.

The concert was disappointing.

My mother bugs me.

The math test was a killer.

The food at the party was incredible.

Those girls are snobs.

The jocks think they're cool.

He looked guilty.

He eats like a pig.

The weather made me nostalgic.

The relationship changed.

The drive in the car was uncomfortable.

School is boring.

Teenagers should not have curfews.

My friend was steaming mad.

This school has great school spirit.

The pizza tasted good.

The loss was devastating.

The living room was a warm, inviting place.

She acted older than her age.

People make or break a party.

Advertisements can be misleading.

The F grade should be abolished.

Camping is a rewarding experience.

My parents are great people.

Reality set in.

She changed.

The weather was perfect.

A student's life is hard.

The streets were crowded.

The puppy was a terror.

He is artistic.

She is creative.

The afternoon was a romantic one.

The principal was effective.

The game was a close one.

The book was intriguing.

Haste makes waste.

They lived happily ever after.

The climb was exhausting.

The roller coaster was the scariest ride at the fair.

The crossword puzzle was tricky.

The new student was lonely.

The fire drill went miserably.

The substitute teacher was strange.

The speaker got everyone's attention.

Before assigning daily sentences, evaluating them, and initiating the full program, you may find it useful to examine the kinds of changes that are likely to occur in students' writing after several weeks of training. In becoming familiar with certain predictable patterns, you will know better how to measure individual growth and change, as well as how to encourage continued development.

With this in mind, let's examine the daily writing progress of two very different students. First, we'll evaluate the writing of a high school freshman, a below-average writer who has little interest in composing; we'll evaluate his first daily writing of the year and compare it to one written two weeks later.

TELLING SENTENCE:
The new students were lonely.

It was the first day of school and there were two new students, Dick and Dan, who had moved over the summer. They were brothers and this was a new city and school which they had come to, and in this school they would have to make friends because neither of them knew anybody or anyone.

—Lance Moreno

This piece is composed entirely of generalities. The writer explains the cause of the loneliness—a new city, a new school, the necessity for making new friends—but unless he shows us some foreign streets, strange faces, and unusual customs that support these reasons, he is not *showing* loneliness adequately. Perhaps if this writer contrasted "playing pool with the old gang at Mike's Pizza Parlor" to "the eyes avoiding his unfamiliar face in the study hall," the reader might better appreciate the realities of "new city, new school, new friends." Here is the same student's writing two weeks later:

TELLING SENTENCE:
The crossword puzzle was difficult to solve.

The sixth row down got me stuck. It was plain to tell that this crossword puzzle was rough. The puzzle as it was, was made for a 12th grade level, and it made me feel as if I was in the 6th grade level. Intellectual words such as "the square root" of 1,091,056 in four digits and others. The next one was a five-letter word for phyladendron, which was "plant" to my surprise. I, as a normal person, had a very hard time trying to figure out what an Australian green citrus fruit was with four spaces. Instinctively I gave up the whole game, as it was too frustrating to cope with.

—Lance Moreno

This selection illustrates a marked improvement in generating examples. The writer introduces his subject by *telling* that the puzzle was rough, but immediately proves his claim with a series of specific illustrations—twelfth-grade level vs. sixth-grade ability, intellectual words like *square root*, names of exotic plants and fruits that call for specialized knowledge. His writing is more enjoyable to read because of the examples he added. Notice also that his paragraph is longer but never rambles or leaves the point. Finally, although he does use telling sentences, "this crossword puzzle was rough," and "it was too frustrating to cope with," he is remembering to include the examples that *prove* those claims. Two weeks earlier he never once used an example. It is clear to me that the student has captured the point of the exercise; his use of *telling* sentences along with *showing* sentences in the paragraph is *not* incorrect. The only rule in the daily sentence "game" is that a student not use the original words of the given *telling* sentence.

For purposes of contrast, let's examine the writing of an above-average, college-bound writer. It is interesting to discover what happens to a writer who already uses detail and example consciously as he composes. The following writings were done by an advanced sophomore. The first paragraph is his very first "showing, not telling" exercise of the year; the second shows his growth and change over a two-week time span.

TELLING SENTENCE:
The room was vacant.

> The next show didn't start for another hour. As I repositioned the spotlight in the upper balcony, the squeaks of the rusty screws seemed to echo throughout the desolate building. I walked down the aluminum stairs that resounded with the sound of rain beating on a tin roof throughout the auditorium. I then opened the curtains to the large, lonely stage which looked dark and forbidding. As I put up the sets and decorated the stage, I guess it would seem to anyone walking in, that the room was very much alive with color and objects. But to me, even the set and decorated auditorium looked bare.

—Mark Thomas

Indeed, we have here a rather original approach; while most students wrote about rooms void of furniture and decoration, this student writes about a room empty of people. Everyone in the class thought his paper was the best response because no one else "did it like he did." When encouraged to explain what they meant by "did it like he did," they finally got around to identifying the quality: *vacancy* can have more than one meaning, and while people often think of vacancy as the absence of objects and possessions from a place, this writer thinks of it as the absence of people, an interesting alternative.

But, does the cleverness of the approach mean that the writer *showed* adequately? Does he thoroughly re-create that empty auditorium? In the first half of the paragraph, the writer carefully gives his attention to taking the reader through the experience. Like many students trying to master a skill, he concentrates very responsibly at the start of his piece. It's as though he's saying to himself, "I should really *show* that vacancy. What made me feel alone?" And indeed, he generates the specific examples: squeaks of rusty screws that echo throughout the auditorium because there is no audience to buffer the sound; aluminum stairs that rattle like rain beating on tin because, again, there is no crowd to muffle the sound, so instead it reverberates through the vast room. I would guess that the writer spent more time creating those first few sentences than he did composing the rest of the paragraph. In the first half, he is *there*, experiencing the event; then he loses that careful attention and reverts to *telling* the rest. With the sentence "I then opened the curtains to the large, lonely stage," he abandons his use of specifics, relying instead on vague adjectives like "dark and forbidding," or general nouns such as "color and objects." He would have carried his piece to a more fully developed close had he written: "I guess it would seem to anyone walking in that the room was alive—the spotlights illuminating the stage, the neon sign blinking 'cafe' in vibrant blue, the skyscraper backdrop looking more like reality than like an acrylic painting. But to me, because the actors weren't hustling and bustling across the stage, touring the nightlife of New York, the set seemed bare."

Within two weeks, this student increased his observational skills considerably. In addition, he was able to sustain his use of vivid details throughout a much longer piece of writing.

TELLING SENTENCE:
The roller coaster was the scariest ride at the fair.

As I stood in line, I gazed up at the gigantic steel tracks that looped around three times. The thunderous roar of the roller coaster sounded like a thunder cloud that has sunk into my ears and suddenly exploded. The wild screams of terror shot through me like a bolt of lightning and made my fingers tingle with fear. Soon I heard the roar of the roller coaster cease. As the line started to move forward, I heard the clicking of the turnstyle move closer and closer. Finally I got onto the loading-deck and with a shaking hand gave the attendant my ticket.

It seemed like I barely got seated when I felt a jolt which signified the beginning of the ride. While the roller coaster edged up the large track, I kept pulling my seatbelt tighter and tighter until it felt like I was cutting off all circulation from the waist down. At the crest of the hill, I caught a glimpse of the quiet town which lay before me and gave me a feeling of peace and serenity. Suddenly my eyes felt like they were pushed all the way back into my head, and the town had become a blur. All I could see was a mass of steel curving this way and that as the roller coaster turned upside down. I was squeezing the safety bar so tight that my fingers seemed to be embedded in the metal. I could see the landing-deck, and I let out a deep breath that had been held inside ever since the first drop. As the roller coaster came to a halt, I felt weak and emotionally drained. When I stepped off onto the deck, I teetered a bit to the left, but caught my balance quickly when I saw my friends waiting for me at the exit gate. I tried to look "normal," while trying to convince them in a weak voice that, "Oh, it was nothing."

—Mark Thomas

This writer now stays with the entire experience from beginning to the end. At every step of the way, he tries to re-create exactly what he remembers feeling. In effect, he has developed more writing discipline. Even though he makes general claims, such as "I felt weak and emotionally drained," he remembers to support these feelings with specific evidence: "When I stepped off onto the deck, I teetered a bit to the left. . . ." And, though he *tells* us he "tried to look 'normal,'" he proves this with dialogue: "Oh, it was nothing."

Some teachers or critics may feel that the writer is *overdoing* the description; some may feel he is laboring too hard over the attempt to be specific. I will agree that students often do get carried away with description; however, I would much rather have them overdescribe than underdevelop. With regular response and evaluation from teachers and peers, students prone to overdoing it can learn to cut back and edit.

So far, then, we've discovered two important results of the daily practice:

1. After several weeks, students tend to write more—either because they are finding it easier to generate more writing, or because they are working harder on the assignment (or both).

2. Students gain control over a wider range of writing techniques.

I have noticed that the time we spend evaluating writing during the first minutes of class becomes a period of *entertainment* for many students, rather than a time of nervousness or embarrassment as you might expect. Since they realize they will be performing for the rest of the students regularly, they often seem to compete for attention. I think it helps that I call the ritual a *game* and liken the exercise to charades, because after a short while, students relax and begin to have fun with their renditions. One major benefit of this pleasurable class atmosphere is the change that often takes place in students with negative attitudes. The sort of student I have in mind is the one who challenges every assignment with "Why do we have to do this? What does this have to do with real life?" One such student showed this attitude from the very first assignment of the year; when asked to elaborate on the *telling* sentence "The new students were weird," she would volunteer only one sentence. She knew what constituted a paragraph, but passed judgment on the value of the exercise by simply scribbling out the following:

> **The new students started screaming and jumping up and down as they entered the room.**

For a first writing, I will not select this student's paper to be read aloud; I will pass it over in search of a more developed response. If by the second and third days this writer is still giving me only single sentences, I most likely will continue avoiding her papers. If, however, by the fourth or fifth day she still believes she's "getting by," I really won't have to do a thing beyond reading her paper to the class. They'll predictably respond: "Is that all? She should write more." I'll agree with them and assign the paper a C, giving the "innocent" the benefit of the doubt. My hope is that her peers' evaluation will inspire her to write more. In this particular case it worked. Watch what happened to her over a series of days.

> DAY 2 TELLING SENTENCE:
> *He has a good personality.*
>
> **He always says "hello" to everyone he passes and he constantly has a smile on his face. He is kind to everyone and never degrades anyone.**

DAY 3 TELLING SENTENCE:
She is creative.

Not only could she sing and play the guitar, but many of her paintings were displayed in her room. In addition, it was a pleasure to smell and taste the gourmet foods she prepared in her kitchen.

When I read this piece aloud, the students told her they liked the mention of "gourmet foods" as an indication of someone's creativity; they thought that detail was an attribute most people don't usually associate with creativity. (Most high school students stick to such arts as painting, weaving, collage-making, and pottery-making as a measure of someone's creativity.) Then they suggested she write more. By the fourth day, she wrote the following:

DAY 4 TELLING SENTENCE:
The drive in the car was uncomfortable.

Sitting in the back seat of the small economy car while driving through the hot and humid desert was a miserable experience. The 110-degree weather along with the 80 percent humidity added somewhat to the stickiness of the situation. Though the seven of us were squished together, we managed to entertain ourselves by letting the sweat run down our bodies and dribble to our feet.

When I read this paragraph, the class roared with laughter! This piece, though brief, is filled with voice and spontaneity. Her one fabulous detail at the end, "entertaining ourselves by [watching] the sweat run down our bodies and dribble to our feet," demonstrates the comic relief that people are apt to look for in seriously uncomfortable situations. This piece of writing reminded us how people band together in tough times and create their own forms of release. The student, having received her applause and genuine appreciation, was a bit more willing to write and share after that incident. The following paragraph illustrates the length and quality of her writing two weeks later.

TELLING SENTENCE:
The pizza tasted good.

As I stared at the pizza set on the table, the colorful combination of cheese, meat, and spices suggested a pleasurable taste ahead. The aroma of the hot, bubbling mass made my mouth begin to water. As I took a bite of the crispy pizza, I savored the taste for a brief moment. My tongue curled around the mellow, warm cheese; my taste buds thoroughly relished the tangy Italian sauce, and as a result, made my saliva glands work faster. When I bit into the reddish-brown pepperoni, I was amazed at the spiciness. All these different sensations combined into one pleasurable experience.

As we've witnessed in the preceding writing samples, students initially rely simply on increased use of specifics and lengthened paragraphs to improve their writing. As they become accustomed to the practice and begin to experience some security or personal growth in generating examples, I can almost predict when an imaginative student will challenge the conventional means of developing ideas. Perhaps because the writing becomes less of a chore and more of an enjoyment, one student or another will "try something different," will test the limits of satisfactory elaboration. In much the same way that, after playing Hamlet every night, an actor can suddenly discover an entirely new and fresh way to express despair, so my students find, without my solicitation, original ways to express their ideas. The following interpretation of our *telling* sentence "The pizza tasted good" is an example of one student's stretching different muscles.

I felt a little apprehensive that morning. I wasn't sure if, after so many years of separation, my brother and I could spend an entire day with one another and enjoy it. Pulling on my jeans, I tried to think of a few conversational topics that would interest us both, just in case conversation came to a standstill. I wondered if he could be thinking of the same thing. "Funny," I thought, "maybe I have no reason to worry; maybe we will have too much to talk about—maybe."

After just a few minutes on the Berkeley campus, I realized that all of my worrying and topic planning was unnecessary. Courtney and I had so much to share, so many years to catch up on, and of course, he was certainly expounding helpful, fascinating, or just plain factual information about Berkeley. He even took me to his favorite Mediterranean Cafe. Together we sipped their rich and aromatic coffee blend as he told me about the many hours he had spent there, reading the morning paper or engrossed in some outlandish novel. Of course Courtney was excited. He couldn't wait to give me a grand tour of "his" alma mater. He wondered if "his" old pepper tree was still as majestic as ever, and if "his" studying area in the Botanical Gardens was still as beautiful as he remembered. The campus came alive with Courtney's nostalgic memories of his old chemistry lab in the Life Sciences Building, or the old Greek Theatre where he enjoyed Shakespeare, Bach, and Sophocles.

By lunch, I knew that Courtney and I would never be at a loss for words. More importantly, I knew that there was a strong bond between the two of us—something that even time could not erase—love. Together we sat Indian-style on the grass just below the Campanile. The stringy pizza we had purchased for lunch brought childish grins to our faces, and through the warm silence, we both knew that pizza had never tasted so good.

—Meg Caldwell

When I read this particular paper aloud, students were not quite certain how to respond. Some wondered whether the writer had fulfilled the challenge, because she actually used the original *telling* words "The pizza tasted good" at the end of her piece. They wondered if she should have shown, in more detail, the kind of pizza she and her brother shared. Since she was an extremely articulate person, Meg retaliated with questions, asking the class members whether or not they had ever experienced a luscious meal without the benefit of company. She asked, "Didn't you ever have prepared for you your favorite meal—let's say a steak—and find that you were left at home to eat it alone? Aren't there some times when we find that food tastes better because of the company we have?" I followed her defense with, "Can anybody share a story in which the experience of eating food changed because of the company you were with?" Someone volunteered a story about disliking refried beans; she had always grimaced at the thought of eating that "mushy paste." Then she went on a date with the boy of her dreams, and he took them to eat tostadas at a nearby Mexican restaurant. Without realizing it, she was soon reveling in the food because she was so enthralled at simply being with her fantasy friend at last. From then on, she developed an adoration of tostadas—refried beans and all—because their time spent together was so fondly memorable. This student writer reminded us all that the taste of food is often influenced by the mood we are in or the company we keep. The classroom attack on Meg's *showing* piece halted as students sat in quiet contemplation. They had discovered a concept they already knew but had never articulated: there are ways of showing ideas other than the most literal ways. Sensory experiences involve more than immediate physical sensations.

This piece of writing became an important lesson, and it came without my instruction. My experience with this training program has shown that the use of effective student compositions as models for learning has much more impact on the growth of student writers than all the lessons in textbooks. Students more readily emulate the successful writing of other students than they do that of professionals. From that moment on, in that particular class, many students felt compelled to be different, to probe for deeper solutions. They were excited by this writer's discovery because it became their discovery, too. The following night, after I assigned the *telling* sentence "The living room was a warm, inviting place," many students focused on *people* as making a living room warm and inviting, rather than fireplaces, leather sofas, or shag rugs.

If you are looking for a similar breakthrough in your own class, you might use this same assignment, "The pizza tasted good." After reading some of your students' papers aloud, present Meg's alternative response on the overhead projector or as a handout to stimulate a similar class discussion. (A reproducible copy appears in the Appendix.) Year after year, I contrive the same situation: after reading aloud the standard responses about pepperoni, mushrooms, cheese, and tomato sauce, I use this same student's paper as a model for discussion. And every year, it sets the students thinking in new ways as they recognize the value of pushing deeper for their elaborations.

CHAPTER FOUR
Evaluating the Showing Paragraphs

In this chapter I'd like to share some effective and non-effective paragraphs written in response to five different *telling* sentences, collected from students in my classes. You may find it useful to present these sample paragraphs as models, either on the overhead projector or as handouts (or both), as you train your students to evaluate the differences between the two versions of each assignment. (You will find reproducible copies of these models in the Appendix.) In my classes, I make a habit of sharing one effective and one non-effective response on the overhead projector once a week. I call this session "the paper of the week," and I get students to articulate what makes each version successful or unsuccessful. As I write their comments in wax pencil on the transparency, they write identical responses on copies at their desks. This weekly ritual prepares them to be better critics in their response groups; it also gives me the chance to help them explain to themselves what makes a composition work.

TELLING SENTENCE
My room was a mess.

My room was so cluttered, full of junk. My mother wanted to kill me. You had to step over everything and it made it hard to walk. She told me that I was a slob and that I didn't take care of my things. But I told her I didn't have time to clean. Everything was thrown and scattered around the room and it was completely a disaster!

This paragraph illustrates a distinct lack of specific description. The writer tries to create a sense of drama by having his mother want to "kill" him and call him "a slob." He wants to convince us of the disorder by showing that his mother is very angry. In other words, he feels that if we as readers see how furiously his mother reacts, then we are likely to believe the seriousness of his offense—this room *must* be pretty untidy!

It certainly is an acceptable technique to have another person react in alarm in order to show the degree to which the room is unorganized; this is one form of effective showing. It is also effective to show that the person has "to step over everything." However, the writer relies exclusively on these techniques without picturing the chaos. He is asking us to trust that the room is indeed a clutter. He needs to let us *see* the room, needs to take us on a tour. The following writer does just that; he becomes our guide on an adventure.

TELLING SENTENCE:
My room was a mess.

To enter the room, I was forced to squeeze in the small door opening, nearly getting stuck because heaps of dirty clothes obstructed the path of the door. Once inside, I had to concentrate fully on every step so that my shoes wouldn't become tangled in the laundry and cause me to fall. Steps later, after freeing my leg from a malicious pair of blue corduroy pants, I noticed that under the spot vacated by those pants was a matted piece of green shag carpet, the only piece of carpet not being smothered by clothing in the entire room. The next thing to attack me was a Pink Floyd poster only partially pinned to the wall. The feeling of my head coming into contact with a foreign object made me whirl about in apprehension, swinging my elbow out and knocking it with force against a drawer jutting out from the half-empty clothes chest. Howling in pain, I flung myself on the bed, long parted with its sheets, and wondered if I wouldn't be safer waiting in another room.

—Brent Sprowl

At this point it is probably needless to analyze, in close detail, the techniques this second writer uses to show messiness. The careful reader knows what this student is up to. He wants us to experience the disorderliness by watching him almost fall on his face as he avoids clothes, laundry, falling posters, and drawers jutting out. The success of this piece is based on the writer's ability to recall details from his own life and make them identifiable, and therefore amusing, to someone else. This writer has a real sense of audience; he wants us to picture the event as he felt it. The writer of Response A assumes that "the reader will know what I mean, so I don't really have to describe too much." It is also safe to say that the writer of Response B seems to delight in writing more than the first writer does. It is my guess that when writer A catches on to the power of detail, he too might enjoy composing a bit more.

TELLING SENTENCE:
Those girls are snobs.

Those girls are so stuck-up! Whenever I'm around they act like they don't even know me. They ignore me. It really hurts my feelings because they think they're so special and I'm not. They never include me in anything they do and they treat me like I don't exist.

This writer relies on *telling* statements for the entire paragraph. She keeps repeating that she is excluded from the group's activities, but never once gives examples of the kinds of gestures, words, or actions they use to convey superiority. To be stuck-up, to ignore and not to include someone else, are certainly forms of being snobs, but the writer is not yet taking us through an experience. In her expansion, she continues to generalize the other girls' condescension.

TELLING SENTENCE:
Those girls are snobs.

While two girls slowly strutted themselves past me, I heard a soft sound much like the hiss of air being let out of a tire. Their eyes slowly shifted around following my every move. It took a second, but it finally hit me like a pie in the face that they were talking about me. One of the girls raised her finger and darted it towards me. As she did this they quickly exchanged glances and the sound of giggling now replaced the whispering. I rolled my eyes in their direction, catching their amused expressions. With my glance they lifted their hands, flung their hair back over their shoulders, straightened their posture, lifted their noses, and pompously walked off.

—Nancy Marshall

As though she were a camera, this writer records every significant mannerism and gesture that illustrates snobbish contempt. Notice the attention to sound—hissing, whispering, giggling; all these details point to secret remarks being made. Pointing fingers, exchanging glances, flinging hair over the shoulders—all demonstrate condescending mannerisms. Even the line "it finally hit me like a pie in the face that they were talking about me" shows rejection and humiliation through the sophisticated use of simile. Whatever they were whispering about does not matter; the remark "hit me like a pie in the face" carries the weight of the gossip. This writer must be recalling a time when she herself felt excluded; without the very real experience behind the description, she probably could not have written so effectively.

TELLING SENTENCE:
She was depressed.

No matter how hard she tried, she could not fall asleep. She was still thinking about the test she had taken that day. It seemed to her that she had studied hours to pass the test and still she had gotten a bad grade. The rest of the day she had walked around feeling gloomy and upset. At the end of the day she went running and for that time she forgot, but later her gloominess returned. Now it was midnight and still she could not sleep. What a gloomy day it had been.

This writer re-creates an event that triggers depression—poor performance on a test at school. Indeed, any student would feel dejected upon receiving inferior results, especially when she had studied so conscientiously. The writer is not yet re-creating the depression, however. Instead, she tries to convince us of sadness through repetitions of the word *gloomy* in the phrases "feeling gloomy and upset," "later the gloominess returned," and "What a gloomy day it had been." In effect, she is *telling* the reader over and over the same message she would have conveyed had she used the word *depressed* in its place. The writer is not yet secure in her ability to generate examples of depressed behavior; that is why she repeats *gloomy*—to make certain the reader doesn't miss the point and, more likely, to lengthen the paragraph. This writer needs to search inside herself, remembering a time when she was actually in a similar mood and recalling what she did with her feelings.

TELLING SENTENCE:
She was depressed.

As she stood there looking at herself in the mirror, her image was blurred from the continuous stream of tears that were falling down her face. She inhaled, then exhaled with a large sigh. "Maybe some music might cheer me up," she thought. She trudged over to the stereo and switched it on. A sweet mellow love song was playing. She angrily flipped it off and threw herself face first onto her bed. Lying there she grabbed her pillow and wept once again.

—Susan Richter

This writer has the reader *live through* a sample moment of depression. The content of the paragraph is based entirely on individual actions and gestures that reveal a hopeless attitude: blurred vision from continuous tears; exhaling uncomfortably; trying to talk herself out of the mood with music from the stereo, then *flipping off* the soothing sound, suggesting she cannot be soothed; finally giving up trying to relieve herself, throwing herself face down onto the bed.

In this student's version, we have a series of definite actions that, in total, present a fully developed idea. From acknowledging her sadness in the mirror, to trying to alleviate it, to giving in with a final outburst of tears, we are led through the experiencing of strong emotion. This writer probably recalled a despondent moment in her own life, because her details seem entirely realistic. Notice also that the writer does not need to give any background information regarding the cause of the girl's sadness; students do not need to narrate full stories. The challenge is to get immediately to the *feeling* and re-create it.

TELLING SENTENCE:
The relationship changed.

Her eyes were like those of a young puppy's moistened around the corners. Her mouth formed a careless line down at the edges. The facial color was no longer glowing with health but now wan. The flowing blonde hair seemed to sag like the limbs of the weeping willow. The once square shoulders now drooped like a basset hound's ears.

Many students might read this paragraph and exclaim about the tremendous *showing* it does. They might praise the lack of any *telling* statements at all, and I would agree with them. This writer clearly shows the contrast between a once glowing, radiant personality and a now listless, defeated person. The rhythm of the sentences, creating the impression "once it was that way, but now it's like this," shows how carefully the writer has constructed the idea of change. Nevertheless, we should point out to students that the showing details we use in our writing need to develop the main idea, and in this case the description does not. We know that the woman described has changed, but there is no evidence of a *relationship's* altering. Basically, we see the *effects* of change on an individual, but we never see the *cause* from which this change evolves. Students need to be reminded that good *showing* alone does not constitute effective elaboration; the descriptive details must explain the assigned idea in order to work.

The following writer, in contrast, is careful to suggest the idea that change is occurring in a relationship:

TELLING SENTENCE:
The relationship changed.

The girl ran across the grass, clutching a worn football in her hands. Close behind her ran a boy, desperately trying to catch the girl. With one giant leap the boy grasped her shoulders, bringing them to the ground in a tangled maze of limbs. Their laughter filled the yard as they both tried to get up.

Slowly the laughter faded, and the yard became quiet. They looked at each other with questioning eyes. Softly the boy placed a hand on the girl's shoulder and slowly leaned over to place a gentle kiss on the girl's lips.

There is no question that the writer has shown a significant change in attitude between these two animated characters. We observe two children magically change to adolescents as they alter their display of affection toward one another. In the first paragraph, we see the roughneck playfulness between a young boy and his tomboy companion: "With one giant leap the boy grasped her shoulders, bringing them both to the ground in a tangled maze of limbs." And in the next paragraph we see the creeping realization unfold: they look at each other with questioning eyes; the boy now places a hand on her shoulder slowly, in contrast with his earlier abruptness. This writer focuses on the change in their laughter, from loud boisterousness to soft seriousness, and on the change in their physical affection, from rough playfulness to tender caressing. This writer has achieved a dramatic contrast by focusing primarily on body language and gestures to reveal feelings, a technique rather sophisticated for a young student writer.

TELLING SENTENCE:
The room was romantic.

The couple looked lovingly into each other's eyes as they sat on the sofa. They had waited all day to be together. He had thought of her all day at work, and she had thought all about him, too. They were going to be married soon. At last they were together and could share their evening together.

This writer offers an effective opening sentence to establish the romantic mood in the room. By starting out right away with a physical gesture—a romantic gaze—he gives the suggestion of an attraction and a longing between the couple, and because they are seated on a sofa, in the evening, we can imagine a setting and a relaxed tone. After the introduction, however, the writer focuses more on the status of the couple's relationship than on the qualities that make the room romantic. Even though the feelings the couple have for one another contribute to a loving atmosphere, the image of the room itself as romantic is rather weak. The writer might have emphasized the room's influence more—or the couple's influence on the room—to dramatize the romantic setting.

TELLING SENTENCE:
The room was romantic.

The sun, rising over the lake, created a rosy glow in the living room as it shone through the window, and the unseasoned wood in the fire gave the room a musky smell as Christy sat down on the couch. She snuggled closer to her husband, that word was going to take some getting used to, and took a sip of coffee. A honeymoon to her family's cabin in the Sierras was a wonderful idea, and now as she fell deeper into the couch and her daydreams, she could hear the ticking of the cuckoo clock on the wall, her grandfather's gift to her mother and father on their wedding day. So many memories, so much of a future.

—Dave Evans

This writer draws on a number of techniques to show a romantic room. First, the writer uses lighting from an early morning sun to cast a "rosy glow" in the room. The sunlight in this case might suggest new beginnings, hopefulness, and promise. In addition, the writer describes a pleasant scent permeating the room—the "musky smell of unseasoned wood" hints at a freshness and vitality in the air. Later in the paragraph we learn that the room is in the family cabin in the mountains and brings with it a sentimentality and tradition. On the wall is a cherished cuckoo clock—"grandfather's gift to her mother and father on their wedding day." By bringing in the sentimental object, by "hearing" its ticking, the writer suggests a longevity in the family's marital relationships, perhaps a foreshadowing of love and commitment—an ultimate romantic condition.

In addition to the physical descriptions used to convey romance, the writer uses sophisticated sentence patterns to emphasize the romantic mood in the room. The opening sentence closes as Christy takes her place on the couch, riding on the heels of sunlight and smell into the room. It is as though she and the fresh air of the morning have arrived all at once. In a single line, the writer establishes setting, tone, mood, and action. Also, the writer crafts another interesting structure—a parenthetical clause—to hint at the bride's nervous excitement. By inserting the clause "that word was going to take some getting used to" next to the word "husband," the writer suggests a sort of giddiness and awkwardness as the woman takes her place in family tradition. This little excess in the sentence—because it interupts a perfect pacing—draws attention to the romantic newness of the marriage. When discussing this model with students, you might point out the way different sentence patterns work to achieve different dramatic effects.

When I find successful student writers approaching these assignments with such effective approaches as the ones demonstrated in this chapter, I often stop and highlight the student's original technique. In effect, I continually devise new lessons on interesting techniques for developing ideas, based on the inventive approaches of my own students.

Teachers of writing, both in English classes and in classes outside the language arts arena, might, as I have, begin collecting their own samples of effective and non-effective responses to various assigned compositions. In this way, they collect their own stock of models based on their *own* writing curriculum. In preparing students to develop satisfactory responses for term papers, for example, the social studies or history teacher might put on the overhead projector a sample elaboration of the *telling* sentence, "Roosevelt and Wilson were different kinds of leaders." He could show his students the sort of development he is looking for in an assigned topic; he could show them what he would not accept. By regularly sharing with students both effective and non-effective compositions, any teacher who demands writing can help prepare the students for more successful major essays.

CHAPTER FIVE
Variations for the Daily Workouts

The English department of an entire school might decide to adopt the daily-sentence idea, only to find that after the first year or even the first semester, the assignment begins to lose its appeal for students, and hence its impact on their writing. This is likely to occur whenever students who master a particular response are asked to go on making the *same* kind of response day after day.

The solution to this problem is to use the *principle* of daily practice, but to change the particular skills being practiced, regularly offering new challenges to students. The daily practice paragraph and all its associated activities, from classroom discussion to peer-guided revision, provides a *method* for teaching and learning, but it need not be limited to a single instructional goal. The rest of this chapter discusses some alternatives, all based on the "showing, not telling" approach.

Undoing Clichés

Once the students become familiar with the daily sentence exercise, after they've become used to developing ideas about subjects close to their experience, I introduce into the program some variations on the assigned sentences. One alternative that proves fruitful is asking students to develop the idea inherent in a cliché. I discovered the use of this variation in answer to my increasing frustration with their use of clichés to demonstrate feelings and attitudes. When more than one student wrote "A chill ran down my spine" to show terror in a frightening situation, I suggested they develop that sentence as their assigned daily workout. I wanted them to think seriously about what that statement claims. Here is one such response.

TELLING SENTENCE—CLICHÉ:
A chill ran down my spine.

Watching the Creature Feature, I saw the monster's distorted head and immediately threw my hands to my face and screamed in terror. I shivered violently and noticed the beat of my heart racing to an incredibly high pulse. A gust of cold air rushed through my body, causing me to pry my hands from my face to try to warm my upper arms. Doing this, I noticed goosebumps covering my entire body. The hair on the back of my neck became perpendicular to my skin.

Finally, I overcame my fear and took a breath of relief which caused me to shiver again with another little convulsion. But that was the last of it, and the last of the movie. I turned it off immediately.

—Kerrie Ely

This writer traces the experience of being suddenly taken by an event. Notice that she does not find it necessary to describe the monster in detail, but instead goes immediately to the fear it arouses. For these daily challenges, I ask students to get right to the core of the idea—in this case, the "chill"—and to resist the temptation to tell lengthy stories. Often students begin with a once-upon-a-time introduction and do not get to the main idea until the close of their compositions. This writer stays with the actual experience to the end.

I do not mean to demean the value of storytelling as a way of revealing feeling and sentiment; students need to think about situation and circum-stance to trigger an assigned emotion. It is my experience, however, that writers often become distracted with storytelling, developing plot and situation *in place of* the central idea. They dramatize an intriguing event, then, in a sentence or two, explain the resulting feeling, believing they have *shown* the assigned generalization. I encourage students inclined to storytelling to weave the dominant impression *inside* their story, so that the central feeling itself governs the plot.

The following story, used to reveal another cliché, shows an expert use of plot to enhance the dominant impression.

TELLING SENTENCE—CLICHÉ:
She really put her foot in her mouth this time.

Cindy glared at the boy walking out of the office doors. She leaned on the switchboard that her friend, Nancy, was operating. "I think that Pete Dawkins is a stuck-up jerk! He walks like the coolest thing since Richard Gere." Cindy said this loud enough so that the people standing nearby could hear. They looked at her angrily.

Nancy looked up and asked, "What's wrong with him?" Cindy studied her fingernails and said, "He's just like Barbara; she thinks she's hot, too!" This was again overheard by the people standing nearby and they walked away shaking their heads in disgust. Nancy looked at her coldly as she fingered the microphone of the school P.A. system. "Listen, can we change the subject? You're always talking about other people." Cindy gave a loud sigh and removed a piece of lint from her blouse.

"OK," she sighed again and looked up at the ceiling. "You know what Mr. Horton gave me on that term paper?" Nancy rolled her eyes. They came to rest on the microphone. She giggled. "Well?" Cindy asked. "He gave me a D! He only gives good grades to those cheerleaders."

There was a soft click as Nancy switched on the loudspeaker. "Besides that, have you ever seen anyone as weird as Horton? Polyester suits! He's just a big, fat . . ." Her words stopped abruptly, eyes becoming large with fear, head cocked stupidly to one side as she listened to her own voice echo across the campus.

—DeAnna Ertel

In this situation, the storytelling is essential to the overall impression. We see that Cindy is the sort of person who is accustomed to getting away with snide and rude remarks about other people. Though friends who overhear her react angrily, there is still complete confidence in the way she handles herself in front of them. As she studies her fingernails, and removes a piece of lint from her blouse, we see her casualness in front of others; she couldn't care less what classmates think of her outspokenness.

With this introduction to her character, the writer sets the stage for the resulting irony in which the girl's composure is replaced with chagrin. She is at last caught off guard as she criticizes a teacher in front of the entire school. When she realizes that her words are echoing across campus, her shame is apparent. Her stopping abruptly and her "head cocked stupidly" reveal the girl's remorse. This time she has indeed put her foot in her mouth.

Encouraging Brevity

Storytelling is clearly a preferred strategy among many student writers; by making a plot entertaining, a writer gains attention easily. The following expansion of a cliché demonstrates an effort sure to elicit the laughter and approval of the class.

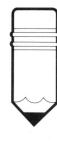

TELLING SENTENCE—CLICHÉ:
He was the picture of health.

He leaned his muscular body against the racquetball court door. He casually removed his wrist weights and wiped the beads of sweat from his sharp-featured face. A group of interested females feasted their eyes on the athlete, bent over to remove his ankle weights.

I let a nonchalant glance last a bit longer than what is considered "safe." I pretended that his wonderfully thick legs weren't headed in my direction although I couldn't help but notice the large, toned set of biceps connected to the pair of hands resting on my table.

I stopped tying knots in my tennis shoes and found no reason to deny his proposal of our having lunch together. He tilted his tanned face toward the waitress and ordered two raw-egg coolers sprinkled with wheat germ, and a "Bran Muffin, Baked Liver, and Brussels Sprout Delight for two." As I searched for strength to stand, I sputtered, "Make it one—I've gotta run!!"

—Susie Marino

As more and more students come to enjoy our daily ritual of sharing their *showing* paragraphs, they try to be comical, often strange, as a way of securing a favorable response from peers. Many, at first, do not have the self-assuredness to try writing a short paragraph or a few rich sentences that display a dominant impression. So, as time moves on, I emphasize brevity more and more, especially in developing clichéd ideas. Where initially I encouraged increased detail, now I pull them back, asking for conciseness and economy. I indicate that I am not asking students to belabor a point, giving tedious description; rather, I am seeking a quick, concise response that gets to the point almost immediately.

Here is another student's response to the cliché, "He was the picture of health." Notice this writer's brevity in relaying the assigned impression.

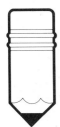

He was off again to the racquetball courts, running full-speed, leaving the Nautilus room far behind. Dodging through the corridors, leaping over sofas, and sliding down banisters, he soon found himself at the entrance to Court Thirteen.

—Matt Innes

The writer's setting, of course, provides an excellent introduction to character. By mentioning the racquetball court and the Nautilus room, the writer sets the stage for his athletic figure to emerge. Then, he relies on careful verb selection—*running, dodging, leaping, sliding*—to convey the character's agility and speed. This two-sentence description alone is adequate in suggesting the picture of health. As writers mature, they need to recognize this type of quality over quantity.

For practice in undoing clichés, here are some additional *telling* sentences you might assign:

It was right on the tip of my tongue.

It went in one ear and out the other.

I knew it as well as the back of my hand.

She was caught between a rock and a hard place.

The situation was as plain as the nose on your face.

Everybody and his brother were at the party.

They were as poor as churchmice.

He was as sneaky as a snake in the grass.

We were as busy as bees.

It was enough to make your hair stand on end.

Then it hit me like a bolt out of the blue.

They're as different as night and day.

It was as easy as taking candy from a baby (falling off a log).

She is as pretty as a picture.

This time I knew I was in hot water.

I was on cloud nine (in seventh heaven).

I could hardly believe my eyes.

The grass is always greener on the other side of the fence.

When my students practice undoing clichés, I have noticed that frequently they rely on *other* clichés to develop the assigned idea. They are not necessarily aware that they are introducing equally trite expressions as they do their describing. For example, when I assigned "A chill ran down my spine," or "I was frozen with fear," I discovered students using the following phrases to aid their descriptions:

My blood ran cold as ice.

My body felt as stiff as a board.

I was glued to the spot.

I was nailed (or cemented) to the floor.

I was paralyzed with fear.

My body was in a state of shock.

When students use these hackneyed phrases in place of original description, I need to make them aware of the problem. I take care not to belabor the point, because I don't want to make them hesitant to write another word for fear of seeming unoriginal; but I do ask that they tune their ears to overused phrases, staying alert to expressions that might lack power. Through this awareness, they might begin distinguishing their own unique phraseology from common, tired expressions.

Developing Vocabulary

Since my students are responsible for studying weekly vocabulary lists, I try to create *telling* sentences that carry with them words from the assigned lists. In this way, students are likely to remember, even internalize, more of the words because the writing exercises have forced them to develop the word meanings.

Here are five words taken from a study list my students use in preparing for the SAT college entrance examination: *abase, abate, factitious, ignoble, meretricious.* The following *telling* sentences use each word in context:

The student who cheats *abases* himself.

The rain *abated.*

That *factitious* smile convinced me she was not sincere.

She came from an *ignoble* background.

Her *meretricious* manner seized our attention.

Here are some student models that develop these assigned sentences.

TELLING SENTENCE:
The student who cheats abases himself.

The girl managed to pry her desperate eyes away from her friend's paper and glanced up at the teacher. Her eyes met the piercing glare of the teacher's eyes and her heart skipped a beat. Her worst fears were made true as the teacher began to slowly rise from her desk. The student felt the red rising in her cheeks.

The teacher began to slowly walk towards her. As she approached the student, their eyes met again for an instant and the student saw the furious look. She knew she was about to be made an example of. Without a word, the teacher snatched up her paper and shrieked, "You were cheating!" Her classmates, who had been quietly working up until then, oblivious to what was going on, simultaneously jumped three feet out of their seats. The girl felt her stomach drop. Now she not only had to face the teacher's glare but also the laughter-filled eyes of her peers. She felt their staring eyes boring into her and could not raise her own eyes from the worn carpeting in front of her desk.

—Greg Konrath

A shorter version:

This is what happens when you cheat!! She spoke sternly, staring at me with accusing eyes. I shifted in my seat but couldn't seem to find a comfortable position. I could feel my face burning, exuding guilt. Wiping my sweaty palms on my jeans, my hands suddenly seemed like foreign objects, and I couldn't find a place to put them. The stares of the other students bored holes into me as they exchanged hushed whispers. Throbbing heartbeats swelled my throat, making me unable to speak.

—Mish Denlinger

TELLING SENTENCE:
The rain abated.

The flooded streets were gradually draining. People on the streets were now walking casually with their umbrellas instead of dashing from building to overhang, trying to survive the windblown rain. All that could be heard now was the soft pitter-patter on my umbrella. This was a relief to my ears compared with the previous thunder and howling wind.

—Burt Dixon

TELLING SENTENCE:
That factitious smile convinced me she was not sincere.

Her smile slid into place in the same pre-rehearsed, teeth-clenching way. It was as if her face had been frozen or poured into a mold to have her lips pinned back, baring gleaming, perfect teeth. I walked away, wishing all that plastic would melt.

—Heidi Howell

TELLING SENTENCE:
She came from an ignoble background.

A child sat alone on the pale green tile floor of a one-room apartment. Her dearest possession stood in her arms. She softly sang "Miss America" as she pranced the rag doll down her imaginary runway. Her escape into make-believe abruptly became reality. The ruthless cries of unmerciful children shattered her state: "Christeena don't have a father . . . Christeena don't got a mother!"
The children playing below the window were far from a game to Christeena. Out of frustration she suddenly threw her beloved old doll against the window sill. The child now sat shamefaced in an empty corner and sobbed brokenheartedly into a closely-embraced pillow.

—Susie Marino

TELLING SENTENCE:
Her meretricious manner seized our attention.

Entering the hotel just moments before her was the unmistakable fragrance that had become her trademark. That unique blend of spices, the deep, almost dusky, Oriental fragrance of her dark brown perfume and the delicate, clove-scented tendrils of smoke that hung in the air around her long, black cigarette holder, announced her presence. As she came into sight, gasps could be heard from the guests scattered about the lobby. Removing her long fur coat, she put even the crystal chandeliers to shame, their delicate dancing prisms fading out of the limelight as the intricately beaded, silver folds of her dress were exposed.

Smiling cooly through well-defined crimson lips, she took a silver cartridge pen from her thin, black handbag and signed the guest register.

—Suzanne Coffee

Each of the foregoing examples surely helped the student writers understand and master the meaning of a word not otherwise in their vocabularies. Similar *telling* sentences can be created from *any* word list to increase students' verbal acumen.

Developing Reading Comprehension

In order to reinforce my students' understanding of particular assigned readings, I have them develop responses to *telling* sentences derived from the major themes of short stories, novels, poems, or plays we are reading. After the first chapter of *Call of the Wild*, for example, I might assign the *telling* sentence "Buck is an intelligent dog," leading students to describe the dog's unique, humanlike characteristics. Students are asked to use details and descriptions from the chapter to support their ideas. In this way, I teach them that *showing* writing, in addition to explaining our own perceptions of the world, can be used to clarify an author's message or point of view. After students have read the first two chapters in Hemingway's *The Sun Also Rises*, I want them to understand why Jake Barnes disapproves of Robert Cohn's way of living. Therefore, I assign the *telling* sentence "Jake disapproves of Robert Cohn" and ask them to prove the claim, using evidence from the chapters for support. Here is one response:

TELLING SENTENCE:
Jake disapproves of Robert Cohn.

Jake disapproves of Robert's definition of "really living" which includes running off to wild and exotic places to have romantic, adventurous experiences. Now that Robert has made a success of himself, having just received wide acclaim for his newly published novel, he wants to keep his life "interesting." Robert is not happy in his current surroundings—Paris—and therefore feels he should constantly be changing them to obtain happiness. He says, "I can't stand to think my life is going so fast and I'm not really living it." He does not realize that he is actually escaping from his "unhappiness" which originates from within his own mind rather than from his surroundings. Jake is looking at Robert through the eyes of experience, knowing that in order for Jake to shed his unhappiness and loneliness, he must stay settled in a single place. Jake says to Robert, "You can't get away from yourself by moving from one place to another. Why don't you start living your life in Paris?" In this way, he is suggesting that Robert should divert his attentions toward his inner thoughts and work his problems out. Jake does not enjoy seeing his friend—a man of 34—so naive.

—Lori Cox

This writer uses evidence from the story to support her ideas. She mentions briefly the individual philosophies of each character's attitude toward living, then supports those claims by quoting from dialogue between the two men.

You might also assign as *telling* sentences memorable lines from selected readings, lines that you would like students to remember long after the reading is completed. For instance, having students *show* the meaning of Shakespeare's "All the world's a stage," or Dickens's "It was the best of times, it was the worst of times," increases the likelihood of their understanding a metaphorical concept or a paradox more permanently. By asking students to develop and struggle with difficult concepts as they encounter them in their reading, we can help make those ideas become part of their own knowledge of the world. Rather than having students take notes as we lecture to them our own interpretations, we suggest that they come up with their own. During our follow-up discussions, as we read several "showing, not telling" pieces aloud, we can assess the workability of different student interpretations; we, as teachers, can then feed into the discussion our own ideas.

While my classes are reading *The Great Gatsby*, for example, I feel it significant to have students understand Nick's position about socializing with the very rich. In chapter 2, while attending one of Tom Buchanan's private parties in New York City, Nick makes the assessment: "I was within and without, simultaneously enchanted and repelled by the inexhaustible variety of life."[1] This line is central to comprehending Nick's character development, because throughout the story he fluctuates between feelings of attraction and repulsion towards the elite society. It isn't until the end of the novel that he takes a course of action in response to his confusing experiences in the East. This line is also a concept with which teenagers can readily identify; they are often attracted to the glitter of the popular crowd, yet just as often become disillusioned with the reality of some trendy lifestyles. And so I ask them to put themselves in Nick's place at Tom's party. I ask them to *show* the thoughts that led up to Nick's thinking that memorable line. In this way I guarantee the comprehension of the abstract concept. Here's how one student, taking the role of Nick, expanded on that character's thoughts.

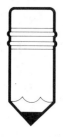

TELLING SENTENCE:
I was within and without, simultaneously enchanted and repelled by the inexhaustible variety of life.

I sit upon the cushioned armchair, surrounded by the warmth of new and engaging people. I watch Myrtle as she tells an amusing story about a woman who came to look at her feet and charged some exorbitant price. Using her entire body to make her drunken anecdote come across, Myrtle laughs loudly as the other women titter gaily. I smile at her broad, demonstrative actions.

I am also a stranger, walking the worn pavement beside the frosted apartment building. The brilliant yellow lights from the room above attract my unworthy eyes. I pause and wonder what wild carousing is going on.

1. F. Scott Fitzgerald, *The Great Gatsby* (New York: Charles Scribner's Sons, 1953), p. 36.

Myrtle drops down next to me and tells me about her magical meeting with Tom. She explains how she was immediately attracted to him because of his shoes. When Tom approached her, she said she felt she'd have to call the police, but Tom knew she was bluffing. Her hot breath warms my face as she says that you can only live once. My whole body is already warmed by the stinging whiskey.

I sit quietly in another room, stunned by what I see. I hear nothing but garbled whispers about Tom and how lucky he is to have Myrtle, and how sad it is that they can't be married because, "well of course you know, Daisy doesn't believe in divorce." Oh, and isn't it just grand that Tom and Myrtle are so in love. I feel cold in the room and cold towards these people and their private little "affairs."

—Clare Blackmer

This writer shows Nick's wavering. She makes him a participant at the party and an observer to it at the same time. She uses the actual facts and incidents from the scene in the book to develop his train of thought, making the actual *showing* very realistic.

It is one thing to hold a class discussion on the meaning of a significant passage from a work of literature; it is another thing to have each student explain the meaning to him- or herself. Frequently it is the same students, an enthusiastic few, who volunteer their oral interpretations in discussion. By assigning important ideas as *telling* sentences, you can guarantee that *everyone* will grapple with the concept, then have the opportunity to compare their ideas with others.

Showing Ideas Through Single Sentences

To improve students' sentence style, I often ask them to *show* me their assigned generalizations through *single* sentences. When students must deliver full development of an idea in a limited number of words, they will most likely increase their use of concrete language; they will also learn to incorporate more sophisticated subordinate structures in order to embellish independent clauses. I have had a great deal of success using the ideas of James Gray outlined in his "Teaching the New Rhetoric," an article highlighting Francis Christensen's work on the English sentence. Gray, founder of the Bay Area Writing Project and the National Writing Project, suggests methods for having students imitate certain rhetorical patterns inherent in the twentieth-century prose style, a style termed by Christensen the *cumulative sentence style:* ". . . students examine variations of the cumulative sentence in scores of sentences written by a number of professional writers and imitate these methods of modification in sentences of their own. In the most important step in the process, students apply these now-familiar structures by writing longer, extended sequences."[2]

---

2. James Gray, "Teaching the New Rhetoric" (an unpublished article available from the Bay Area Writing Project, University of California, Berkeley, prepared in 1969).

Students learn to identify verb, adjective, and noun clauses, then imitate those structures in sentences of their own. They study the effective use of appositives, the precision in parallel phrases, and watch how they can manipulate language to enhance their own styles. Any teacher of composition would do well to read Gray's latest publication, *Sentence and Paragraph Modeling,* a work co-authored by Robert Benson, composition instructor at San Francisco State College.[3] The methods and strategies outlined in this manual are extremely effective in getting students *immediately* writing more sophisticated sentences and paragraphs.

The following *showing* sentences—single-sentence versions of the daily expansion exercise that were assigned after much sentence modeling practice—illustrate more effective use of concrete language and complex sentence structure than students usually produce in the early stages of the program.

TELLING SENTENCE:
The jocks think they're cool.

A small group of boys clad in shorts and tank tops stand inside the shady entrance of the cafeteria, puffing up their chests to full capacity as they proudly recall last Saturday's drunken exploits.

—Suzanne Coffee

TELLING SENTENCE:
Mother Nature absorbed us.

A bluejay, flapping its wings frantically, comes to a sudden stop on a sturdy tree branch, squawking wildly, demanding attention, and without hesitation flies to another tree twenty feet away, still shrieking.

—Jim Butler

TELLING SENTENCE:
The children were having fun.

Tumbling off the couch, letting out banshee-like screams, the small children fell to an imaginary death at the foot of the torn and tattered "cliff."

—Jesse Brennan

TELLING SENTENCE:
I was annoyed.

The blue Ford pickup came bouncing down the winding dirt road, grinding to a halt beside me, the dust rising and writhing up into the air, curling its way into my eyes and making them itch.

—John Ertel

---

3. James Gray and Robert Benson, *Sentence and Paragraph Modeling* (Berkeley, Calif.: Bay Area Writing Project, 1982).

TELLING SENTENCE:
The soldier was impressive.

He was a stocky, barrel-chested man in his thirties with thick muscular forearms, a jagged scar running along his forehead, a Purple Heart and Vietnam Service Ribbon emblazoned on his chest.

—John Ertel

Modeling Paragraphs

In addition to having students model and imitate the intricate sentence patterns of published writers, I have them model whole paragraphs. While working to narrate an idea in someone else's style, students are likely to internalize different rhetorical devices for expressing their own ideas. In these modeling exercises, I ask students to imitate, part of speech for part of speech, a paragraph from a famous work of literature. When we're studying Fitzgerald, for example, I will ask them to imitate a passage representative of his distinguished style. They invent their own descriptions based on the exact sentence patterns of the assigned paragraph.

To introduce this technique, I ask them first to imitate a rather simple sentence pattern—let's say, "The cat ran through the yard." Students come up with sentences like, "The car drove down the street," or "The Popsicle dripped in my hand." In this case, a noun, a verb, and a prepositional phrase have been substituted in the exact order of the original sentence. After practicing a few additional sentence patterns, I ease them into the more difficult task of imitating major passages from literature. One typical passage I might use is this one from Fitzgerald:

We walked through a high hallway into a bright, rosy-colored space, fragilely bound into the house by French windows at either end. The windows were ajar and gleaming white against the fresh grass outside that seemed to grow a little way into the house. A breeze blew through the room, blew curtains in at one end and out the other like pale flags, twisting them up toward the frosted wedding-cake of the ceiling, and then rippled over the wine-colored rug, making a shadow on it as wind does on the sea.

The only completely stationary object in the room was an enormous couch on which two young women were buoyed up as though upon an anchored balloon. They were both in white, and their dresses were rippling and fluttering as if they had just been blown back in after a short flight around the house. I must have stood for a few minutes listening to the whip and snap of the curtains and the groan of a picture on the wall. Then there was a boom as Tom Buchanan shut the rear windows and the caught wind died out about the room, and the curtains and the rugs and the two young women ballooned slowly to the floor.[4]

4. Fitzgerald, *The Great Gatsby*, p. 8.

Following is a student paper based on this model. Although his sentences do not always match perfectly, part of speech for part of speech, this writer's approximations are close enough, delivering to the reader the essence of the Fitzgerald style.

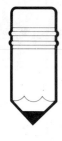

FOOTBALL GAME

I jogged through the tunnel onto the bright green football field, boxed in on both sides by the stadium seating. The seats were filled and overflowing with noise from the fans that seemed to be spilling onto the field. A violent wind whipped through the stadium, blowing empty popcorn boxes out of the stands and onto the field like autumn leaves blowing from the trees, lofting them up toward the powder blue of the afternoon sky, and then letting them settle on the green plastic of the astro-turf, like feathers floating to the earth.

The only lifeless object in the stadium was a player dressed in blue, slouched on the rusty bench like a sack of potatoes. His oversized blue jersey bagged and flapped in the wind as if it were many sizes too large. I must have sat for a few minutes, listening to the whistle of the wind and the grunts of the players on the field. Then there was a screech of brakes as the motionless player was set in the back of the ambulance, and the doors slammed shut on the field, and the whistle of the wind slowly died to a hush, and the grunts of the players were just an echo and the lifeless body winced in the ambulance bed.

—Will Hayes

Another passage I use for an imitation assignment is this, from Hemingway:

I wondered if there was anything else I might pray for, and I thought I would like to have some money, so I prayed that I would make a lot of money, and then I started to think how I would make it, and thinking of making money reminded me of the count, and I started wondering about where he was, and regretting I hadn't seen him since that night in Montmarte, and about something funny Brett told me about him, and as all the time I was kneeling with my forehead on the wood in front of me, and was thinking of myself as praying, I was a little ashamed, and regretted that I was such a rotten Catholic, but realized there was nothing I could do about it, at least for a while, and maybe never, but that anyway it was a grand religion, and I only wished I felt religious and maybe I would the next time; and then I was out in the hot sun on the steps of the cathedral, and the forefingers and the thumb of my right hand were still damp, and I felt them dry in the sun.[5]

---

5. Ernest Hemingway, *The Sun Also Rises* (New York: Charles Scribner's Sons, 1954), p. 97.

When students encountered this passage in their reading, they wondered whether this single-sentence paragraph was evidence of improper grammar and usage. They wondered whether this sentence was, in fact, a run-on. With all the *and*'s and all the commas, they were confused about the correctness of the sentences. Instead of lecturing on the reasons Hemingway chose this rhetorical structure, I asked students to imitate the passage, seeing if they could discover their own answers to their questions. Here is one result:

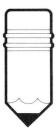

> I struggled with my decision of what I would wish for, and I decided that I might wish for an 8-track player, so I wished that I would get an 8-track player, and then I was pondering over what 8-track tapes I needed to buy, and thinking of buying 8-tracks made me think of Styx, and I wondered when they'd have their next concert in our area, and regretting I missed their last concert in Oakland, and about Erin telling me how excellent they were, and as all the time I was leaning over the table with my face glowing because of the candles on my cake, and was thinking of myself as wishing, I was a little embarrassed and regretted that I took so long to blow out the candles, but realized it was too late to do anything about it now, at least for the moment, so I despairingly watched my ice cream cake, unknown to me that it was an ice cream cake, steadily flow onto my mom's lace tablecloth, but that anyway it was a luscious cake, or shall I say milkshake, and I only hoped that I could have blown out the last candle before it sunk into the lump of ice cream and maybe I might still get my wish if it meant not having good luck; and then I began ladeling up as much of my cake as was possible into the numerous bowls, and the candles flowed into the bowls with the ice cream, so I took them out and I licked the ice cream off of them.

> —Kathy O'Connor

Imitating this style, the students came to understand why Hemingway chose to include all the character's thoughts in a single sentence: the technique shows that the entire reverie happens in a single instant. In fact all of us can, in a momentary instant, think a variety of thoughts; this technique emphasizes the mind's ability to roam and wander in a few seconds. Because students imitated the sentence first, we had a strong foundation for the resulting discussion. Students came to realize under what circumstances a long-winded sentence might prove effective.

Imitating Other Styles

Toward the end of the year, after students have practiced word-for-word imitation of different author's styles, I ask them to go one step beyond this and write papers in which they emulate the characteristic styles of several of the authors they've studied during the year. For this assignment, they are working without specific model paragraphs. Since my juniors focus primarily on American authors, I ask them to demonstrate their understanding of differences in style by retelling a well-known fairy tale or nursery rhyme in the style of three selected authors. Students narrate the stories of "Jack and Jill," "Little Miss Muffet," or "Cinderella" as if the story had been written by F. Scott Fitzgerald, Mark Twain, Ernest Hemingway, J.D. Salinger, or John Steinbeck; they choose any three.

Following is the story of "Little Miss Muffet" as told by one student in the style of Fitzgerald in "The Splended Spider," in the style of Hemingway in "The Spider Also Scares," and in the style of Salinger in "Catch 'er in the Web."

THE SPLENDID SPIDER

In my younger and more vulnerable years, my mother gave me some advice that I've been turning over in my mind ever since.

"Whenever you feel like complaining about your curds and whey," she told me, "just remember that all the people in this world haven't had the advantages that you've had."

She didn't say any more, but we've always been unusually communicative in a reserved way, and I understood that she meant a great deal more than that. In consequence, I'm inclined to eat only curds and whey, a habit that has opened up many curious natures to me and also made me the victim of not a few stomachaches.

One morning, I resolved to eat my accustomed breakfast outdoors. I walked through the large porch into a bright green-colored garden, fragilely bound into a circular shape by a white picket fence constructing the entire circumference. The flowers were dew-kissed and glistening against the fresh grass outside that seemed to grow a little way up the porch. A breeze blew through the garden, blew leaves on one tree and on another like light flags, rustling them together, enclosing all empty spaces and then moving them apart, making a tree shadow once again upon the ground.

The only completely stationary object in the garden was a small tuffet on which my cousin, nicknamed Miss Muffet, was sitting, eating *her* breakfast of the "delicious" curds and whey. She was wearing white and her dress was rippling and fluttering as if she had been hung outside to dry. I must have stood for a few moments listening to her slurping and smacking of the cereal and the clinking of the spoon against the bowl. Then there was a scream as my cousin saw a spider and watched it creep towards her, causing her relaxed breakfast to be interrupted.

At any rate, Miss Muffet's lips fluttered, she nodded at me almost imperceptibly, and then quickly tipped her head back again—the spider had obviously sped up and given her something of a fright.

I looked again at my cousin, who continued to scream in a high-pitched voice. It was the kind of voice that the ear tries to shut out, as if each burst is an arrangement of three out-of-tune pianos with a back-up set of pots and pans. Her face was frightened and alive with bright things in it, bright eyes and a brightly flushed complexion, but there was terror in her voice as she turned and ran into the house.

THE SPIDER ALSO SCARES

In the morning it was bright, and they were sprinkling the streets of the town, and we all had breakfast in a cafe. Across the street we witnessed a scene which we found amusing. We were all a little tight.

A three-legged stool, called a tuffet, was occupied by a girl. The girl who had sat down, her name was Miss Muffet, found toward the end of last summer that her figure was going, and her attitude toward food changed from one of careless choice and decision to the absolute determination that she should have curds and whey. She began eating.

After a while we heard a shriek from across the way and then we saw the girl running down the street. A spider had come along and frightened her. We continued talking and drinking.

"Oh, Justin," Bridget said, "she could have had such a damned good breakfast this morning."

"Yes," I said. "Isn't it pretty to think so?"

CATCH 'ER IN THE WEB

If you really want to hear about it, the first thing you'll probably want to know is where I met her, and what I was doing when I saw the whole thing, and where it all happened, but I don't feel like going into it, if you want to know the truth. That kills me. You try and tell someone a simple story and all and they have to know the whole crummy background before they're even interested.

Well anyway, where I want to start telling is that day in the park. I was walking by when I saw this girl sitting on a stool-thing eating her breakfast. I asked her name and she said Miss Muffet. At first I thought she was being smart. I hate it when people feel like messing around and give you a phony name like that and all. I can't get too mad though cuz it's something I'd do. Anyway her name really was Miss Muffet and there she was eating her breakfast in the middle of the park. I can't believe she'd really sit there and do that. I mean, you'd have to be a damn moron to sit and eat breakfast where everyone can watch you. But there she was, munching away on the most god awful stuff you ever saw. It was all watery and lumpy at the same time and it damn near makes me puke now just to think about it. I asked her what it was and she said curds and whey. I *knew* that wasn't a lie cuz something that looked that bad would have to have a name like that.

Well anyway, she just kept on eating and I kept sitting on the end of the bench across from her thinking what I'd do today. I'm still sitting there and all when this damn spider crawls right up my leg. That kills me. Spiders think they can walk anywhere anytime they want to. They don't care what you're doing or anything, they just crawl right up and stare at you. Well, I took the damn thing and dropped it on the ground. I didn't see where it went.

Then I knew where it went. I heard the loudest scream coming from that dopey girl that I ever heard. She goes and drops her crummy bowl all over the ground and runs off cuz of that stupid spider. That *really* kills me. Girls are always so scared of spiders and all. They just look at them and you'd think they were shot twenty times in the head or something. Girls. They kill me.

—Cathy Peterson

When students imitate and later emulate the distinguishing styles of major authors, not only do they come to appreciate the talent and craft of the writer, they also learn specific rhetorical devices for delivering ideas. Students consider the varying impact of different sentence lengths, of descriptive and nondescriptive language, of direct and indirect narrations. In short, they learn to tell their stories in new and different "voices." When Cathy emulates the styles of Fitzgerald, Hemingway, and Salinger in her Little Miss Muffet tales, she sees that for Fitzgerald the scene must be portrayed as a painting, filled with scenic descriptions to highlight the action; for Hemingway, the emphasis must be on action, on stating facts without cumbersome detail; for Salinger, she must digress, using interior monologue to reflect the attitude of the narrator toward the incident, to the extent that the digression becomes more prominent than the incident itself. Through regular practicing of other writers' styles, students discover new options and can adopt whatever techniques feel right for their own emerging styles.

Making Generalizations

A final variation on the daily workouts is having students perform a reversal of the *telling* sentence, *showing* paragraph exercise. Instead of assigning a generalization that must be developed, I distribute elaborated paragraphs and ask for generalized or "topic" sentences. Students need just as much practice in *summarizing* bodies of facts or details as they do in developing them. Though students tend to think their homework assignment is rather easy with only a single sentence to create, they often find the task more arduous than they originally believe. They must write an abstract statement that provides meaning to or explains the significance of *all* the collected facts and details. Following are two models with accompanying generalizations by student writers. The first paragraph is from Mark Twain:

SHOWING PARAGRAPH

The house was a double log one, with a spacious floor (roofed in) connecting it with the kitchen. In the summer the table was set in the middle of that shady and breezy floor, and the sumptuous meals—well, it makes me cry to think of them. Fried chicken, roast pig; wild and tame turkeys, ducks and

geese; venison just killed; squirrels, rabbits, pheasants, partridges, prairie chickens; biscuits, hot batter cakes, hot buckwheat cakes, hot "wheat bread," hot rolls, hot corn pone; fresh
corn boiled on the ear, succotash, butter-beans, string-beans,
tomatoes, peas, Irish potatoes, sweet potatoes; buttermilk, sweet
milk, "clabber"; watermelons, muskmelons, cantaloupes—all
fresh from the garden; apple pie, peach pie, pumpkin pie, apple
dumplings, peach cobbler—I can't remember the rest. The way
that the things were cooked was perhaps the main splendor—
particularly a certain few of the dishes. For instance, the corn
bread, the hot biscuits and wheat bread and the fried chicken.[6]

TELLING SENTENCE:
The meals of summer were heavenly.

Certainly not all paragraphs are void of *telling* sentences to begin with. As
a result, when I choose a *showing* paragraph, I am likely to delete a significant
telling sentence to see whether or not students invent similar summary
sentences. Below is one paragraph I have used from a book by Nancy Friday.
The original paragraph began: "When I was nine I went to a private summer
camp, a beautiful plantation home on an island, hung with Spanish moss. *I
had my first case of homesickness, impetigo, and rejection by a best friend.*
Her name was Topsy and she came from Atlanta." (Italics added.) I identified
the material in italics as a *telling* sentence that generalized the entire
paragraph, so before presenting it to students, I omitted the *telling* sentence
and paraphrased the beginning of the following line to keep the sense of the
story accurate. What I gave the students read as follows:

SHOWING PARAGRAPH

When I was nine I went to a private summer camp, a
beautiful plantation home on an island, hung with Spanish
moss. . . . [My best friend there] was Topsy and she came from
Atlanta. We slept together, we ate together, we jumped
hand-in-hand off the diving board on the big oak pier together,
and we made a pact to do everything together, especially to be
best friends forever. One day a mother arrived and left her little
girl at the big house. She was put into our room. Topsy and I
eyed her during lunch, conspicuously leaving her out with our
giggles, as we left out everyone from our secret world. By supper
time I was the one on the outside. They whispered when they
looked at me, sharing secrets you would think they'd shared for
years. Their friendship was born on the strength of my
exclusion. That night I lay in my bed and sang "Onward
Christian Soldiers" to myself to keep from crying. My head
ached, trying to know what I had done.[7]

TELLING SENTENCE:
I felt rejected and believed it was my fault.

6. Samuel Langhorne Clemens, *The Autobiography of Mark Twain*, ed. Charles
Neider (New York: Harper and Row Publishers, Inc., 1959), p. 4.

7. Nancy Friday, *My Mother, Myself* (New York: Dell Publishing, Inc., 1977), p. 202.

Recently I have noticed the need for increasing my use of these *reverse* "showing, not telling" exercises. Students often have difficulty interpreting a set of facts or details, a problem that shows up most prominently in their major compositions. For instance, a student is likely to *show* very well that Jake Barnes in *The Sun Also Rises* is unemotional while his good friend Robert Cohn is extremely emotional. Because students have been trained to prove their claims with a thorough use of quotations, they manage to include a rich variety of examples. I have begun to realize, however, that they are less talented in interpreting their quotes, in drawing meaning from their evidence. For instance, students noting the difference between Jake and Robert ought to be able to deduce from the examples that Jake remains unemotional when his pain and internal suffering are too great to bear; his "unemotional response" is more a *denial* of his feelings; Robert Cohn, on the other hand, finds more peace when he lets go of his emotions and states them outright, but he often gets himself ridiculed for sentimentality. A *conclusion* that might evolve would be, "Hemingway shows that there are both rewards for and drawbacks to expressing one's feelings freely."

Students need much practice in drawing such conclusions, so lately I have increased the number of reverse exercises I use, asking students ever more frequently to create *telling* sentences for elaborated paragraphs. In fact, it has become as important to assign *telling*-sentence resolutions as it has to assign *showing* paragraphs. I believe that in this way, we can improve students' critical thinking capabilities and in the long run, push them toward writing more thoroughly developed essays.

3 Preparing for Longer Compositions

CHAPTER SIX
Structuring Through Comparison and Contrast

After their initial practice with all aspects of the daily sentence, students must begin working toward writing major pieces of narration and exposition. So, I begin using the daily exercises as a way to practice what might be new or unfamiliar techniques for developing main ideas. Instead of assigning random topics for development, I now deliberately choose topics that build toward a particular theme or mode of writing. In this way, students will have the opportunity to rehearse the different structures they will be required to develop in their major compositions.

Structuring a comparison essay is one of the most important writing lessons that students can master. History instructors frequently ask students to contrast two decades or two leaderships; science teachers might have students compare two chemical reactions or two biological cycles. When faced with discussion questions on essay exams, students can usually rely on this kind of structure; the comparison/contrast pattern gives them something to *do* with the facts they've studied. At some point in the year, I use the following series of practice exercises in my English classes, preparing students to write comparison/contrast compositions on themes derived from major works of literature.

The final assignment is not always the same. Sometimes as students begin reading *The Great Gatsby*, I want them to focus on the recurring attention to the difference between illusion and reality. Many of the characters have a vision of what it takes to achieve success and fulfillment, but learn through the course of the story that they have directed their lives inappropriately. As students discover this emerging theme, I have them compose personal essays portraying a time in their own lives when they discovered that reality did not live up to their fantasies. This serves as preparation for their final composition on this theme in Fitzgerald's writing.

Other times, following the reading of the same novel, I have students compare and contrast Gatsby's quest for Daisy Buchanan with the quest for the American dream. During our preparatory class discussions, students notice the emphasis placed on money as the key to happiness; in their compositions, then, they take the idea further, comparing it to the relationship between money and happiness in our own culture.

I have also used the comparison/contrast unit with another novel, *The Catcher in the Rye*. Since Holden Caulfield, seventeen-year-old narrator of the story, struggles with many of the problems that all teenagers face, I have my students compare and contrast their own views of the world to Holden's.

As you can see, all three assignments make an attempt to connect the major themes of the novel to the students' own lives and the lives of people around them. Whenever students can *see themselves* in the lives of the characters, they are more likely to appreciate the value of literature and will perhaps enjoy reading on their own even more.

Regardless of the choice of final assignment, my students have the same training to prepare them for structuring a major paper through comparison and contrast. (The models I use for instruction also appear as reproducible pages in the Appendix.)

Preparatory Exercises

My first assignment in this unit is the *telling* sentence, "Saturday is different from Sunday." Asking students to write about subjects very familiar to them is good preparation for more difficult comparisons. After reading aloud alternative interpretations, we share and discuss especially successful structures. Here is one such student model:

TELLING SENTENCE:
Saturday is different from Sunday.

Without the help of an alarm clock, at 8:30 sharp Saturday morning, I wake up brimmed with energy and ready to take on any activity that floats my way. The sun is pouring bars of golden liquid in my window and the blue jays are singing merrily at the top of their musical voices. Anticipating a whole day to do whatever I want, I eagerly throw on my clothes and spring down the stairs. After a light breakfast I grab my old familiar cut-offs and my favorite beach towel, jump in the convertible, and with a delightful screech of the wheels, fly off to spend a beautiful day running and laughing in the sun.

My mother is shaking me and saying, "It's past 11:00. Get up; there's work to do." With a deep groan I open my bloodshot eyes and am immediately blinded by the terrible glare of the sun beaming hot and stuffy directly on me. Very slowly I claw my way out of bed, and in a drained, limp state of semi-consciousness, stumble sheepishly down the stairs. My family, faces cheerful and repulsive, is having breakfast. Just the aroma of eggs turns my stomach, making me feel queasy. Instead, I trudge to the cabinet, fumble with a bottle of aspirin, and with a glass of warm water sloppily gulp three down. Then, still hung over and depressed, I sit down and stare straight ahead, thinking about the agony of mowing the lawn.

—Brent Sprowl

Classes are usually impressed by the vividness of this student's composition, achieved almost exclusively through concrete details. They enjoy hearing this version because they can identify with the writer's outlook for each day. Many of them agree that Saturday is the day for playfulness, while Sunday is the day for responsibility.

This model composition also uses a typical form: one paragraph devoted to Saturday's activities, one paragraph to Sunday's. I have found that the majority of students will use this structure—A in one paragraph, B in the other—when responding to this assignment. It seems to be far easier to take one day at a time and show the activities of each day than it is to talk about two days at once. However, I have also noticed that most students have no real connecting thread between their two analyses; often Saturday is handled as one list of typical activities, Sunday as a different one. What's significant about the sample above is that this student unites his composition by describing *the same series of events* in both paragraphs. In effect, both days are identical in that he awakens, gets out of bed, goes down the stairs, considers breakfast, then leaves for the day's activities. In this way, the two days are actually very comparable. The irony comes, of course, in his contrasting outlook each day: Saturday is joyous, Sunday is bleak. By altering the connotations of the verbs in the two paragraphs—sun *pouring* bars of golden liquid versus being *blinded* by the glare of the sun, *springing* down stairs versus *stumbling, throwing* on clothes versus *clawing* his way out of bed—the writer achieves a strong *implied* contrast.

Since I can count on the fact that most students will not know how to design paragraphs with this *parallel construction*, I use this particular model on the overhead projector to demonstrate one effective option in designing comparison/contrast essays. *Parallel sequencing* gives a paper built-in organization. If a student sets out to contrast himself with Holden Caulfield, for example, he would do well to use identical situations as a basis for comparison. If he describes Holden's attitude toward school, he should describe his own position; if he analyzes Holden's handling of depression, he should certainly disclose his own mood management. The similarities and differences between the two individuals will then evolve naturally.

For the next assignment, I have students practice this parallel construction by having them develop the *telling* sentence, "My mother is different from my father." I ask for two paragraphs designed in parallel sequence. Here are two student samples:

TELLING SENTENCE:
My mother is different from my father.

My mom was sitting hunched over in front of her sewing machine, working on a dress or something. She worked steadily and silently, paying no attention to anything around her. Needles, patterns, and scissors lay on the sewing machine within her reach.

My dad stood by his work bench holding a piece of a carburetor up to the light. Whistling almost constantly, he walked to and fro, collecting tools as he needed them. Scattered all over the bench were tools and parts already used.

—John Jensen

This writer describes the differences in his parents' hobbies and the way they perform them: his mother works silently, completely engrossed in her sewing; his father works audibly, whistling and moving as he goes along. The unifying thread between the two characters is their fondness for their individual hobbies. Though this composition is rather short, it fulfills the assignment nicely. The student demonstrates his understanding of the parallel sequence.

Here is a longer model.

TELLING SENTENCE:
My mother is different from my father.

Even though my eyes were on the road, I could tell she was smiling. She knew that she shouldn't smile and laugh when I tell a dirty joke, but she had thought it was funny. My mom and I drove in silence for a while, thinking about the joke; then I asked her a question and the conversation flowed once again. We talked unhesitatingly about my friends, school, or anything else that might be weighing down our thoughts. We talked as friends.

The heavy silence was broken as I reached over and clicked on the radio as I drove, my father sitting in the passenger seat of our Volkswagen bug. Even though the radio played, there was still the uncomfortable silence one feels when he thinks he should say something but he can't think of anything to say. First he would talk, asking a question or commenting on something, then I would answer. Then another stretch of silence would engulf us—drown us. We talked in uncontrolled, unpredictable spurts as if desperate just to break the strangling void between us.

—Jenny Reed

This model shows the dramatic effect that parallel construction can have on a piece of writing. By situating her parents alone, next to her in the car, she provides a dramatic setting that enables her to contrast the two characters while dealing with only one at a time. The common point of reference is the car, but more symbolically, their spiritual proximity to their daughter.

To ensure that students understand the technique, I ask them to practice parallel sequence once again for the following night's homework. For this assignment I let students devise their own *telling* sentences. The models that follow show three slightly different approaches to parallel sequence. In the first model, the student shows the difference between his geography and English teachers through a careful, point-by-point analysis. Another student contrasts her Spanish and geometry teachers by parallel presentation of a single personality difference. In the third model, the writer describes a variety of characteristics as she contrasts her two dogs.

TELLING SENTENCE:
My geography teacher is different from my English teacher.

Uttering phony excuses, my geography teacher straggles into class five minutes late with a newspaper stuffed under one arm. Dragging a chair up to his desk scattered with papers, coffee cups, and last Sunday's comics, he slouches into his seat and paws through the disaster on his desk for the day's assignment. Crying "Eureka, I found 'em," he yanks some papers from the depths of the mess, volunteers someone to hand them out, puts his feet up on his desk, and settles down to read the newspaper for the rest of the period.

My English teacher is in class early, sitting stiffly in her chair with the day's assignment already in hand. The moment the tardy bell sounds, she sharply states "Class has begun," causing everyone to stop talking and focus their complete attention on her. Rising formally from her seat behind her immaculate desk, complete with a stapler, Scotch tape, a ruler, paper clips, erasers, pencils, and pens, she personally distributes the assignments. Once done, with an ominous glance at the class, she stiffly sits back down to grade papers with her unmerciful red pen.

—Brent Sprowl

TELLING SENTENCE:
My Spanish teacher is different from my geometry teacher.

As my Spanish teacher handed out progress reports, I prayed that she would somehow miraculously skip over me this time. But to my disappointment, there she stood a few moments later, with that wide-toothed grin of hers that resembles that of the Cheshire cat. She seemed to thrive on the chance of ruining someone's weekend by sentencing them to bring home those belittling "snitch" notices. And I swear her eyes seemed to light up with an almost triumphant excitement as we all grumpily signed our reports at the bottom as instructed.

Funny though, because my geometry teacher had seemed

genuinely sorry about the progress reports he gave out. Just handing them out seemed to put him into a somber mood, as if he had somehow failed in educating us. As each new report would surface, he would call us up individually and explain to us why we were getting a report and what we could do to raise our grade. He seemed to understand our point of view about our almost certain punishment to come from our panicky parents, worrying that they were raising terrible juvenile delinquent children who got progress reports. So he would always include a good comment about our strong points. He seemed to hate giving progress reports almost as much as we hated to get them.

—Kathy Olsen

TELLING SENTENCE:
My dog B.J. is different from my dog Pal.

My dog B.J., a year-old black labrador, upon command comes running through the house, tennis ball in mouth, and running over like a bulldozer on new asphalt. I lie there with her pink tongue licking me like a child does a lollipop. It's really disgusting. I look into the living room and see her dog bowl and food scattered all over the brown, plush carpet. She runs down the hall and comes galloping back with one of my new black pumps in her mouth, the heel all deformed and raggedy. She drops it and runs to play.

Pal, a sedate seven-year-old Doberman pinscher/German shepherd mix, comes clicking across the ceramic tile to see me. He sniffs my hand and nudges his muzzle against me as a sign to pet him. He picks up the ball that B.J. dropped and carries it back to his dog bowl, the food neat and still in place.

B.J. comes trampling inside from the garden and carrying a small bush that my mother had just planted. She drops it on the linoleum and looks at me with her mud-streaked tongue hanging out, and grabs ahold of Pal's tail, chewing. Pal looks at me with his big brown eyes and if he could talk I know he'd tell me, "This is so degrading."

—Kelly Debelak

I am not revealing here only the best papers in the class; once students learn this technique of organization, their writing improves dramatically. When I begin reading aloud sample papers, students are so captivated by the writing quality that they encourage me to read *everyone's* aloud! Obviously I don't have time to read 35 renditions. Instead, I distribute copies of them around the room, asking students to write individual comments and volunteer particularly memorable pieces to be read aloud.

The next preliminary comparison/contrast exercise introduces a more challenging technique: *the integrated comparison.* In this structure, the writer must weave back and forth within a single paragraph, disclosing similarities and differences at the same time. Without becoming monotonous in this zigzag fashion, "A is like this, while B is like this; A does this, but B does that," the writer learns how to emphasize the points of comparison. The class first examines a sample paragraph using integrated comparison, such as the following description of two unusual birds:

> There are two species of Sooty Albatrosses (Brown and Antarctic), both of which are quite similar in appearance. They both have dark plumage, a long, wedge-shaped tail, and long wings that are very narrow. On the underside of its body, however, the Antarctic Sooty Albatross has paler plumage than the Brown Albatross, and it flies less gracefully. On their bills, both species have a groove called a *sulcus*, which divides the lower segment of the bill; but, the sulcus of the Brown Albatross is yellow or orange, whereas the narrower sulcus of the Antarctic species is blue. For nests, both species build up a low cone of earth, hollowed out on top.[1]

The emphasis of this paragraph is on the distinguishing differences between two very similar birds. In contrast to the A-in-one-paragraph, B-in-the-other sequence, where a writer simply presents parallel descriptions and leaves the reader to extract the similarities and differences, this integrated structure demands that the writer make explicit the points of comparison. In the albatross paragraph, for example, had the writer devoted one paragraph to the Brown Albatross and another to the Antarctic, the reader might have had to reread both paragraphs to extract the major differences. This integrated structure is particularly effective, then, when we wish to emphasize to our reader a particular conclusion about the differences or similarities in two separate items. With this structure, the writer *interprets* the set of data and announces that interpretation outright to his or her audience.

Next, we examine the use of the *transitional expressions* that improve the coherence of the paragraph and make the contrasts clear. In the integrated comparison, a writer must use these expressions more frequently than in the parallel A-B structure. So, I list on the board for discussion additional expressions that signal similarity or difference:

TRANSITIONS FOR SIMILARITY	TRANSITIONS FOR CONTRAST
similarly	but
likewise	however
equally	on the contrary
in the same way	on the other hand
in addition	while
also	whereas
too	in contrast

Finally, we discuss the economy of compiling sets of characteristics into a single paragraph. If a writer has only a few details, the single structure works

---

1. Norman A. Britten, *A Writing Apprenticeship*, 4th ed. (New York: Holt, Rinehart and Winston, 1977), p. 149.

best; a larger body of necessary and interesting details calls for more paragraphs, most likely in the parallel A-B structure.

At this point, after close examination of the albatross paragraph, I ask my students to imitate the structure of that paragraph, supplying their own items for comparison. Their *telling* sentence becomes: "There are two kinds of _____, (X and Y), both of which are quite similar in _____." I want them to replicate the sentence patterns in the albatross paragraph as precisely as possible. I want students to acquire the *feel* of a tightly organized paragraph, in this case a comparison, using transitions to disclose similarity and difference. This assignment requires that during pre-writing, each writer discover the distinguishing differences of his or her chosen comparison in order to be able to imitate the albatross format. The writer may use the same transitional expressions and create descriptive phrases similar to the model paragraph ("are quite similar in appearance," "on the underside of its . . .," "whereas . . ."), or may even duplicate the exact structure and sequence, part of speech for part of speech. The process is the same as for the modeling and imitation I described in chapter 5, "Variations for the Daily Workouts."

Following are two student imitations of the albatross pattern:

FROSTED MINI-WHEATS

There are two flavors of Frosted Mini-Wheats (brown-sugar and cinnamon), both of which are quite equal in nutritional supplements. They both are made from 100% whole wheat, have frosting on one side only, and cost the same amount of money. On the frosted side of the wheat biscuit, however, the sugar coated Mini-Wheat has a smoother and lighter texture than that of the cinnamon frosted wheat biscuit, and it has a sweeter taste. On the uncoated side of the Mini-Wheats, both biscuits have hundreds of criss-crossed wheat fibers; but the fibers on the cinnamon coated biscuit are darker, whereas the smaller fibered, brown sugar coated Mini-Wheat is lighter in color. For breakfast, both flavors of Frosted Mini-Wheats give one a good supply of daily nutritional needs.

—Jan Galloway

TENNIS

There are two ways of playing tennis (singles and doubles), both of which are played using similar techniques. They are both played on a regular tennis court, scored the same way, and require the same amount of skill. When playing singles, however, one needs to cover more area of the court due to the fact there's only one player. In the serving procedures, both the singles and the doubles players must serve the ball into the same area; but the doubles players stand one at the net and one at the baseline while serving, whereas the singles player stands alone at the baseline. In order to be good, both types of tennis require a lot of practice and dedication.

—Kelly Look

Upon completion of this exercise, each writer is required to read his or her paper aloud. Because the paragraphs are short, this reading takes practically no time. After listening to some thirty imitations, the students have probably internalized the transitional shifts that create the smooth-running texture of the integrated comparison paragraph. In addition, they begin to grasp the usefulness of more sophisticated punctuation: parentheses—"(Brown and Antarctic)"—for incorporating a list within a sentence, and the semicolon for joining closely related sentences that together draw a comparison or make a contrast.

In the follow-up assignment, I ask students to develop the *telling* sentence "My _____ teacher is different from my _____ teacher," using the integrated comparison. I want to see whether or not students can make use of this structure when developing ideas of their own; I want to see whether or not their having imitated the albatross paragraph has influenced their ability to create their own integrated comparisons. Here is a student model; notice how it differs from the earlier paper on the same topic, written in parallel structure.

> **My French teacher and my U.S. history teacher are both working Foothill High School teachers. They are both polite, considerate, and helpful when they are not teachers; between classes or after school has ended, they ask about students' problems and encourage students to continue to get good grades. But when they are confronted by uncooperative students in class, they act differently. My U.S. history teacher becomes rude, loud, and mean as her jaws clench and her face turns ugly from loudly berating the class. My French teacher becomes quietly distressed, calm, and patiently waits for cooperation as her lips silently purse and her eyes stare at the ceiling. Teaching causes teachers to become Jekylls and Hydes.**
>
> **—Wendy Yee**

In this response, the writer integrates both similarities and differences. After mentioning the courtesy and friendliness both teachers display with students outside the school environment, she emphasizes their personality changes *within* the school environment. The significant difference appears when the writer shows how each teacher tolerates misbehavior. While one becomes "rude, loud, and mean," the other becomes "distressed," but calmly and patiently waits for the behavior to alter. Finally the writer grips the reader with her forceful ending: "Teaching causes teachers to become Jekylls and Hydes." With this conclusion, she in effect issues a new, more refined *telling* sentence based on the significant differences of these two instructors. In place of the assigned sentence, "My French teacher is different from my U.S. history teacher," she has created a better, more specific generalization. In fact, I have noticed that students often end up with superior generalizations after they have worked on developing simplistic ones; through the act of explaining to themselves the meaning of an abstract concept, students often clarify the idea, focus it into a more crystallized form. In this way, they are learning to interpret a body of ideas more deeply, more critically.

Here is another example of a student's discovering a better *telling* sentence as a result of having synthesized his ideas into a single *integrated comparison.* For this assignment I posed the following telling sentence: "Though Fitzgerald's and Hemingway's stories start out similarly, they end up rather differently." This assignment came after thorough discussions of *The Great Gatsby* and *The Sun Also Rises.*

> *The Great Gatsby* and *The Sun Also Rises* start at the same point and end up with two different solutions to a problem which is virtually the same. Both men, Jay Gatsby and Jake Barnes, have a dependency problem on a woman whom they cannot have. Upon finally coming to grips with this reality, Gatsby is destroyed while Jake grows within himself. The drastically different endings seem to indicate that Fitzgerald felt that it was wrong to hold onto an unattainable dream for so long, and that only disaster could stem from staring at one "green beacon" and ignoring the rest of one's life. Hemingway shared this idea, but expressed that it was never too late to change, and that after you have made all your mistakes and stumbled in ignorance, the sun also rises, and there is a new day in which new opportunities can be found.
>
> —Pat Terry

This integrated comparison is effective because it states specifically what makes both plots similar—the hero's dependency on a woman—and shows also the resulting, contrasting outcomes—one man dies; the other moves on. The student then concludes something, interprets the meaning of these differences: that perhaps one author felt there was little redemption in holding onto a dream for too long, while the other believed there was always time to change. This writer has seen the value of summarizing the points of his examples. He has given meaning to the abstraction that "each author is different."

Another practice assignment for this unit—sometimes the last before the final essay—requires students to compare and contrast pairs of words that have similar denotations but varying connotations. Besides providing students another chance to rehearse structure, this exercise also requires them to explore the precise definitions of words. I present the class with a list like the following:

WORDS WITH SIMILAR DENOTATION AND CONTRASTING CONNOTATION

rebel/revolutionary	curiosity/nosiness
wisdom/knowledge	skinny/trim
pride/conceit	nuts/insane
attractive/beautiful	jealousy/envy
hate/dislike	brainy/intelligent
rug/carpet	lady/chick

Students select one of these pairs for the writing assignment. If students prefer to compare a pair of words not listed, I allow them to choose their own, provided they clear the words with me first. I need to make certain that the pair represents the proper combination of similar denotation and contrasting connotation. One very successful student paper from this assignment follows.

LADY—CHICK

A lady and a chick, while both representing the female sex, have many contrasting attributes. In fact, it is not likely that one would find them together. A lady, for instance, might be found in a shaded parlor reading Shakespeare or on the verandah sipping a cool drink. A lady is respected and admired, from afar by men, and in loving friendship by women. Even her physical appearance bespeaks refinement. Her hair may be pulled neatly back from her face, revealing well-scrubbed skin and clear, bright eyes. She presents a soft, smooth voice at all times, no matter what may ruffle the serenity of the moment. At times, however, a refined laugh may escape from rosy lips showing pearly white teeth.

A chick represents a different group of the female sex. She has the normal attributes of a woman, but what she does with them is the deciding difference between her and a lady. The chick might be seen on a hot Saturday afternoon slinking down the street, poured into tight jeans that have seen better days. Slogans like "I'll try anything once" or "So many men, so little time" adorn the front of her shrink-to-fit T-shirt. She, too, may be admired by men, though in contrast with the lady, *not* from afar. The chick's appearance, like the lady's, is representative of her personal attitudes and values. She may look out on the world through frizzy, unkempt bangs, her eyes ringed with last week's eye makeup. Whereas the highest compliment to a lady may be a whispered word from the most eligible bachelor in town, a chick receives her compliments from total strangers in roaring cars who wolf-whistle as they screech by.

After a long day of socially acceptable activities, visits, trips to the library, cooking lessons, the lady comes home. About the same time, the chick flops down on her waterbed after a long guitar-playing session in the park. Now they both like to think a bit. If one could hear their thoughts at this moment, one may understand one very important similarity. The lady's secret wish is to be blatantly whistled at and the chick thinks how nice it would be to just once be called a lady.

—Lisa Andersen

This student's essay is effective because she uses the structures we discussed in class appropriately. She uses A-in-one-paragraph (discussing the lady) and B-in-the-next-paragraph (showing the chick). In addition, she matches characteristic detail for characteristic detail (parallelism). If she mentions the lady's pulling her hair "neatly back from her face, revealing well-scrubbed skin and clear bright eyes," she counters that description in paragraph B with the chick's looking "out on the world through frizzy, unkempt bangs, her eyes ringed with last week's eye makeup."

The writer also successfully employs the integrated comparison (A, however B). In the middle of the second paragraph, she shifts into distinguishing or emphasizing the most interesting differences. She begins weaving back and forth between lady and chick, saying, "Whereas the highest compliment to a lady may be a whispered word from the most eligible bachelor in town, a chick receives her compliments from total strangers in roaring cars who wolf-whistle as they screech by."

Her last paragraph also uses the integrated comparison to bring the essay to an especially effective climax. She continues identifying major differences between the lady and the chick, then jolts the reader with her final ironic revelation. This stunning turning point indicates that both females long for a little of what the other has, a revelation highlighting the similarities between the two characters.

I believe that most comparison/contrast assignments work toward the discovery of this sort of irony. Two items that seem so dissimilar on the surface are often discovered to have properties in common, and items that appear to be identical show more contrast when examined more carefully. Students come to discover this sort of irony as they practice again and again drawing conclusions about their comparisons. I do not tell them in advance that comparison/contrast often produces irony; I prefer to let them discover this through repeated practice. With this discovery, they are perhaps in a better position to plot out their final assignments. They have, it is hoped, learned the effectiveness of drawing such parallels and contrasts.

Another student takes a different approach in designing his word-contrast essay. Rather than lecture about the characteristic differences between a rug and a carpet, he delivers his interpretation by narrating a fictitious story, the subject of which discloses the distinctions he sees between the two forms of floor covering.

RUG—CARPET

As I drove up to the unfamiliar landscape of the early twentieth century house, I had a feeling that this was not going to be one of my best days. As I was told by my boss, the key to the house was in the mailbox. I walked up to the ominous door and turned the key. The door opened and two decades of stale air blasted up my nostrils. I fought my way into the house, past the wall of air, to see the one sight I had hoped not to see. I had been sent by my boss to put new carpet in the ancient house. The sight before me was the rug that had been put in the house when it was built. Before I put the new carpet in, I had to remove the old rug.

I set to my work, beginning to pull out the old rug. The rug was holey and was almost ready to fall apart from the amount of dust and grime built up over the years. I pulled up the rug at one of the corners, only to be cut by one of the rusty staples around the edges. I knew there had been a dog living in the house because the smell of old urine made me gag as it was released in the air with each tug. There was mold growing on the bottom of the rug from water that had been spilled a long time before. I finally succeeded in pulling out the ancient rug and gladly took it out of the house.

I dragged the new carpet from my truck into the house and cut it to the size I needed. The carpet had just been received from the manufacturer, so it had that certain freshness that comes with newly woven yarn. The smell of the carpet was like that of a load of newly washed clothes. The clean carpet was now ready to be put into the house. I stapled down the edges of the stiff material with ease. The handling and installation of this new stock was a breeze compared to the pulling up of the old smelly rug. I stood back to look at my masterpiece which had turned the old dump of a house into an honorable mansion.

The carpet was so new and clean it outclassed the old rug. It was like comparing a royal cloak to the ragged jacket of a beggar. In time, the new carpet will become an old rug, because one cannot stop time from taking its toll, not even on new carpet.

—John Gregerson

Again, this writer makes use of both parallel and integrated structures to make his points. In the first half of his story he shows the texture, smell, and condition of the rug; in the second half, when he installs the new carpet, he is careful to describe those qualities, too. The smell of dog urine is contrasted with the smell of recently washed clothes. The old rug, "ready to fall apart," is certainly different from the new stiff version. At the end of the piece, the writer delivers the ironic notion that it is only a matter of time before a carpet will age and become like the old rug, "the ragged jacket of a beggar." Here the writer integrates his thinking, joining similarities and differences together.

Although there are certainly other and perhaps more accurate interpretations of the word *rug* as contrasted with *carpet*, for instance, *throw rug* or *area rug* as opposed to *wall-to-wall carpet*, this student's creative response is still acceptable for it develops a common association with the word *rug*—that we are likely to choose a less flattering word than *carpet* to describe a once lovely but now worn piece of floor covering.

Finally, here is an essay written to contrast the words *curiosity* and *nosiness*. This writer, like the previous one, also creates a scenario to dramatize the difference between the two terms.

CURIOSITY—NOSINESS

The mirrored door of the medicine chest is ajar and the drawer beside the bathroom sink isn't securely closed. A hand towel is crumpled into a damp heap on the counter and the hot water is slowly dripping, wasted, down the sink. The party brought many people through the bathroom; some wanted to "freshen up," some to throw up, and most merely to relieve themselves. Alone in the bathroom, behind a locked door, there were two kinds of guests—the curious and the nosy.

The worried person searching for another roll of toilet paper and the pre-teen hunting for mouthwash or toothpaste were curious, out of necessity. The first person didn't look to see if the spare roll was Charmin or bargain brand. He didn't care. The twelve-year-old eating toothpaste out of the tube was only concerned with getting the smell of Budweiser off his breath. He didn't even notice whether or not the cap was off the tube. Curiosity left the little smudgy fingerprints on the mirror and checked the scale after eating all those Ruffles loaded with onion dip. And it was only a curious little guest who went in the shower to figure out how to work the faucet and to find out if one could see out of the glass shower door.

The nosybody peeked into the bathtub to see if the harried hostess had skipped over a bathtub ring. Like comparison shoppers, nosies sniffed the towels for the "Downey fresh smell" and fussed over the soap, trying to guess whether it was the remains of a bar of Safeguard or expensive perfumed guest soap. They read labels on prescriptions in the medicine chest and formed opinions on their host's heart condition and whether or not their hostess was on Valium. Nosiness "borrowed" lipstick and mascara and noticed if the towels didn't match.

Throughout the night, this bathroom door had opened to the symphony of rumbling water pipes and guests had emerged feeling a trifle better, make-up repaired, bladder emptied, or stomach as the case may be, or hands washed for dinner. Once they left that bathroom, the curious forgot the taste of the Crest and the nosy no longer cared if the towels were Downey fresh. Back in the midst of the party, people ate, drank and were merry once more. Only behind the closed bathroom door did curiosity and nosiness define themselves into terms so clear.

Simple and basic interests such as understanding an unfamiliar faucet mechanism or the need for finding more toilet paper motivate a curious person to peek around a strange bathroom. The driving force that makes a nosy person snoop is the satisfaction he gets from being included, in a perverse sort of way, in somebody else's business—somebody else's bathroom. Knowing the deepest, darkest secrets of his host's medicine chest makes the nosy person feel important—part of the family almost—when he finds they use the same brand of shampoo as he, or makes him feel superior when he finds they need to rely on tranquilizers to get through their lives.

—Tegan McLane

In this case the parallelism occurs through the common setting—the bathroom at a party. Notice how the actions within the room, behind closed doors, do not necessarily parallel each other. Using the scale and browsing through the medicine chest do not appear in both paragraphs; actually very few of the private gestures match, but they don't have to. The way people handle themselves within the confines of the same setting proves the contrast sufficiently. Here then is another way of using parallel sequence—providing a common experience from which to disclose contrasting behaviors. Finally, notice the writer's careful attention to interpretation. In her conclusion she points out that the curious seem to operate out of innocent interest or even necessity, while the nosy enjoy feeling accepted by or superior to other people.

Contrasting Illusion/Reality

If the major comparison/contrast assignment I have in mind for the class involves the theme of illusion and reality in *The Great Gatsby*, students complete one last preparatory exercise before writing their final essay. For this assignment, I ask them to write about personal experiences that demonstrate how reality does not always live up to fantasy. I want them to be composing this at the same time we are moving through the novel; if they reflect on their own lives as they read about the lives of the characters, they are likely to understand the character's condition more deeply. As a model for this assignment, I have students read the following excerpt from *Life on the Mississippi* by Mark Twain. In this short piece, Twain shares two contrasting visions of the Mississippi River.

THE MISSISSIPPI

Now when I had mastered the language of this water [as a pilot], and had come to know every trifling feature that bordered the great river as familiarly as I knew the letters of the alphabet, I had made a valuable acquisition. But I had lost something, too. I had lost something which could never be restored to me while I lived. All the grace, the beauty, the poetry had gone out of the majestic river! I still keep in mind a certain wonderful sunset which I witnessed when steamboating was new to me. A broad expanse of the river was turned to blood; in the middle distance the red hue brightened into gold, through which a solitary log came floating, black and conspicuous; in one place a long, slanting mark lay sparkling upon the water; in another the surface was broken by boiling, tumbling rings, that were as many-tinted as an opal; where the ruddy flush was faintest, was a smooth spot that was covered with graceful circles and radiating lines, ever so delicately traced; the shore on our left was densely wooded, and the somber shadow that fell from this forest was broken on one place by a long, ruffled trail that shone like silver; and high above the forest wall a clean-stemmed dead tree waved a single leafy bough that glowed like a flame in the unobstructed splendor that was flowing from the sun. There were graceful curves, reflected images, woody heights, soft distances; and over the whole scene, far and near, the dissolving lights drifted steadily, enriching it every passing moment with new marvels of coloring.

I stood like one bewitched. I drank it in, in a speechless rapture. The world was new to me, and I had never seen anything like this at home. But as I have said, a day came when I began to cease from noting the glories and the charms which the moon and the sun and the twilight wrought upon the river's face; another day came when I ceased altogether to note them. Then, if that sunset scene had been repeated, I should have looked upon it without rapture, and should have commented upon it, inwardly, after this fashion: This sun means that we are going to have wind tomorrow; that floating log means that the river is rising, small thanks to it; that slanting mark on the water refers to a bluff reef which is going to kill somebody's steamboat one of these nights, if it keeps on stretching out like that; those tumbling "boils" show a dissolving bar and a changing channel there; the lines and circles in the slick water over yonder are a warning that that troublesome place is shoaling up dangerously; that silver streak in the shadow of the forest is the "break" from a new snag, and he has located himself in the very best place he could have found to fish for steamboats; that tall dead tree, with a single living branch, is not going to last long, and then how is a body ever going to get through this blind place at night without the friendly old landmark?

No, the romance and beauty were all gone from the river. All the value any feature of it had for me now was the amount of usefulness it could furnish toward compassing the safe piloting of a steamboat. . . .[2]

In this piece, Twain *begins* with his interpretation or his conclusion, then reminds us of the contrast again at the closing—that the original vision of the romance and beauty of the river had changed, leaving only the "usefulness it could furnish toward compassing the safe piloting of a steamboat." In the middle of the piece, Twain contrasts the two visions, using parallel sequence: if he mentions the jewel-like quality of the water's surface, "the red hue brightened into gold, through which a solitary log came floating, black and conspicuous; in one place a long, slanting mark lay sparkling upon the water; in another the surface was broken by boiling, tumbling rings that were as many-tinted as an opal;" he counters in the next paragraph with the more practical considerations: "This sun means that we are going to have wind tomorrow; that floating log means that the river is rising . . .; that slanting mark on the water refers to a bluff reef which is going to kill somebody's steamboat one of these nights . . .; those tumbling 'boils' show a dissolving bar and a changing channel. . . ." Twain's piece serves as an excellent model to help students prepare their essays because it reinforces both the parallel sequence and the integrated comparison; students see a well-known writer using these same strategies they have been practicing.

Here is one result of this assignment, a humorous student essay contrasting the illusion and reality of owning his first car.

WHAT A NIGHTMARE
(OR HOW TO LIVE WITH A *MINI* MUSCLE CAR)

And ever since that day . . . Oh, hi. I was just telling these people about my new car; you see it? Over there, behind that green station wagon. No, not the Cadillac, the other one. Yeah, that little Volkswagen that looks like an Army surplus mini tank. Why would I own a car like *that*, you say? Well, why don't you just pull up a chair with these nice people and I'll start my story from the beginning.

When I was little I had always dreamt about owning my own car. Maybe a sleek, bullet-like sports car or a large powerful

---

2. Samuel Langhorne Clemens, *Life on the Mississippi* (1883), Signet Classics (New York: The New American Library, 1961), pp. 67-8.

muscle car with enough brute force to blow the gates off Fort Knox. But until last July I had never had the chance to own my very own dream machine. Nor had I made up my mind as to what kind of car I would most like to buy.

I have always daydreamed about the most perfect and extravagant car I could ever own. One would fall head over heels if he would ever purchase the car about which I had so fondly fantasized. I would begin with one of the two most sought after muscle cars in history, a Mustang Mach I or a '57 Chevy. Into one of these I would drop a 454 Chevy engine with titanium valves and pistons. I would then place upon this massively mountainous mound of majestic metal an aluminum Edelbrock intake manifold. As its counterpart in crime I would add a Holley four-barrel carburetor. As no great undertaking should end, I would slap on a pair of Hooker headers to top off my fantastic, featherlight, fireball of a power-pac. As a finishing touch I would place in this awesome auto an all-aluminum Hurst four speed "Lightning Rod" transmission. I dreamt about this car day and night, making mental images of it in my mind.

It finally arrived—the day I would be able to buy my own car and turn it into a mean street machine. It was a hot summer day in July. My father, who is a mechanic at Shamrock Ford, came home from work and said that they took a car in on a trade at the shop and that he could buy it for a low price. My eyes got as big as balloon tires. Without hesitation, I said, "Yes, I want it; how much?" I didn't even know what kind of car it was; I was too caught up in just buying it. The phrase that was to follow dropped in my heart like a lead weight. It was as if my life had ended and the world was as lifeless as a black velvet coat in a darkened closet. My father said, "Now hold on a minute; let me tell you about it first. For one, it's a '72 Volkswagen Super Beetle with a few dents, ripped seats, a bad radio, and it needs a new generator. I can buy it for $55 and we can use the generator out of our other Volkswagen to replace the burnt out one. Now what do you want to do?" After I thought about what I could do with it for a while, I gave him my answer. I told him I would buy it, fix it up, and possibly sell it for enough to buy the car of my dreams.

When he brought it home the next week, I couldn't believe my eyes. It was hideous! It was a faded red color with crash marks in the back and the left front fender. It looks like someone threw rocks at it from a bridge while the car was going 60 mph, if it could go that fast. The interior was, if possible, in even worse shape. The back seat, of which half was missing, was torn beyond recognition. The front seats looked as if they had just exploded. Well, if one would take the Hefty bags off them, he could try his best to recognize them as such. After seeing this, my hopes and dreams were shattered forever.

I've had this "car" now for about three months, and when I look back on its former appearance, all I can do is laugh. If one could see a picture of it now as compared to then, he would have to wipe his eyes and look again. It now boasts a fine running, clean engine, new mags and tires, new upholstery, and as of this week, a desert camouflage paint job. I put in a stereo a few days ago but it is an old one. It still works great, but my speakers are shot and as soon as the stereo is replaced I might consider this my new dream car. I figure by the time I receive my license next month, this car will be exactly the way I want it to be. I guess you could call this a sort of riches to rags to riches type of story!

Hey guys, wake up! Damn, they fell asleep during the best part; I was just about to tell them about my dream *house*.

—Andy Persson

Andy points out the difference between illusion and reality almost exclusively with *showing* details. Through parallel construction, he sets up the perfect vision of his dream car, then counters beautifully with the more sobering description of his actual first purchase. As he moves from his initial, startled reaction to the used Volkswagen ("It looks like someone threw rocks at it from a bridge. . . . The front seats looked as if they had just exploded.") to his reconditioning work ("It now boasts a fine running, clean engine, new mags and tires, new upholstery, and . . . a desert camouflage paint job."), we feel his gradual change in feeling toward the "new" automobile. He is carefully preparing the reader for his brief though significant conclusion: "I guess you could call this a sort of riches to rags to riches type of story!" Without directly stating it, the writer implies that *he*—without necessarily anticipating the outcome—has seen a dream shattered, then rebuilt through his own diligent and careful laboring. The original, glorified vision is transformed into a more realistic achievement. Ironically, his "new car" ends up retaining the magic of his former vision; we get the feeling that he is almost more in love with his "surplus mini tank" than with the "Mustang Mach I." If Andy had stated this conclusion directly, something like "Although both cars are certainly different in design and power capability, I learned that I could make a dream machine out of any beat-up leftover," he would have ruined the appeal of his "riches to rags to riches" line. Therefore, his closing interpretation, though subtle, is certainly powerful enough. With his next line, when he suggests we might have fallen asleep during his story, he insinuates that we might have preferred a more glamorous ending to the "fairytale." But we also get the feeling that he is not disappointed, but rather excited with discovering a valuable lesson about perseverance—so much so that he is moved to tell us about the tale of his "dream *house*." Here he implies that he perhaps learned a similar lesson, transforming an overrated vision into a simpler reality.

The Final Expository Essay

Through all these preparatory exercises, let's not forget where the students are headed. At the same time that we've been exploring and practicing these alternatives to comparison/contrast structure, we've been reading and discussing the assigned novel. In fact, I have assigned students to panels that lead the class in discussion of the reading. Panelists invent their own provocative questions, asking the rest of us to respond. This way of organizing a discussion proves quite effective because students enjoy being authoritative. They also seem to spend more time analyzing the text because they want their questions to be challenging for the rest of us. (I also spend some time leading my own discussions, particularly when I feel some major points have been overlooked or when I want to introduce a provocative idea.)

When the novel has been read and thoroughly discussed in class, I make the final composition assignment. Students have known all along that the paper will involve comparison/contrast thinking; by now they are ready to structure a longer paper along those lines.

Here is one student's essay in response to the assignment to compare Jay Gatsby's quest for Daisy Buchanan with the quest for the American dream.

TWO DREAMS

When the founders of this country came to the new world, they were looking for a fresh start. They were looking for the fulfillment of a dream; searching for a place where they could start a new life and shape a better future. Their ideals were high, and they were spiritually enriched by the promise that this new land, America, seemed to hold for them. Gatsby, too, is like these early explorers. Just as the "green breast of the new world" promised new hope for the explorers, so does the "single green light, minute and far away" promise to Gatsby that he may obtain his dream.

So Gatsby's dream, to win the love of his fantasy girl, starts out fresh and pure like the dream of the new explorers. However, Gatsby becomes enamored with the idea that the money will win her love, and from this point on, his dreams will begin to decay and eventually crumble. So hungry to obtain his money is Gatsby, that he goes about it illegally. "He and his friend, Wolfscheim, bought up a lot of side-street drugstores here and in Chicago, and sold grain alcohol over the counter." He tries to win his girl by impressing her with a display of money. His house, "a colossal affair by any standard," and all the furnishings therein—"Marie Antoinette music-rooms and period bedrooms swathed in rose and lavender silk, shirts piled like bricks (as is gold) that lost their folds as he tossed them, and covered the table in a many colored disarray," were bought and displayed solely in the hopes of attracting her. "Can't repeat the past? Of course you can, old sport!" Gatsby also believes that with his money he can recapture the past and the innocence of youth.

In these views, Gatsby is demonstrating the characteristics of the American dream. Obsessed with materialism, Americans now believe money can buy love, happiness, and can forever capture youth and beauty. Hence they buy expensive cars and wave big bankrolls to impress prospective mates. They shower themselves with jewelry, wear status-label clothes, go to lavish parties, and take trips to Hawaii in order to be happy. They spend thousands of dollars on make-up, hair restorers, wrinkle creams, exercise equipment, and memberships in exclusive European health spas; all in order to keep that image of youth and beauty. Just as this country is supremely confident that money can buy anything or solve any problem, so was Gatsby confident that money could fulfill his dream.

Ironically, Gatsby's obsession with materialism eventually destroys him. His car, "a rich, cream color, bright with nickel, and swollen here and there in its monstrous length with hat-boxes and supper-boxes," is the ultimate American status symbol of money and affluence. It eventually causes his death. Not only does the car, symbolizing money and materialism, cause Gatsby's death, but also Myrtle and George Wilson's, who were only fringe acquaintances. Their deaths symbolize the destruction that money can bring to those only remotely connected with it.

This parallels the moral decay and destruction of American society because of the obsession with money. Americans have become so engrossed in material aspects—big houses, two cars in every garage, two television sets, three telephones—that they have let spiritual goals and morals disintegrate in the race to "keep up with the Joneses."

In writing this novel, F. Scott Fitzgerald chose Gatsby to symbolize the American experience. Gatsby's dream, starting out as a spiritual quest, "the following of a Grail," and its subsequent corruption, is the personification of the course of the American dream. Fitzgerald wishes to show to us the decline of America, from the fresh "green breast of the new world" to, because of gross materialism, nothing more than a "valley of Ashes."

—Alycia Clatworthy

Like the writer of the dream-car essay, this student makes effective use of parallel sequence but makes more use of integration. She explains, first, the similarity between both dreams. Both begin as a search for a better life—Gatsby will be happier with Daisy; Americans crave comfort and security. "Just as the 'green breast of the new world' promised new hope for the explorers, so does the 'single green light, minute and far away' promise to Gatsby that he may obtain his dream [winning Daisy]." Next, in separate paragraphs she details the course of each dream. Gatsby thinks he needs money to impress Daisy, so he becomes obsessed with getting enough to win her approval. Similarly, Americans think money will buy them the happiness and security they long for.

In an additional set of parallel paragraphs, this student interprets the consequences of each obsession. For Gatsby, money has indirectly caused the death of Myrtle and George Wilson as well as his own, symbolizing the destructive powers of materialism. For Americans, dependence on money for happiness has indirectly allowed "spiritual goals and morals [to] disintegrate in the race to 'keep up with the Joneses.'" Finally, Alycia integrates these likenesses, suggesting how a personal vision might be derived from a larger, collective one—that the corruption of one man's dream is the corruption of all our dreams. Instead of taking the "green breast of the new world" and turning it into a garden of paradise, we have shaped a gross materialism and become "a valley of ashes," an insightful connection between the two dreams.

When I use this unit in conjunction with *The Catcher in the Rye*, students know in advance that they will be asked to compare and contrast their own personalities with that of Holden Caulfield. So, while we're reading the text and while we're regularly practicing ways of developing comparisons, the students are keeping pre-writing lists of similarities and differences. I tell them that whenever they notice a striking similarity or a powerful contrast, they should add it to their lists. This way, when they begin composing the final assignment, they'll have a large body of details upon which to draw.

A student list might look something like the following:

SIMILARITIES

1. Holden becomes bored with school; this happens to me a lot.

2. Holden wants to be on his own in "the big city." I often wish I could go to San Francisco for the weekend and be on my own.

3. Holden wants to appear older than his age; I often feel this way too.

4. Holden becomes depressed constantly. Things like the nuns having beat-up suitcases really makes him feel sorry for them; I know exactly what he means.

5. Holden appreciates the innocence and spontaneity of children; I often look back on my childhood and wish I were still as innocent as I was then.

DIFFERENCES

1. Even though I get bored with school, I stick with it; I couldn't just drop out and run away to San Francisco. I might like to, but I couldn't. My parents would kill me!

2. Holden goes to bars and tries to get served. Although I'd love to try this, I never would; I guess I'm the type who will wait until I'm 21.

3. Holden rarely snaps out of his depressions. I get depressed, but I can bring myself out of it by doing things I like to do and not dwelling on things.

4. Holden never wants childhood to end; he wants to "catch" kids before they fall over the cliff into adulthood. I just can't see that this makes sense. We all have to grow up and learn from experience. Instead of facing the struggles of experience, Holden wants to retreat into childhood.

When the students compose their final papers, they begin seeing the application of the various rhetorical structures we've been practicing. They see that they might set up parallel sequences, citing examples and situations from Holden's experience as well as their own. They see also that they'll need to use the integrated comparison to explain or interpret the differences or similarities. This interpreting is probably the most difficult part of their composing process;

it demands that they *make meaning* from their investigations; they must draw conclusions about their findings. Most students do not develop successful integrations the first time around. Summarizing and tying together the major points takes time and thought. With their rough drafts in hand, students meet in response groups to talk out their ideas and get encouragement and direction. (More information on how response groups can help in this stage of the writing process can be found in section 4, "Training in Revision Techniques.")

Here now is a final comparison/contrast essay written for *The Catcher in the Rye*. Notice how this writer has learned to use the structures presented in the preparatory exercises.

BEING A TEENAGER

Holden Caulfield is the typical teenager. He's lost, like many others, in a huge world and can't find his place. Every teenager at one time or another feels scared from not knowing what the future holds for him. These feelings that Holden feels are shared by most teenagers across the world—including me.

While trying to find himself, Holden looks deep into other people and sees phoniness. He watches people in bars, at school, and at the Lutz's party. "You never saw so many phonies in all your life, everybody smoking their ears off and talking about the play so that everybody could hear and know how sharp they were," Holden reflects.

It seemed, while I was reading the book, that I was looking myself straight in the face. When I'm at a large party, I watch people say things like "How nice it is to see you again!" then duck behind a large group and avoid coming in contact with the person for the rest of the night. Adults tend to do this an awful lot. They try to be polite and not let the person know that they don't like him too much, but instead what they really are doing is hiding their individual personalities and thus melting themselves into society.

Children, on the other hand, rarely act phony. They can go right up to someone and say, "That shirt's ugly" if they feel it is. It may be a bit rude and not too nice, but if an adult was to compliment the shirt, the person might wear the ugly shirt to a formal dinner. Holden and I both feel that because of this freedom children have, they are a special part of this world.

Another reason we look at children so highly is because, as teenagers, we're being torn from childhood to adulthood. When we look at adults and their phony personalities, the carefree happy life of a child is much more appealing, so we tend to envy them, knowing we can't go back. I watch children jump on and off one step for fifteen minutes, and they never seem to get bored. It gives me a happy feeling inside to think that even though I can no longer have fun playing on a single step, somebody can laugh and giggle each time he hops off. Holden feels this way with his sister, Phoebe. One particular example is when Phoebe is on the carousel. Holden reflects, "I felt so damn happy all of a sudden, the way old Phoebe kept going around and around."

It seems as though Holden and I are a lot alike because we dislike adults' phoniness and appreciate children more, but one thing we see differently is change. Holden needs time to figure himself out. It seems to him that everything and everyone is changing—the ducks are gone for winter, and Jane Gallagher has grown up and may no longer leave her kings in the back row to defend herself. Holden wants to stop time because of his fears of the future. Holden shows this best when he talks about the museum he used to go to almost every Saturday.

"The best thing, though, in that museum was that everything always stayed right where it was. Nobody'd move. You could go there a hundred thousand times and that Eskimo would still be just finished catching those two fish, the birds would still be on their way south, the deer would still be drinking out of that same water hole . . . Nobody'd be different."

I can understand Holden's fears for the future because I have them too. I don't know where I'm going after high school. I'll probably end up in some strange college, although school doesn't appeal to me much. The boredom of the everyday routine and the kids who act ridiculous because they don't know how else to act—too young to act like adults, too old to act like children— always seems to turn me off. I feel as though this world is a huge place and I'm just a small speck bound to get stepped on by many pairs of huge feet. The thought of this makes my knees shake a bit, but I don't feel that we should make the world stop like the world of the Eskimo and birds in that museum, because not knowing what lies ahead is exciting, too. Holden, unfortunately, is too scared to see the excitement.

Holden's and my feelings for the future and for adults and children are all formed because of this gap between childhood and adulthood. We are thrown into this space and expected to overcome these frightful feelings by ourselves. The few people society allows us to receive help from—parents and friends—can never seem to get rid of this fright. They just discuss with us our feelings at that moment, whether it be frustration with friends or the lack of freedom, yet they can never seem to get rid of this fear of the future. Most teenagers feel these feelings of fright for the future and confusion about adult personalities, and society refuses to see it, so every generation goes through this in-between space, not knowing and wondering.

—Sherry Ward

This writer analyzes both the similarities and differences between Holden and herself, and she does so quite thoroughly. Her piece is rich with examples both from his life and her own. She organizes her paper neatly around a sequence of parallel structures, weaving back and forth between his attitudes and hers. At first she presents the similarities—in fact we learn later on that she and Holden are, for the most part, very much alike. If she discusses Holden's attitudes toward phoniness, she sides with him by disclosing her own; when she shows his appreciation of children, she gives an example from her own experience to show she agrees with him. By taking several pronounced characteristics one at a time and comparing herself to him, she proves that she really does understand his situation.

At the same time, she moves toward integration, tying together the similarities and differences into a significant revelation—that, though they are both afraid of adulthood and the future, she feels that we shouldn't "make the world stop like the world of the Eskimo and birds in that museum, because not knowing what lies ahead is exciting, too." The significant difference between Holden and Sherry is that he is too frightened to see the excitement in growing up. This conclusion constitutes an insightful closing to her essay; it makes a stunning point.

I would have preferred that this writer show us more of her own excitement toward change; had she given us one or two instances of how she transforms fear into curiosity and excitement, she might have rounded out her piece more effectively. Her final paragraph, for example, is a little weak; she ends up introducing a whole new idea about the way parents counsel teenage problems and doesn't fully develop her point. However, this writer had made so much improvement as she moved from rough to final draft, it made no sense to ask her to revise once again. While I feel it is necessary and right for students to work carefully with revision, if we force them *every time* to make everything perfect, revising is apt to become too tedious, and we risk losing them. Writing then becomes too much of a bother. I reward my students when I see them making progress in the form of noticeable changes, and in this case Sherry developed her ideas and examples far more thoroughly in this final draft than in her earlier attempt; she slowed down and took the time to support her feelings with specific instances from her own life as well as Holden's. She has demonstrated a stunning ability to *use* the preliminary exercises in parallel structure and integration to build an effective final paper.

CHAPTER SEVEN
The Argumentative Essay:
A Study in Concessions

Students need both instruction and lots of practice in developing arguments for controversial topics. In social studies classes, teachers frequently ask the students to support their personal opinions about historical controversies. Students often feel handicapped, not knowing how to organize such difficult assignments. Usually they have one or two major points, or at least some emotional reactions to a given situation, but they feel at a loss to say anything else. I remember feeling this way myself in school when our teacher introduced the term *capital punishment* and asked that we write a paper taking sides, defending our own positions. Most of us felt that killing was wrong, but beyond that we had no idea how to defend our viewpoints. The teacher's only response to our bewilderment was to tell us *to think.* When our parents were unable to help us, we ended up plagiarizing other written material.

Indeed, having to "think for ourselves" in order to develop critical-thinking skills is a necessary step on the road to growth and awareness. However, teachers need to set students on the right path, guiding them through proper questioning, directing them toward sources that will help them identify the *facts* they will need to consider in their papers.

Preparatory Exercises

When I first taught high school, the chairman of the English department announced that sophomores had to do a Pro/Con Essay. Students were to give the varying positions on such controversies as the drinking age, abortion, the draft, and nuclear disarmament. When I collected the final papers for these assignments, I sensed a notable lack of motivation and conviction. Students cranked out the same arguments that have been printed in articles and pamphlets for years; there was little creative or personal thought. As a result, I began to search for areas in which controversy *does* affect the adolescent, *personally,* in day-to-day experiences. It is my firm conviction that the best writing comes from a place of engagement, of caring about a topic, so I asked my students to begin making lists of problems they encounter with their parents or their friends. On the blackboard I wrote the issues they came up with—curfew, length of time on the telephone, doing homework, who they could date, and so forth. Everyone in class could relate to these general items. Then I asked them to become more specific about their particular conflicts. I asked them to select one particular issue that they would like to have resolved once and for all. Issues like the following surfaced:

My mother says that five minutes is long enough for a phone call on a school night.

My mother says I can't wear this certain brand of musk (perfume/after-shave) in the house because it smells up the entire place.

My father won't let me grow my fingernails long; I have to go through inspection once a week!

My mother says I'm too thin and that I have to eat more at every meal.

My father says I have to pay for my own car insurance.

My parents won't let me get a job while I'm still going to school.

Once students have decided on their issues, I begin training them to develop their arguments. Their first *telling* sentence of the unit is, "Lunch period at Foothill High School is too short." This controversy is one with which everyone can identify. Students and faculty have been complaining about our 30-minute lunch for *years.* There is hardly enough time to get through the cafeteria line and settle down to eat before the first bell for fifth period rings across the campus. Students who have P.E. fourth period are often in the showers and lose ten minutes of the already short lunchtime getting dried and dressed. Students who have to do make-up work during the lunch period have a limited number of minutes to take tests, an unfair amount of time compared to the usual 50 minutes that students had originally. And since many of these students have jobs after school, there is not time to stay and do the make-up work when school is over.

When students turn in their *showing* paragraphs the following morning, many of these supporting arguments appear in their paragraphs. Indeed, they know only *one side* at this juncture. After sharing aloud several papers, I ask students whether or not there are any *advantages* to the short lunch break. Some offer that "at least we get out of school earlier," or "getting out of school earlier means I can hold down a job with more reasonable hours." I introduce at this time, then, the idea of *concession*, the notion of admitting to some points on the other side of the argument. Opponents, I explain, are more likely to listen to us if we acknowledge their positions as well as our own. But that is as far as I go at this time—simply introducing the idea.

For the next night's assignment, I ask them to develop the *telling* sentence "Teenagers should have their own telephones." Usually I can predict the results I will receive: very few students concede *any* points. Even though I have suggested that admitting a few points on the other side can strengthen an argument, few students actually put this idea to practice on the subsequent assignment. Unless I direct students to employ this strategy specifically, they usually prefer to argue their sides completely. Such statements as "I won't interfere with anyone who might be needing the phone," or "Then I can talk for as long as I choose," are the mainstay of most papers.

Therefore, I begin *training* students to organize more effective arguments. At this stage, I plunge them fully into the idea of concession. I want to show them the benefits of their admitting to reasonable points on the other's behalf. I ask them, for the time being, to assume the roles of their parents in their particular controversies. I ask them to place, at the top of their papers, a typical "one-liner" they hear their parent say when stating his or her opinion on the issue at stake. In other words, I ask them to isolate the *one* line they hear over and over as their parents express their concerns. Here are some examples:

"Five minutes is long enough for a phone call on a week night!"
"Are you wearing that musk perfume again? I thought I told you not to wear it in this house!"
"If your fingernails get any longer, I'm going to cut them off!"
"If you want your own car, *you'll* have to pay for the insurance!"
"While you're in school, homework and studying will be your job!"

Sometimes I've encountered the student who claims he gets along with parents and friends and has no memorable differences with them. This is a good time to have everyone read aloud his or her particular controversy and the resulting one-liner. We move quickly around the room, having everyone state one issue briefly. Usually someone else's problem triggers an idea in those who are stuck. Students who first claimed there were no issues usually arrive at something after they've heard many different personal controversies. If there are still a few without ideas, I talk to them privately, helping them to discover something with which to work. I ask them to think of one time they might have disagreed with their parents' attitude toward a particular problem having to do with chores around the house, with homework, with socializing with friends. If a student remains insistent that he cannot arrive at a controversy, I ask him to consider differences in opinions with friends or school officials. I ask him whether or not he feels any difference in values on the subject of dating or loyalty in friendships; I ask him if he disagrees with any teacher's grading philosophies or ways of handling classroom discipline. With this sort of specific questioning, students can usually discover a suitable topic.

In the next step, students quickly write down the details of their problems. I give them about fifteen minutes to simply describe the issue briefly. When they are finished, I ask them to pair off and exchange these written descriptions. I emphasize that each partner must become very familiar with the other person's issue, because for the remaining minutes of the period, each partner will assume the role of devil's advocate in that issue. However, rather than taking the parent's role, the partner takes the *student's* side. For the time being, each student will play the role of his or her *own parent*, pretending that the partner is the teenager coming to argue. I have the students engage in a Socratic dialogue in writing, arguing the issue back and forth in a paper exchange, each challenging the other's point of view.

To get started, I have each student write the parent's one-liner at the top of a clean sheet of paper. This opening attack represents the viewpoint of the student playing the parent's role. When the student hands this paper to the partner, that partner answers the attack (posing as the teenager) and makes a further challenge. Usually asking a *question* is an effective way to continue the argument. For approximately 25 minutes, students engage in this written exchange. I ask them to keep working at it even when they feel as though they've run out of argumnents, for I want them to stretch and consider as many sides of the issue as possible. Each partner should try to outdo his opponent's point of view.

Admittedly, some issues are irresolvable; some students can, at best, only surrender to compromise. Bringing the dialogue to a closure of compromise, then, is a reasonable alternative for those who feel they can't win.

Following this approach, students are forced for a long period of time to be in their parents' shoes, developing the arguments their parents would uphold. Thus they are forced to see and understand their parents' concerns in great detail, for they must defend those viewpoints very specifically.

Usually we start out doing one partner's issue at a time, but I have found that after five minutes have passed, students understand the procedure and can easily begin exchanging responses on the second partner's issue as well. That is, they're exchanging both issues at once, which saves time and also keeps their attention on the task, as no one is left sitting and waiting for the partner to finish.

Following is a sample student controversy with its explanation of the issue and the resulting dialogue.

MY ISSUE:

I talk on the phone to kill boredom and loneliness. My parents don't realize this. They know I'm a bit lonely since my

sister has gone to college, but they don't realize how much. Because my parents and I aren't very close, I need to talk to friends. The most convenient way is by using the telephone. My father, concerned mostly with calls that might be trying to come in, does various things to keep me from talking too long, which to him is anything more than ten minutes. He thumps my head, attempts to hang up, and picks up the other receiver and slams it down two or three times. All of this he does in the middle of my conversation. I feel as though we should come to a resolution if at all possible. I feel as though I'm responsible enough to know when I'm ready to get off the phone without running up a huge bill.

—Sherry Ward

Working with her partner, Kathy Huber, Sherry takes the role of her father while Kathy argues the teenager's point of view.

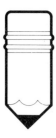

Parent: You see your friends at school. Why do you have to talk to them on the phone? It's irresponsible!

Teenager: But Dad, can't you see that there's nothing else to do? I'm so bored all the time and my friends cheer me up!

Parent: Don't you think you could be a bit more understanding? There are other phone calls that may be more important than yours. Why can't you think about other people, too?!

Teenager: I do, Dad, I do! But you never get phone calls; people call you at the office. It's not like the phone isn't for me, too, anyway.

Parent: Nothing you talk about on the phone should last any longer than ten minutes, if that. What can you possibly talk about to friends you've seen all day that would take any longer? Why can't you just take care of business, then get off the phone?

Teenager: Dad, you can't talk about anything deep or even important at school. Classes weren't made to talk during, and there's *no* privacy at all during any breaks. Besides, it's not like you pull someone aside and say, "Let's talk about what it means to be alive." Be serious!

Parent: You mean you spend time on the phone trying to figure out what it means to be alive? Come off it! Get smart, girl! You'll never figure that out, no one will! Ever! So why do you have to spend so much time on the phone? I obviously explained you can't figure out the answer to that, so what else could you possibly talk about?

Teenager: I'm just using that as an example. I'm just saying that there are important things that can be discussed; it's not like we giggle and gossip all the time. I take as much time as I feel I need. I think I'm really quite old enough to know what is excessive. Dad, just get off my back!

Parent: Don't talk to me that way! You should know better than that, young lady! As for your taking as much time as you need, you *need* too much time!

Obviously students delight in imitating their parents; they're outstanding actors when it comes to delivering the authentic comebacks they've heard again and again. When they're pushed to explain their concerns, however, they have to probe more deeply for effective responses. The student above has to admit that there might be more important calls than hers, and that she *could* take care of some of the conversation at school. The student who plays devil's advocate can be an equally effective actor, because most students have encountered similar issues in their own family battles. Students often tell me afterwards that this Socratic dialogue helped them acquire new angles they could take up with their parents; their partners have offered retaliations more sophisticated than their own! Occasionally students will conclude that their parents are right; there is no way to argue against their viewpoint. However, students who work toward compromise in their dialogues leave the classroom with healthy new ways to approach their problems.

For their next homework, I ask students to create paragraphs that summarize the major concessions and arguments of their controversy. Now they may be themselves once again, assuming their own sides. But they must, in the first half of the paragraph, concede those points they feel they have to; then, in the last half of the paragraph, they can counter with their own major points. For a conclusion, they are asked to state a course of action or a direction the problem should take. They can restate a stronger point of view, more clarified than their original view of the issue, or they can propose a compromise.

I provide students with sample rhetorical structures for developing their summary paragraphs. They insert their own arguments into one of the following rhetorical patterns:

> It is true that . . . However, . . . Therefore, . . .
>
> Certainly, . . . But . . . In short, . . .
>
> Admittedly, . . . On the other hand, . . . So, . . .
>
> Of course, . . . Nevertheless, . . . As a result . . .
>
> Obviously, . . . On the contrary, . . . Finally . . .

I caution students to be thorough in their concessions, for experience has taught me that students often think the mere *mention* of the opponent's point of view satisfies the need for concession. For example, some students think the following is satisfactory concession:

> It is true that I should do my homework, *but* . . .

A better attempt at concession would be as follows:

> It is true that I should do my homework. Because I want to go to medical school, I want to get into a reputable pre-med program, one that has high standards of admission. If I don't keep up my grades, there's little chance I will get into the college of my choice. However, . . .

Here are two model paragraphs in which students use the rhetorical format properly:

> **It is true that some rock music contains lyrics that are both provocative and rebellious. In fact, one form of rock music, punk**

rock, concentrates purely on antisocial subjects as a basis for its songs. However, rock music itself is not enough to make a teenager rebel against society. Even though some lyrics contain hints of social rebellion and moral decline, the average teenager does not take this seriously and concentrates more on the musical value of the songs rather than the inner meaning of the lyrics. In conclusion, I feel that even though lyrically rock music shows hints of anarchy and social rebellion, it is *not* a threat to society.

—Eric Shaffer

This paragraph is strong in its appeal, for the writer is willing to admit that people might misread a teenager's enchantment with punk rock music. He shows that he understands why a father, for example, might worry about his son's direction, given the meanings of these antisocial lyrics; however, when he argues that most teenagers enjoy the "musical value" over the "inner meaning of the lyrics," he offers a reason to put his opponents' fears to rest. Many people enjoy the melodies of certain songs without even becoming acquainted with the lyrics. We see that this student's argument is a logical one and is given even more credibility by his willingness to concede to the other side.

Here is another:

It is true that, when using my room, my brother does sometimes clean up after himself. There have been times when he has used it every day for a week and kept it clean by putting things back in order. On the other hand, there are times when he has left my room in a total mess. I have walked into my room to find records and books spread all over the bed and I have had to clean it up myself. I think that if he uses my room freely, he should have to clean it up and leave it just the way he found it. Therefore, although he is able to keep my room clean most of the time when he uses it, I think he should be able to keep it clean *every* time he uses it or should not be permitted to make himself "at home."

—David Allen

Notice how each writer's paragraph could serve as an introduction to a longer essay. The argument for permission to enjoy punk rock music could later include sample lyrics that prove the antisocial nature of the songs; it could also include examples of friends at parties engaged in dancing, unable to discern the words as they dance. In the same way, the paragraph arguing one student's right to a clean room could later include descriptions of his brother's pattern in returning the room to tidiness; he could contrast the times the room was left in order with the times it was left in chaos. In other words, this preliminary paragraph assignment should only *summarize* the main points. Students can attend to the specific details later in the body of the essay that culminates this unit of study.

Students now form groups to exchange their paragraphs. I direct them to counsel each other on the effectiveness of their concessions. If a writer has made only a token concession—"I know I should do my homework, but . . ."—the group should point out this underdevelopment. The group members also scrutinize the logic of the argument, deciding if the points make sense and are not too emotional.

An essay that shows students how this rhetorical framework is employed effectively is one devised for use with Sheridan Baker's *The Practical Stylist.* This essay argues for having all classrooms carpeted—perhaps a dry subject, but nevertheless an easy essay to understand. Students see the "It is true that . . . However, . . . Therefore, . . ." format at work in each paragraph of the essay.

CARPETED CLASSROOMS

    I should start by admitting that as little as five years ago carpeted classrooms would rightly have been regarded as a fanciful and expensive luxury. The carpeting then available would have been costly, difficult to maintain, and would have required frequent replacement. Now, however, because of improved materials, the arguments in favor of extensive use of carpeting seem a great deal more plausible. New indoor-outdoor synthetics—stain resistant, fade resistant, durable, and inexpensive—have made carpeting seem much less a luxury than a reasonable, even desirable, alternative to tile floors. Briefly, there seem to be three central arguments in favor of the extensive use of carpeting.

    First, of course, carpeting is clearly desirable for aesthetic reasons. Now, admittedly, there is a great variety of attractively colored tiles available, and the days of the drab, institutional grays, greens, and browns in tile are—happily—over. But, even though tile may approach carpeting in terms of color, it still has a hard and unattractive texture. Carpeting, on the other hand, is colorful, attractive to touch, and comfortable to walk on. It goes a long way toward creating a pleasant atmosphere all of us would like to work in, both in and out of class. Richly colored carpeting, such as the bold reds often used in banks, restaurants, department stores, and commercial offices, would make our facilities far less "institutional." Bright carpeting can easily make attractive an area that would otherwise seem Spartan and sterile. In short, carpeting seems desirable simply because it is more attractive to look at and walk on than tile.

    The second argument in favor of carpeted classrooms is essentially pragmatic: carpeting serves a useful acoustical function. It is true, of course, that the flexible backing and roughened texture of new tiles available on the market make them far less noisy than tiles available just a few years ago. Just as there have been advances in the carpeting industry, there have also been significant advances in the tile industry. Carpeting, however, is an excellent sound dampener; it cuts noise from crowded hallways, absorbs annoying background noise in classrooms—scuffing feet, scooting chairs, coughs—and makes busy space less noisy and, therefore, much more practical. In industry, if not in schools, one frequently finds carpeting being used because it makes heavily used areas more functional by reducing noise.

    A final argument in favor of extensive use of carpeting is that, over a period of time, carpeting appears to be no more expensive than floor tile. Certainly it is true that the cost of carpeting is initially much higher than the cost of tile, and it does need eventual replacement. So, if one calculates only the initial cost, tile is admittedly cheaper than carpeting. On the other hand, the cost of maintaining carpeting is minimal when compared to the cost of maintaining tile floors, which need frequent washing, waxing, and dusting. The new synthetic carpet materials are resistant to stains and fading, and all that one needs to maintain them is an ordinary household vacuum cleaner. The tile floor, unfortunately, needs frequent scrubbing and waxing if it is not to look dull and yellow with accumulated wax. And not only is this a laboriously slow process, but also, in large institutions, it is impossible to do without large and expensive scrubbing machines. In short, if one computes the cost of tile and carpeting only in their initial investment, tile is clearly cheaper. If, on the other hand, one computes the cost overall, the differences between the two disappear and carpeting becomes a legitimate economic alternative to tile.

Were it not for the obvious advantages in appearance and acoustics of carpeting over tile, one could perhaps argue fairly in favor of conventional flooring. After all, the cost differences figured over a very long period, say 20 or 30 years, are genuinely unpredictable. We simply haven't yet accumulated enough experience with the new synthetics, and perhaps it will turn out in the end that the cost of carpeting figured over a quarter of a century is a good deal higher. Perhaps we will discover that, after a decade or so, the cost advantages of carpeting evaporate. To this point, however, our experience with synthetic materials is essentially affirmative. And so, given the clear edge carpeting has over tile aesthetically and acoustically, and given its apparent economic justification, carpeting for classrooms seems completely sensible.[3]

We spend class time discussing this essay, finding each concession and each counterattack, and exploring how the concessions actually strengthen the writer's argument.

The Final Persuasive Essay

Students can now begin plotting their arguments for the final assignment. Having analyzed the careful organization of the carpeted classroom essay, they can decide how they will design their own arguments, using the "conceding, arguing, deciding" framework. At this juncture I ask students to turn in rough drafts of their arguments.

Having tried this assignment for several years now, I am prepared for what will happen at this stage of the writing process. Even though students may think they have their arguments all accounted for, they will not necessarily recognize whether or not they have been logical. For instance, one

---

3. Sheridan Baker and Dwight Stevenson, *Practice in Exposition: Supplementary Exercises for the Practical Stylist*, 5th edition (New York: Harper & Row, Publishers, Inc., 1981), pp. 15-17.

student, defending herself against her parents' attack that she never makes her bed, countered with: "Well look, Jane Bradley next door is in juvenile hall every week; I'm not doing anything so terrible; why are you on my case?"

This writer thought she was being completely logical; she had no idea she was dodging the point in question. Because many students *are* immature in their logical arguing, we need to introduce them to some of the terms of fallacious argumentation. The following six terms are ones I explain thoroughly to young writers to help them anticipate faulty reasoning.

1. *Red herring.* This is the term used to describe an irrelevant issue that is introduced to distract the reader (or listener) from the issue at hand. Also known as ignoring the question, or dodging the question, or "What does that have to do with the price of beans?", this form of faulty logic is very common in students' argumentation. It's very tempting to try bolstering our position by alluding to another issue that is more easily argued. We might do this by bringing up a "worse case" that makes our own position look good by comparison. When the girl defending her own behavior brought up Jane Bradley's weekly return to juvenile hall, she was introducing just such a red herring. Another typical red herring: "So I've been forgetting to do my chores. I drove Jesse to his piano lesson, didn't I? And I started dinner the night you worked late. And I picked up Dad's clothes at the cleaners. I was even nice to Aunt Gloria when she came over, even though you *know* how much she bugs me. You don't appreciate anything I do!" True or not, it's still dodging the issue of the chores the girl hasn't been doing.

2. *Begging the question.* This means reasoning in a circle. Instead of giving real evidence to support a particular point, the arguer makes a statement that assumes as *already proved* the very issue he or she is supposed to be proving. For example, if someone claims that "All high school students should be required to learn how to operate a computer because we live in a computer age," the speaker is evading the issue—or begging the question—by assuming as true that the term "computer age" means that everyone needs to know how to operate a computer to be a part of, or to survive in, these times. Instead, the arguer should give specific reasons *why* knowing how to operate a computer would perhaps make life in an advanced technological society easier or more comprehendable.

3. *Faulty cause and effect—"Post hoc ergo propter hoc."* The commonly used Latin name for this fallacy means "after this, therefore because of this." This form of illogical thinking occurs when we suggest that just because one thing happened *before* another, it necessarily *caused* the other to happen. For example, a father might blame his son's low grades on the teenager's recent car purchase, saying, "Ever since you bought that car, your grades have dropped. Therefore, you may not use the car until your grades change." This father is using *faulty cause and effect* reasoning. There needs to be actual evidence to prove the claim, even though the claim may appear logical. Is the son going for drives in the car during the time he used to spend doing his homework? If so, then the car is not to blame for the lower grades; *not doing homework* is the real cause.

4. *Argumentum ad hominem.* Another Latin term, this means literally

"argument to the man." A person who uses *argumentum ad hominem* distracts the reader from the issue by attacking the *people* involved in the issue instead of the issue itself. For example: a student, instead of arguing fairly for the need to have a longer lunch hour at school, directs her attention to the newly appointed principal and sputters, "We can't have a longer lunch on this campus because our principal is opposed to excessive socializing. Everyone knows he is the strictest disciplinarian in the city!" Instead of sticking to the matter under discussion (that the lunch period is too short), this student moves into an attack on the principal. That's *argumentum ad hominem.*

5. *Either/or, the false dilemma.* This form of fallacious thinking occurs when we present only two options as the possible results of a controversial issue—assuming (wrongly) that there are only two sides to an issue. For example: a student claims that "those who do not attend the Friday night football games have no school spirit." This student is suggesting that school spirit is defined in limited terms: either a person attends all school sports functions or is a traitor to the school's best interests. This student has created a false dilemma; to make his argument logical, he needs to find other reasons that members of the student body ought to attend the weekly games.

6. *Glory or guilt by association.* This is a transfer technique by which we attempt to associate our issue with other strongly positive or negative concepts to make the reader (or listener) accept our ideas. For instance: a student suggests that "liking punk rock music is the same as condoning drug use." This student implies that all punk rock music enthusiasts indulge in drugs; he is associating a strongly negative concept—drug use—with a form of music he does not like. In effect, he is asking his audience to reject the avant-garde sound—not for its own qualities, but for its "guilt by association" with the drug scene—an association that is not necessarily valid. When glory by association is used, the arguer tries to associate his or her issue with positive feelings of something else that most people approve of or respect. For example, if a teenager tells his parents that "owning a motorcycle is as American as apple pie and Chevrolet," he's trying to get them to believe that motorcycles are an upright and wholesome American tradition. The "all-American" associations in fact have nothing to do with the issue of owning a motor bike, but the teenager is trying to equate owning a bike with patriotism—a positive association with his issue, or "glory by association."

Although these fallacies may seem straightforward, they are often very difficult to put your finger on in a piece of writing. One good resource I use to further illustrate the six terms is the amusing "Speech by Senator Yakalot to His Constituents." This fictional senator's flowery and exaggerated speech is rife with the sort of logical fallacies I want students to learn to recognize. Students enjoy the speech and have a good time picking out the errors—or tricks—of faulty reasoning.

SPEECH BY SENATOR YAKALOT TO HIS CONSTITUENTS
My dear friends and fellow countrymen in this great and beautiful town of Gulliville, I stand before you today as your

candidate for state senator. And before I say anything else, I want to thank you wonderful people, you hard-working, right-living citizens that make our country great, for coming here today to hear me speak. Now, I'm at a disadvantage here because I don't have the gift of gab that a big-city fella like my opponent has—I'm just a small-town boy like you fine people—but I'm going to try, in my own simple way, to tell you why you should re-elect me, Al Yakalot, next election day.

Now, my opponent may appear to you to be a pretty nice guy, but I'm here today to tell you that his reckless and radical policies represent a dire threat to all that we hold dear. He would tear down all that is great and good in America and substitute instead his own brand of creeping socialism.

For that's just what his ridiculous scheme to set up a hot-meal program for the elderly in this town amounts to—socialism. Sure, he says our local citizens have expressed their willingness to donate some of their time and money to a so-called senior citizens' kitchen. But this kind of supposed "volunteer" work only undermines our local restaurants—in effect, our private-enterprise system. The way I see it, in this world a man's either for private enterprise or he's for socialism. Mr. Stu Pott, one of the leading strategists of the hot-meal campaign (a man who, by the way, sports a Fidel Castro beard), has said the program would be called the "Community Food Service." Well, just remember that the words "Community" and "Communism" look an awful lot alike!

After all, my friends, our forefathers who made this country great never had any free hot-meal handouts. And look what they did for our country! That's why I'm against the hot-meal program. Hot meals will only make our senior citizens soft, useless, and dependent.

And that's not all you should know about my opponent, my fellow citizens. My pinko opponent has been hopping around the state in his little puddle-jumper, whining about the size of cars that most Americans have chosen to drive. He says that if he is elected he will force all government employees out of regular-sized cars and squeeze them into those little gas-driven sewing machines. Now you and I know those little things are unsafe. In fact, a recent study shows that in 1959, when more Americans were driving full-sized cars, there were fewer accidents. Obviously, driving full-sized cars means a better car safety record on our American roads today.

My opponent claims that his vicious attack on full-size cars is just an attempt to preserve the beauty of the American countryside. He is supported in his crack-brain crusade to "save the butterflies" by none other than Congresswoman Doris Schlepp, who is sure no beauty symbol herself! And for this, my opponent wants to jam red-blooded Americans into a bunch of mobile can openers (many of which are made in Japan and Germany, countries we licked in the last war), rather than allow them the comfort of full-sized cars, which have always been as American as Mom's apple pie or a Sunday drive in the country. Why, full-sized cars have been praised by great Americans like

John Wayne and Jack Jones, as well as by leading experts on car safety and comfort.

What's more, full-sized cars are good for working men and women of this country, too. My opponent has tried to sell you the old bill of goods that small cars will save some of our material resources, like chrome, rubber, plastic, and glass. But when manufacturers need greater amounts of these materials to build full-sized cars, that means more jobs for these industries right here in the good old U.S. of A. And when our great American chrome industry suffers, then the men and women working in our chrome factories suffer.

My fellow taxpayers, I'm here to tell you today that if we don't use these God-given resources we are going to be a part of a heartless plot to drive working men and women right out of their jobs. My opponent's plan to cram those unsafe motorized baby buggies down the throats of the American people just won't work—because it is unworkable. Trying to take Americans out of the kind of cars they love is as undemocratic as trying to deprive them of the right to vote. And with the help of the Amerian people I am going to put a stop to it.

I'm mighty grateful to all you wonderful folks for letting me speak what is in my heart. I know you for what you are—the decent, law-abiding citizens that are the great pulsing heart and the lifeblood of this, our beloved country. I stand for all that is good in America, for our American way and our American birthright. More and more citizens are rallying to my cause every day. Won't you join them—and me—in our fight for America?

Thank you and may God bless you all.[4]

I help students find examples in this speech of each of the six terms we have discussed.

1. *Red herring.* When Senator Yakalot opens his speech with assurances that he is "just a small-town boy," not a "big-city fella" like his opponent, this may well be true, but it is irrelevant to the value of either man as a congressional representative. Later, when the senator is discussing the pros and cons of compact cars, he refers to their manufacture in Japan and Germany, "countries we licked in the last war." This is again true—but irrelevant to the issue at hand.

2. *Begging the question.* Senator Yakalot begs the question when he states, "My opponent's plan . . . just won't work—because it is unworkable." He needs to give specific reasons *why* it won't work.

3. *Faulty cause/effect.* The senator sets up an illogical cause-effect relationship in his discussion of auto safety: Because there were fewer accidents in 1959 when people drove larger cars, driving larger cars today would lower the accident rate. The senator is ignoring some other more probable causes of accidents—such as number of cars on the road.

4. *Argumentum ad hominum.* One blatant example of this is Senator

---

4. James MacKillop and Donna Woolfolk Cross, *Speaking of Words: A Language Reader* (New York: Holt, Rinehart and Winston, 1978), pp. 182-84.

Yakalot's cutting reference to Congresswoman Doris Schlepp, "no beauty symbol herself."

5. *Either/or, the false dilemma.* As the senator tells us, "In this world a man's either for private enterprise or he's for socialism." Are there *no* other alternatives?

6. *Glory or guilt by association.* Senator Yakalot tries to convey glory by association to full-sized cars, telling us they "have been praised by great Americans like John Wayne." He uses guilt by association when he suggests that his opponent "sports a Fidel Castro beard."

There are many other examples in the speech, and this is also a good chance to point out to students the weakness of name-calling—something they are apt to do in their own essays. We discuss how name-calling can make a person's argument sound too emotional, even unreasonable, and how it distracts attention from the merits of the argument itself.

Once we've discussed different types of faulty reasoning, I reiterate to students that the purpose of an argumentative speech or essay is to persuade others to *agree* with them; therefore, the supporting reasons must offer convincing evidence that our opinions—our conclusions—are sound. If the arguments are to be acceptable to straight-thinkers, they must first avoid errors in reasoning. With this important lecture, I introduce two student essays, both of which rely on fallacious argumentation. The first, "The Truth About Dirt Bikes," shows a student writer careful in his concessions but sometimes illogical in his arguments.

THE TRUTH ABOUT DIRT BIKES

It is a known fact that off-road motorcycle riding, because dirt bikes use high-performance two-stroke engines, pollutes the air. Also, dirt bikes can tear up the land and can be dangerous to ride. However, dirt bikes are less polluting than almost any other type of vehicle, are fairly easy on the environment, and are not as hazardous as one would think. Therefore, dirt bike riding should not be banned.

Unhealthy polluted air is a big problem in America, and measures should be taken by the government to regulate air quality. However, banning dirt bikes is the wrong way to go about cleaning the atmosphere. Motorcycles in general, according to the government, account for only a fraction of a percent of all the pollution in the air, and dirt bikes are just a very small fraction of all motorcycles. Clearly, the pollution emitted by dirt bikes is extremely limited. A better and more efficient method of controlling car exhaust, jet plane exhaust, or any other kind of gaseous waste generated by transportation or industry would do more to cleanse the air than taking all the motorcycles in the world and submerging them to the bottom of the Atlantic Ocean.

A major concern of environmentalists everywhere is the effects of savage ORV's (off-road vehicles) ripping up tender grasses, mangling bushes and young trees, and killing scores of small animals. To an extent, ORV's do damage the landscape, sometimes severely. However, dirt bikes are certainly not the only type of off-road vehicle; so are four-wheel drive trucks and jeeps. These metal monsters, weighing thousands of pounds, dig up and destroy anything that happens to get in the way of their massive, churning wheels. Comparatively, a dirt bike weighs just over one hundred pounds and has just one small tire delivering power to the ground. It would take a dozen screaming motorcycles all day to do the destruction of one four-wheel drive doing doughnuts for twenty minutes. Also, because dirt bike riders are less protected from menacing thorn bushes, ominous cactus, and jagged rock, dirt bikers tend to stay more on established trails, leaving nature unmolested.

To a mother, letting her son own a dirt bike is like letting him drive a car without brakes. "Why don't you do something safe, like go skiing or play football!" she might shriek at her misguided son. Actually, dirt bike riding is safer than either of these sports, and not surprisingly, one doesn't see mothers fainting when their sons buy a football or ski boots. In southern California, where dirt bikes are more popular, some high schools got together and started school-sponsored motorcross teams. Complete with a coach and league meets, motorcycle racing became a major school sport. After a few years, some interesting facts emerged from this experiment. Year to year there were more injuries from playing football than racing motorcycles.

One reason dirt bike riding is relatively safe is because of the vast expansion and improvement in motorcycle safety equipment. New, sophisticated helmets are able to take poundings that would have reduced helmets of a few years ago to a small pile of carbon and fiberglass soot. Thick leather boots, plastic and leather padded pants, padded nylon jerseys, and space-age plastic goggles and mouth protectors are all part of most dirt bikers' wardrobes. Crashing now sure isn't as painful as it used to be.

Because of the lack of knowledge and bad image associated with motorcycles, public opinion toward dirt bikes is unfavorable. With environmental groups pushing the government to stop off-road vehicle recreation and to enforce regulations to eliminate air pollution, the government is considering a ban on dirt bikes. This unnecessary ban would be a great injustice to dirt bike riders everywhere. The needless ban would be a great crime, depriving many people of the pleasures, thrills, and experiences of off-road bike riding.

At first glance, most students feel this essay is wonderful because the writer spent careful time on each argument; they think his examples in favor of riding a dirt bike are colorful and believable. He sounds to them very knowledgable about his subject; it seems he has even done research to strengthen his own convictions. If we examine his logic a bit more closely, however, we can spot some errors in reasoning.

Like the student who claims her parents overlook her good behavior in comparison with her neighbor who frequents juvenile hall, this writer has us overlooking the "minimal effects" of dirt bike pollution compared with the more dramatic pollution of "car exhaust, jet plane exhaust, or any other kind of gaseous waste generated by transportation or industry." This faulty logic is a red herring, dodging the question by turning attention toward something else the audience is likely to disapprove of or condemn. In this case, the writer distracts us from the real issue of *dirt bike* pollution by bringing up the more monumental problems of auto, jet, and industrial pollution. In effect, he is saying, "See, *I'm* not so bad. Why are you picking on me?"

The writer makes the same error in reasoning when he discusses the dirt bike's minimal effects on the environment. By putting the emphasis on the larger ORV's—"metal monsters, weighing thousands of pounds, [that] dig up and destroy anything that happens to get in the way of their massive, churning wheels," he has us ignoring the question at hand: how much damage is actually inflicted by the dirt bike.

This writer introduces a third red herring when he compares riding dirt bikes to playing football. Although he is clever in his comparisons and careful to present a number of provocative examples, he is still not dealing with the real issues of environmental damage and rider safety, his parents' first concerns. When, in his final argument, he discusses the advances made in motorcycle safety equipment, he is presenting his first really persuasive evidence. Parents might be convinced that with "the vast expansion and improvement in motorcycle safety equipment," it will in fact protect their son more thoroughly than equipment of a few years ago.

Finally, students should see that this writer is perhaps too defensive in his approach. From the very start of his essay, "It is a known fact that off-road motorcycle riding . . . pollutes the air," he never gives us the chance to see his dilemma; nowhere in the essay does he show us the positive side of the coin—his reasons for wanting to ride a dirt bike, his "pleasures" and "thrills." Instead, his entire piece deals with defending an attack.

Of course there are several merits to this essay that we shouldn't overlook. The writer is obviously engaged with his topic, for he painstakingly creates dramatic scenarios: "savage ORV's ripping up tender grasses, mangling bushes and young trees, and killing scores of small animals." And when he makes his point about modern safety equipment, describing the "thick leather boots, plastic and leather padded pants, padded nylon jerseys, and space-age plastic goggles and mouth protectors," we see him taking the time to cite specific evidence in defense of his viewpoint about safety standards. We can believe that this writer has indeed put some serious effort into making his argument work; however, he needs to be educated—perhaps for the first time in his public school career—about logical thinking.

Admittedly, an introduction to logic at this point does *not* mean that students will automatically spot fallacies from here on in. Like any other new, sophisticated concept, this one takes time to learn, and students will need much practice in rethinking the controversies of their experience. Students need exposure to the pitfalls of fallacious thinking even in the junior high years, and they should be asked to write argumentative papers every year as a part of the required curriculum. With practice, year after year, we can better prepare our students for the kind of critical thinking they will be asked to do in college and in the adult world. Providing students with model essays by great writers can also facilitate their growth in critical thinking.

Here is another student essay, written before any training in logical vs. fallacious argumentation. Here the writer argues her right to a messy room.

THE BATTLE OF THE ROOM

I'm sure many a teenager taking up space in the households of today has heard at one time or another those famous words, "Clean up your room." These words (usually coming from a distraught mother) are unfortunately common in my household, with battles occurring after each usage. This typical argument between me and my mother is not one of casual remarks and small disagreements. But, rather one where both parties end in complete rage with doors slamming behind them. The central conflict, obvious mainly to me, is my mother's infatuation with a clean, well-organized room, and my insistence upon a right to keep my room the way I want it, whether it be tidy or in this case "lived-in."

My mother has always been an exceptionally neat, organized person. While I, on the other hand, am sloppy, completely unorganized, and downright messy.

At times when I feel like Felix Unger is vacuuming around my feet, I can realize that it is Mom's house and people do visit. Therefore, dusting the rims of lamps, vacuuming underneath couches, and organizing the sock drawers of her and my brother, really doesn't faze me. But when she lays down her views and demands about my room is when I become most argumentative.

I have been warned time and time again that without organization like clothes hung up in order, drawers all categorized, and dresser clutter free, I just won't make it in life and many losses will occur. Yes, it is true there have been times when a matching shoe was nowhere to be found, or a favorite brush was somehow misplaced. But, more times than not I have found my friendly pair of jeans resting on a chair, rather than stashed away in some closet. Or maybe my nighttime mouthpiece [retainer] thrown freely on a nightstand, instead of sealed up in its container, up high on an organized shelf. These things seem much easier to find when they are out in the open, instead of packed and pushed out of sight.

During the course of our discussions on my four-walled adventure, Mom always brings up the fact that living in this so-called "garbage pit" shows what kind of irresponsible person I really am. If this is to be true, then does she also mean that I am too irresponsible to hold down a job, maintain a car, and be voting in our upcoming elections, in which I will be considered a legal adult?

As it looks right now, Mom and I will be fighting over this issue until I move out or at least go away to college. Because of that, I am even more determined to stand up for my rights for my

section of the house. If only she could realize that through the messiness of my room, my true personality emerges and I am allowed to express myself fully.

When I share this essay with students, they laugh and cheer loudly. When asked to decide which essay is more effective, the dirt bike essay or the messy room piece, they usually select the dirt bike; but when asked to decide which essay they *prefer* to read, they select the one about the messy room. I have to agree with them; even though this argument is not as well organized, is not as carefully worked out in its concessions and defenses, it is written with far more believability and spirit. The dirt bike essay is rigid and defensive; it is so committed to adhering to the "It is true that . . . however . . . therefore . . ." format, that the writer fails to share with us the fun of riding, fails to convey any of the "pleasures, thrills, and experiences of off-road bike riding." In contrast, the writer of the second essay lets some genuine feelings pour out. From the start of her piece, she asks for immediate empathy. With her first words, "I'm sure many a teenager taking up space in the households of today has heard at one time or another those famous words, 'Clean up your room,'" she wins the attention of her audience. We get the clear feeling that this is written in behalf of *all* teenagers who want the rights to their own rooms. She is committed to defending that right, conceding where necessary, but trying to resolve the issue once and for all. Whereas the writer of the dirt bike essay seems committed to arguing fairly, committed to sticking to "the teacher's formula," the writer of the messy room essay is committed to her feelings, committed to a point of view in which she becomes the spokesperson for others. As a result, she grants herself a lot of power. It is as if she is saying, "I'm going to convince all parents everywhere that they should leave the business of the child's bedroom to the child, and here is the logic behind that argument."

In effect, this writer's essay has *voice*. There is a sincere engagement with her topic that allows her own personality to color the argument humorously, sometimes powerfully. "At times when I feel like Felix Unger is vacuuming around my feet, I can realize that it is Mom's house and people do visit. Therefore, dusting the rims of lamps, vacuuming underneath couches, and organizing the sock drawers . . . really doesn't faze me." With lines like these, she seems to be gritting her teeth to bear the consequences of living in her parents' domain. In effect she is conceding, "There will be times when I must abide by my parents wishes," but she does so *believably;* she does not artificially act the compliant, dutiful daughter, but rather responds in true character—a little begrudgingly, as we see with her reference to Felix Unger, a compulsive cleanliness fanatic. The reader sides with her argument here because she has conceded, but has done so in a genuine manner. After all, who *really* enjoys dusting the rims of lamps, vacuuming under couches, and organizing sock drawers?

This writer's defense is not as strong as her concessions, however. Her appeal may be humorous and believable: ". . . more times than not I have found my friendly pair of jeans resting on a chair, rather than stashed away in some closet. Or maybe my nighttime mouthpiece [retainer] thrown freely on a nightstand, instead of sealed up in its container, up high on an organized shelf. These things seem much easier to find when they are out in the open, instead of packed and pushed out of sight." But, with this approach, she suggests that there is no room for order in her life, or (for that matter) anyone else's. If everything were out in the open all the time, some things would in fact get buried and lost; this writer needs to make her point without exaggeration. Though we laugh with her, "Yes, that's true; it would be easier to reach the jeans and the retainer if kept close at hand," we know that this viewpoint cannot really be taken to an extreme. Perhaps she needs to concede that she might pack *some* things away and leave the more frequently used items out where she can get her hands on them.

The argument in which the writer suggests that her mother might think she is "too irresponsible to hold down a job, maintain a car, and be voting in our upcoming elections," is badly underdeveloped. The reader is not certain what the writer means here. She expresses a lot of resentment, but she needs to take the time to explain the logic of her associations. Just as the dirt bike rider called attention to the more destructive power of a four-wheeled ORV in comparison to his own small bike, this writer seems to introduce the more powerful issue of *adulthood* to distract the audience away from the real issue. Thus her argument here is a red herring, in that her responsibility in other areas—working, driving, voting—is really unrelated to her duties in her mother's household. Her argument also involves elements of glory by association and the false dilemma. Using glory by association, she lists the positive signs of adulthood that society grants to 18-year-olds like herself. In effect she is saying, "You call me irresponsible? Why, society says I'm responsible enough to work, to drive a car, and to vote . . . so I *must* be responsible!" With this argument, she additionally creates a false dilemma, asking that her mother see her *either* as an irresponsible child *or* as a responsible, legal adult. She ignores the possibility that a teenager might exhibit conflicting behavior patterns, might be both a child and an adult at different moments. No, she implies, it's one or the other—and she defies her mother to call her a child when society treats her like an adult.

After presenting both of the preceding sample essays to my current students, I suggest that each piece has a little of what the other should have; the dirt bike essay needs more voice and less rigidity; the messy room essay should have better organization and better development of the individual arguments. *Both* need more attention to logic.

After several years of using this assignment, I have learned the merits and drawbacks of teaching students "formulas" for designing essays. In this case, teaching the "It is true that . . . however . . . therefore . . ." structure to thinking *does* give writers a framework in which to work out their arguments and defenses; the structure forces them to concede and to deal with those admissions. Unfortunately, since this careful, structured thinking is difficult, students often labor too long and too hard over the logic of their essays, losing the spontaneity and freshness of conviction that comes with less studied efforts. It is a very talented and creative thinker who manages to keep both logic and spontaneity intact.

This unit in having students deal with personal controversies through the argumentative essay is still in evolution. Each year I try to refine the assignment, try to make it more workable. For instance: now, instead of overemphasizing the formulaic structure, I tell students that using this structure for working out the issue is only *part* of their task in the paper; once they've satisfactorily worked out the concessions and defenses they plan to use, they should let go and *have fun* with the paper. I ask them, for example, to begin their papers with narrations. "Tell your reader what always happens when you walk in the front door. Create the scenario of the typical argument. In this way, you're more likely to grab your reader's interest, attract the reader to your cause." I've noticed with this change in my instruction that I receive far more interesting and engaging papers. Once students have had fun re-creating the scene at home, they become more committed to finishing the paper in a thorough, logical manner. As they finish narrating the stories and ease into the more formal arguments, their papers take on an air of authenticity and believability.

Here is one final essay written at the end of the argumentation unit.

THE TELEPHONE CONVERSATION

"Oh, Marylinn!" I said excitedly through the telephone receiver. "Guess what I did today after school. I got my license! I'm so excited!"

"Wow, that's great! I still hafta . . ." Three clicks of an extension being hung up interrupted her sentence. "What was that?" she asked curiously.

"My Dad," I admitted. "I guess I should get off before he gets too mad!"

"OK . . . Did you hear that Carol got her license yesterday?"

"No! Now we all . . ." I heard my father's recliner thrust forward and his extension slam down, bam, bam, bam, temporarily cutting off my conversation. "Listen, I'm gonna hafta go," I replied apologetically.

"OK. See ya tomorrow. Oh! Are we going shopping?"

"Sure." As we made our arrangements, my father's heavy body stomped up our steep stairs and into the dining room, where I sat finishing my plans. I felt the hard thump of my father's hand on my head.

"Did you hear?" he complained. "You should have been off half an hour ago! You've been on that dumb thing too long lately, young lady!"

Why must he get so upset about my long phone calls? Why is talking on the phone so important to him when he doesn't even use it? I feel the answer to both of these questions is that he just can't understand why I have so many long "unimportant" telephone conversations.

Certainly, the things I talk about may not be "important" to my father or anyone else, and such "nonsense" subjects like when I get my license, what I'm doing for the weekend, or what new movies I want to see could be talked about at school, as my father thinks. On the other hand, those aren't the only things I talk about. Many of my feelings and problems come out when I'm talking to my friends on the phone. It is hard to feel or discuss real emotions like love and sorrow at a place where one's brain is being filled with mathematical equations and atom diagrams. So, I believe that I should be able to say what I wish on the telephone without my Dad's remarks like, "What do you talk about, anyway? You sit there with that black plastic bar up to your ear and mouth, and nothing has ever passed through your lips that is worthwhile!"

Besides my topics of discussion, my father and I disagree on a time limit. We both know that I spend at least twenty minutes per call and that he would prefer no more than ten minute calls. However, his feelings of ten minute calls aren't shared by me. Since my older sister has left for college, I'm the only teenager living at home. My sister, my closest family member, left a year ago. Now, I sit on my warm waterbed and stare at the blue walls of my room, cut off from the rest of the huge house and unseen parents. I need my friends for comfort and reassurance. They are only a phone call away for help. But who can give a helping hand or dry shoulder to cry on in ten minutes? That's not even enough time to explain to my friends what is wrong. Therefore, I feel as though I should be able to talk on the telephone until my conversation is finished.

Although my father is right by saying that I'm on the phone too much, and even though he doesn't believe that most of my conversations are "important," I know that my "nonsense" phone calls have killed a lot of my empty time and saved me from being forgotten. All I ask is that my father give me a chance to have uninterrupted conversations on the telephone, and that he allow me to hang up all by myself when the discussion is over. If this can't happen, I at least hope he'll be willing to treat his sixteen-year-old daughter with a little more courtesy, instead of thumping her on the head like a three-year-old.

—Sherry Ward

By beginning her essay with a scenario that dramatizes her problem, this writer effectively lures the reader into her dilemma. Before knowing either her father's position or her own, we have a glimpse into an "unsettled" situation. She re-creates a typical episode of her father's interrupting her phone conversations; yet, we have no clue as to whose behavior is the more justified—the girl's or her father's. The writer leads us into the problem by suggesting that her father doesn't understand her, and that if he (and her audience) would just bear with her for a few moments, they might see that her phone conversations are not as foolish and everyday as one might think.

Some of her concessions and defenses work well, while others need a bit more development. For instance, she admits that to her father, some of what she considers "important" subjects might seem nonsensical. Admittedly, getting her license, plans for the weekend, and movies she wants to see, are subjects that she could discuss at school; on the other hand, there are matters of discussion that cannot be developed before or after a math or science class.

She suggests that some more serious topics, like dealing with difficult teenage feelings, need time outside the hectic school environment. At the end of this particular argument, she adds impact to her plea by relating her father's typical "What do you talk about, anyway? You sit there with that black plastic bar up to your ear and mouth, and nothing has ever passed through your lips that is worthwhile!" In effect, she portrays her father as narrow-minded and closed to her feelings. And she does this without name-calling or disrespect; she lets the *quote* speak for itself. Later in the essay she reiterates her need for a *friend's* shoulder to cry on in place of a parent's. With the absence of her sister as confidante, she needs friends her own age. At the end of her essay, she demonstrates once again her father's unreasonable behavior of "thumping her on the head like a three-year-old" instead of treating her as a young adult. For a second time she uses his *actions* as a device to strengthen her plea, rather than calling him unfair or intolerant.

As with most students, this writer has the most trouble handling concessions. She tells us, for example, that her father prefers that she stay on the phone only ten minutes. However, she won't concede that he's probably right. Instead, she immediately explains why ten minutes is not enough. There is a concession in the last paragraph, where she agrees that she is "on the phone too much," but she doesn't define what *she* means by "too much." Instead, she continues to emphasize the importance of her need to talk until she's through.

This essay, nonetheless, is more thorough than either the dirt bike or messy room papers. The reader feels the sincerity of her plea (the essay has *voice*) and sees some real logic behind her arguments. The writer leaves us with the realistic notion that perhaps she and her father need to talk more in order to understand each other's point of view. The issue is not resolved, but seems open for further discussion—a reasonable course of action for the both of them.

Here is another student's final essay, one that is stronger and better developed.

MOMMY'S BABY

It's ten after six. I've just driven home from work, and I'm thinking about having a taco before I start my homework. I jump out of the car with a smile on my face and walk through the door—to find my brother standing there, dressed in the pair of plaid bermuda shorts I had bought myself last week, my pink Izod shirt—which has a big brown stain in the middle of it that I have never seen before—and my new topsiders that I paid sixty dollars for last week. My mother is standing just behind my brother in the kitchen. My face goes cold white; the little jerk is doing it again; he's destroying my things. "MOM!" I holler desperately. "Tell him to take those off before he wrecks them all."

She stands there with a blank face. "Bennett, take the clothes off," she says without much emphasis. All he does is shrug and walk into the living room to turn on the TV.

I scream again, "Mom, make him take them off, NOW!"

She replies, "John, don't make this into a big deal again. I don't want to hear about it now." Then she walks away.

"MOM, MAKE—"

"No more!" she interrupts. I walk back to my room, my feet dragging as I go. I feel as though I have been mugged, completely defeated.

My mother buys my brother and me ample amounts of clothing. When we see something we want, or tell her there is something we need, she usually gets it for us, just so long as we don't get carried away. In the past year or so I have compiled a nice amount of clothing. I carefully select each item before my mother purchases it for me. My brother, on the other hand, chooses "fad" clothing and other sorts of clothes which don't last long. I also spend much of my own hard earned money on my clothes. It is for these reasons that I object to my brother wearing my clothing, and wearing it continuously after I have asked him to stop.

At least every other day I find my brother is wearing part of my wardrobe, whether it be a shirt, shorts, socks, and so on. It bothers me. I ask him over and over to stop stealing the clothing out of my closet, but he reacts to these requests as though he were deaf. Since direct confrontation doesn't work, I call in the law. My mother is then requested to command Bennett to quit infiltrating my closet, take off what he is wearing of mine, and return it to its place of origin, my bedroom floor. This usually doesn't work; Bennett shrugs her commands off and continues on with what he is doing. But, this is as far as my mother takes it. When she sees Bennett purposely disobeying her, she doesn't get worked up about it; she tells me to get out of her hair, as though it's no big deal that my brother is destroying my personal property.

It is not as though I am a selfish person. Bennett doesn't have much money, mostly because he is too lazy and unmotivated to do anything for which he will be paid, so I usually pick up the tab for lunches, movies, and other things we do together that cost money. This doesn't bother me much, though, because he usually *asks* me if I will lend him the money. When it comes to my clothes, he usually *doesn't* ask if he can use something; he just takes them as though they were his.

I realize that my parents can't run out and get everything my brother and I want, and I don't expect them to. Raising three children is expensive. My father's income is limited. My mother works hard earning money for the "extra" things we own and do. I know they can't afford to get us duplicates of every item of clothing; therefore, to have certain items, we must share. I feel a person should share his things freely and unselfishly. I would like to think of myself as one of those people.

On the other hand, I feel when a person buys an item with his own money, it should be solely his to keep, which means that person has the right to regulate that item's use, and the lending of that item. Bennett obviously doesn't feel the same way as I. He feels he has the right to wear my clothes and use my things as if they were his own. Items *I* worked for, spent hours trying to earn, my brother uses just as if they were his own. I don't think an item which is earned should be community property.

My parents, who provide us with many of the things we have, don't make Bennett stop taking the clothes that I pay for. It is true that the money I have made thus far has afforded me many nice and desirable things. Bennett should feel he has the right to use some of my things simply because he is my brother, but as the owner of the property, I feel he should first have to ask to use the item before he uses it.

Sharing a person's property is one of the things that makes life enjoyable. When only one person has something to share, though, it turns into charity work. My brother uses my stuff unregulated by my parents, although I plead with them to stop Bennett's stealing of my clothes. I am not asking that my parents stop my brother from borrowing my things; I just want them to make my brother *ask* me if he can use an item before he takes it; therefore, the final decision of the lending of my property is mine.

In resolving this problem I am willing to compromise, but I am not willing to back down on what I feel strongly for. I feel Bennett should be made, by my parents, to ask me first before borrowing an item. This will give me the respect that I feel is rightfully mine as the owner of the property. I don't feel it is an unreasonable request for me to want to know what clothing he has of mine and what he plans to do with it. If this were to happen, I would be more than happy to allow my brother the use of my things. It would put an end to many of my mother's headaches, caused by continuous fighting over the issue, and do away with unnecessary hardships felt by us all.

—John Williams

This essay makes an appeal to two parties; that is, the writer really makes two separate arguments: (1) that Bennett, the younger brother, should not use the writer's clothes without permission, and (2) that the parents should enforce their commands regarding Bennett's use of the clothes. For the most part, the writer remains fair in his concessions and logical in his counterattacks; he sticks to the issues at hand without distracting the reader into other arguments. He shows that he understands both his brother's and his parents' viewpoints by admitting when their actions are justified. For example, the writer (with admirable generosity) can understand his brother's wanting to borrow clothing, especially since the younger boy has little money for himself and the parents can't provide *everything* he might want. He concedes his parents' willingness to provide "extras" for their sons as best they can, and he understands also the limits of their ability to provide. He admits that sharing what he has with his brother seems a necessary part of family life. His major argument is that there should be some limits to Bennett's borrowing of the clothes; to this end, the writer suggests the simple compromise that

Bennett ask permission rather than *assume* he can borrow anything at any time. His secondary complaint is that while his parents pay lip service to their older son's rights to his own clothes, they fail to follow through with any punishment when Bennett refuses to respect those rights. As the writer explains, when Bennett purposely disobeys, his mother "doesn't get worked up about it" but instead tells John (the writer) to "get out of her hair." If the proposed compromise is accepted and upheld by the parents, the writer feels that his family can avoid further repetitive arguments on the subject.

In addition to presenting his issues carefully, the writer of this essay manages to be consistent in voice. He remains strongly committed to his feelings throughout and is not hampered by trying to follow the "it is true that—however—therefore" structure too rigidly.

Given the difficulty most high school students have with this assignment, the weaknesses of this writer's argumentative essay are surprisingly few. He does stumble when he concedes that Bennett doesn't have the money to buy extra clothing; at first he seems sympathetic toward his younger brother's lack of funds, but when he adds "mostly because he is too lazy and unmotivated to do anything for which he will be paid," he weakens his concession by "name calling" and becoming too emotional. His title, "Mommy's Baby," reflects the same negative emotionalism. The writer is also a bit repetitious, suggesting more than once his compromise—that Bennett be made to ask permission before borrowing any clothes. On the whole, however, this writer is straightforward and fair in his appeal.

For most of my students, this is the first time they have ever been asked to write such detailed arguments. That I do not receive exemplary models from even half my students, therefore, does not worry me. What counts is that students have engaged in this sort of careful thinking and applied it to their own experience. We as educators need to increase the number of times our students practice the art of argument and persuasion. As they mature, so will their essays. Just as we do not expect a young actor's first performance in Shakespearean acting to be his best, so we cannot expect our junior high or high school students' early experiences with argumentation to be flawless. We must simply point them in the right direction and ask that they try again and again.

CHAPTER EIGHT
Saturation Reporting: The I-Search Paper

Many teachers are familiar with Ken Macrorie's book *Searching Writing*[5] and have tried having students write the I-Search paper. In this form of research essay, students investigate a topic of interest by interviewing people associated with the topic, by visiting places that allow them to observe people engaged in

---

5. Ken Macrorie, *Searching Writing* (Rochelle Park, N.J.: Hayden Book Company, 1980).

related activities, and by doing some outside reading that enhances their knowledge. Macrorie proposes that when students *experience* the activities and observe people associated with them in a hands-on fashion, they write far more thorough and involving pieces than when they are assigned only outside reading as research. On-the-job reporting and investigating turns student writers into journalists of sorts; the students feel that their topics *matter* and that it is their job to present their findings honestly and powerfully. Every spring I have my juniors, as a final project of the year, compose an I-Search essay based on six weeks of investigation. This turns out to be their favorite unit of the year; the following year, invariably, their senior English teacher tells me they ask if they'll be conducting another research assignment; they claim that the I-Search paper was the best assignment they ever had.

All due credit must go to Ken Macrorie for devising such an inspirational project. He has taken the "saturation report"—a report in which the writer visits a place of interest and records all the actions and sensory details—many steps beyond. In a saturation report, the simple recording of the facts, without interpretation, makes a comment on society today. It is simply a vignette, a microscopic glance at our world, but even so it can make powerful statements about life as we know it. Students, for instance, may choose to observe the goings-on at the local McDonald's, the local lumber yard, or the wig salon at Macy's department store. They visit the chosen place of interest and record the activities, the details in the environment (smells, sounds, visuals), and overheard snatches of conversation. The writers do not analyze what is happening, nor do they react and share their feelings about anything they see occurring; they present simply what they observe. Powerful pieces of description can emerge from this form of reporting.

In the I-Search paper, however, students *use* their visits as research for later interpretation and reflection; they have chosen particular places to enrich their knowledge of subjects they care deeply about, subjects they *want* to write about. Though I take no credit for devising this assignment, I do have preliminary activities and exercises to share, ones based on the daily "showing, not telling" warm-ups. These, like the preparatory exercises I have used in other units, help students rehearse smaller sections of their papers before the "final performance."

Preparatory Exercises

Before making any formal assignment, I like students to have read a particularly effective piece of personal journalism—a piece of research that is exciting to read because of the writer's personal commitment and engagement with his topic. Often we read excerpts from Tom Wolfe and E. W. Johnson's anthology of investigative journalism, *The New Journalism.*[6] In the first section of the book, Wolfe talks about the notion of "detailed realism" and how he came to change his investigative techniques to get to the core of experience. His introduction sets a foundation for understanding the personal journalistic styles of writers such as Truman Capote, Hunter Thompson, Norman Mailer,

---

6. Tom Wolfe and E. W. Johnson, *The New Journalism* (New York: Harper & Row, Publishers, Inc., 1973).

Joan Didion, and Gay Talese. My students read excerpts from *In Cold Blood* (Capote), *The Hell's Angels: A Strange and Terrible Saga* (Thompson), and *Slouching Towards Bethlehem* (Didion). In these pieces, *fact* is turned into narration; the writers tell their findings through fictional techniques. In his *In Cold Blood*, Capote re-creates a scene and dialogue between two ex-convicts; in *The Hell's Angels: A Strange and Terrible Saga*, Thompson re-lives his firsthand experience with a pack of Angels on the Fourth of July holiday; in *Slouching Towards Bethlehem*, Didion becomes intrigued by the environment of San Bernadino, California, and uses a description of the town as the dramatic backdrop for the murder case she is investigating. Additionally, for the past three years my students have read Tom Wolfe's *The Right Stuff*[7] as their final required reading of the year. We watch how Wolfe artfully combines interviews, visits, and outside reading to present his investigation of the lives of the original Mercury astronauts. Students are so inspired by Wolfe's style that when I announce that *they* will be investigating their own subjects of interest, they really are raring to go. It may sound too good to be true, but the combination of having read such electric prose, based on real life, and being permitted to explore the things they genuinely care about, sets a class of high school students wild with curiosity and enthusiasm.

Let me emphasize that students need to know the difference between "topics that *interest* them" and "topics that *engage* them." For example, many students anticipate that you have in mind something serious like "job opportunities" or "the welfare system." Some believe that they're supposed to choose subjects that will have relevance to college—as in possible future careers; others believe that they might impress you if they select "intellectual" topics such as World War II or the Middle Ages. Though some students do have a genuine interest in these topics, the subjects themselves are too broad. If a student selects "future careers," I push him to select *one* career to pursue. Suppose he then chooses nursing; I ask him privately whether he is *really* committed to visiting hospitals, interviewing nurses, and doing outside reading on the subject. In other words, a teacher needs to be absolutely certain that the student *cares* about his or her pursuit. Usually historical topics, such as World War II and the Middle Ages, do *not* make good investigative topics because the student cannot return to those times to investigate them. If a student wants to narrow the topic to World War II bomber pilots, making plans to inverview experienced aviators and to tour preserved aircraft from the war, then that is a different story.

It is crucial, then, that for this unit you consult with each and every student before they finalize their research topics. Following are some of the topics that have proved popular over the past several years and were the ones I found most enjoyable to read. These topics were often out of the ordinary, and for once in my teaching career, I did not mind reading final term papers in June! What's more, the students themselves could not put down each other's reports. Everyone wanted to read everyone else's; so I learned to set aside several class days for silent reading. Sometimes students have enjoyed my offering an award for the best piece of "new journalism"; this gives them even more incentive to turn in papers of excellence. (I have since moved the I-Search assignment back to April or May; if I leave it too close to the end of the year, students seem to let down and not give it their best shot.)

---

7. Tom Wolfe, *The Right Stuff* (New York: Farrar, Straus, and Giroux, Inc., 1979).

SAMPLE TOPICS OF INVESTIGATION

1. *What happens to my college application after it leaves my hands?* This student met with admissions officers at the nearby University of California campus and watched the screening process for college applications. She saw the actual paperwork move from desk to desk, computer to computer.

2. *Chain letters and pyramid parties: Did anyone ever make any money?* This student attended several pyramid parties—his parents hosted one—and interviewed subscribers. He also researched the legality of the pyramid schemes.

3. *Skyscrapers in San Francisco: What is on the top floor of each major skyscraper?* This student rode elevators all day long and interviewed secretaries and guards. She also studied the history of San Francisco's skyscraper architecture.

4. *The rock group The English Beat: What are they like in person?* This student enjoyed private interviews with each member of the band when they performed at the Greek Theatre in Berkeley.

5. *Playing the conga drums with professional players: What would it be like to improvise with them?* This student summoned the courage to attend a weekly outdoor concert of professional conga players and to join them in playing.

6. *What's a typical day for the police? What kinds of scary situations do they encounter?* This student spent six hours riding in a patrol car, observing every encounter that one night-duty police officer had.

7. *Hot-air ballooning: What's it like?* This student rode in a hot-air balloon and reported the experience.

8. *What do people do when they're depressed? What are their outlets?* This student posed her question to all sorts of people. She interviewed people she knew as well as strangers in unfamiliar places. She described each person's character and personal environment and recorded their responses to her question. She did outside reading on the causes of depression and methods of treatment.

9. *What's it like to be a surgeon? How do doctors handle the death of a patient?* This student interviewed doctors and paramedics to learn how they react to saving lives.

10. *What's it like to be among the rich?* Two students spent an afternoon in the financial district of San Francisco, eating at an expensive restaurant during lunch hour, visiting exclusive shops, interviewing people who serve the very rich.

11. *Female veterinarians: What does it take to become one?* This student interviewed three very different kinds of animal doctors, two of whom were women.

As you can see, students can come up with unique and inventive topics when encouraged to strive for individualism; it is worth the time and effort to counsel students carefully to help them arrive at truly meaningful topics.

To get started, I have students brainstorm possible subjects of intrigue. I give them about twenty minutes to jot down ideas freely and spontaneously as they occur. When time is up, I ask them to circle their top three choices; then I move around the room asking each student to read his or her three selections out loud. As each student speaks, I record the three subjects on the board with colored chalk. When I start another student's list, I change colors of chalk. By the end of a period, I have squeezed some ninety topics onto two boards. I tell students that if they see a topic on the board they hadn't thought of but are interested in pursuing, they may add it to their own list. For homework, I ask that the students narrow their selections down to two and put a star beside their first choice. In this way, we have a foundation for discussion when I consult individually with each student; if we find that one topic is really not feasible—especially if we predict parental or administrative disapproval—we'll still have a second choice to consider. For instance, some parents may not approve of their children riding in police cars; some may not want their teenager attending a certain rock concert. During this important consultation period, I need to work out all the obstacles that might be encountered.

When the students have each arrived at a final choice, I ask them to write down, spontaneously, everything they know about their subject already. Here is one such response.

I have firsthand experience with pyramid parties because my parents hosted one. I know that a lot of people in this world are money-hungry, and a lot of people believe they will receive $16,000 pretty soon if they're in on the "pyramid chain" early on. They arrive at our house with fat wallets, ready to invest their $1000 or $500. There are all sorts of people who attend, too. There are wealthy people from the neighborhood who pull up in Mercedes Benzes and there are people I've never seen before who pull up in Volkswagen vans. People wait in long lines outside the door, waiting to be given a number in the chain. They all seem cautious of each other, too. They wonder if this is illegal and if they're going to be caught. The news people have said that these parties are illegal, but others have said they're not.

Some students know a lot about their topics, and some students do not. They probably know more than they think they do, but most write only a few paragraphs for their initial responses.

Next I ask them to write down some of the questions they would like to pursue. I ask them to describe why they've chosen their particular topic and what they plan to uncover in their investigations. The student who described the pyramid parties writes:

I am really curious about what happened to these people. I want to interview them and ask them how they feel about having received their bucks or having lost their money. I want to know what made them risk prosecution. I want to know why they wanted the money so much and what they planned to do with it. If they didn't get any money, I want to know how they feel about pyramid parties and chain letters now.

After these preliminary activities, I announce the major requirements of the final paper. These include the following:

1. Introducing the topic by disclosing how you became interested in your search; here's where you tell your reader what you hoped to uncover.

2. Visiting a place of activity that relates to your search; recording the actions and details of the environment.

3. Interviewing at least *three* people associated with your field of interest.

4. Reading outside literature on your subject and incorporating some of the important information in the body of your report; including footnotes and a bibliography citing your sources.

5. Drawing a conclusion about your findings. What have you learned?

At this juncture the requirements seem monumental. The students wonder how they'll ever put these sections all together. So we begin with one small step: practicing ways to describe places.

Focus on Setting

Since everyone will have to visit an unfamiliar place—and sometimes this place is simply an office or home where an interviewee works or resides—we start examining the way an environment makes statements about those who live and work there. In fact, part of the interview process often involves recording the surroundings in which the character of interest usually works. For instance, the student who interviews the British rock group observes each member of the band in his own private dressing room backstage; the student who plays drums with the professional conga players records the background at Sproul Plaza at the University of California, complete with spectators.

To get the students started with their practice pieces, I assign a random *telling* sentence that asks for a description of a fictitious place—let's say, "The office was well organized." Since we've been practicing "showing, not telling" all year, this simple sort of detailing poses no problem to students; they can easily create wonderfully explicit—sometimes exaggerated—tidy offices. I have them write these paragraphs mainly to compare their results. As we always do in our follow-up oral readings, we contrast the different techniques students found for delivering the same impression. While one student may focus on the order-liness of the items on the office desk, another may emphasize the arrangement of the entire working environment—the shelves, file drawers, plants, dicta-phones, computer terminals, and so forth.

Following our discussion of the alternative techniques, I introduce an activity that emphasizes personality and character development through attention to personal environment. This six-step exercise prepares students to elaborate their next *telling* sentence assignment in a new and unusual way. This exercise is completed during a single class period that culminates in the assigned *telling* sentence. It instructs students in the use of details to evoke character by allowing them to explore how character is revealed in their own experience of themselves and people they know. In a way, I'm killing two birds with one stone: in the act of teaching them techniques for describing environment, I'm also instructing them how to use environment to reflect character.

Step 1. I give each student a copy of the following chart.[8]

Items in my room at home.	What I think these items say about me to others.	What these items **do** say about me to others. #1	What these items **do** say about me to others. #2	What these items **do** say about me to others. #3

Step 2. The students all privately decide on three items of decoration in their bedrooms at home that they consider their favorites. These items could be posters, plants, photographs, pieces of furniture, record collections—anything that can be seen upon entering the room. If some students do not have a room of their own, I ask them to consider the *section* of the room that is theirs.

In the first column, "Items in my room at home," each student lists the three favorite objects. The student should also describe each possession so that someone might be able to picture it in its particular setting. For example, instead of merely listing "the plant on my desk," it is better to say, "the baby African violets growing out of a blue ceramic planter that I made on a potter's wheel"; or, instead of listing "the photograph of my boyfriend on my wall," a student might write, "The poster-size photograph of my boyfriend taken when he made a touchdown for our football team; you can see him smiling wide and raising his arms in pride. The crowd is cheering in the stands behind him."

Step 3. In column two, "What I think these items say about me to others," students suggest what each object might reflect about them. If students have difficulty grasping this idea, I ask them to consider *why* they like that particular object and *why* they chose it as one of their favorites. Each possession should be interpreted individually.

---

8. Adapted from Sydney B. Simon, Leland W. Howe, and Howard Kirschenbaum, *Values Clarification: A Handbook of Practical Strategies for Teachers and Students* (New York: Hart, 1972), pp. 331-32.

I also assure them that this column is a private column; no one will see their personal interpretations. They are to be as honest as possible. For example:

Items in my room at home.

1. *My trophy collection that sits on top of my bookcase; there are football, baseball, and track trophies. I started winning them in junior high school.*

What I think these items say about me to others

1. *I'm successful in many different sports. Others have recognized my athletic talent. I'm proud of what I've accomplished.*

Step 4. When the students have filled in columns one and two, they should fold column one *over* column two in such a way that column two—the private one—is hidden, but column one remains visible. With column two covered, there will be three remaining columns to be filled in. To ensure privacy for column two, I distribute paper clips so that everyone may secure column two tightly in its fold.

Each student then asks a classmate to *evaluate* his or her furnishings. The responding student answers in the first column headed "What these items *do* say about me to others." In other words, after reading the descriptive list in column one, the evaluating classmates should say what they think each item suggests about that person. After responding to all three items, the classmate returns the chart to its originator, who now folds column two over column three, keeping column one still visible, and again paper-clips the folded columns tightly together. The originator then selects another person with whom to exchange charts and follows the same procedure until all the columns are completed. *At no time should any evaluating partner look at the interpretations of other students or of the originator.* Each student deserves original evaluations, not just repeats of another's ideas. This way each student comes away with three separate interpretations of his or her personal environment.

The sample chart shown on the next page was begun by junior Kathy Huber and completed by three fellow students.

Step 5. The students now compare their own interpretations to those of their classmates. I encourage the students to write something they learned from doing this activity. On the back of their charts, they answer questions like these: Did most people see you the way you see yourself? Did your evaluators' impressions differ greatly from your own? Why?

Kathy (whose chart is illustrated here) wrote on the back, after the activity

Items in my room at home.	What I think these items say about me to others.	What these items **do** say about me to others. #1	What these items **do** say about me to others. #2	What these items **do** say about me to others. #3
1) my 8" stars (different colors on each side, about ½" thick, gold glitter on the sides) that I hang on my ceiling at strategic points. My oldest sisters friends (all boys) "starred" our house one night with them.	1) My adoration of anything my sister does. Love of color, they're cheerful and heartwarming. They're positive, like me.	1. that you have a taste for things that glitter, perhaps meaning a taste for rich or expensive gifts.	I think it shows that the might everyone "starred" your house was a memorable night, and that it might have been special for you.	Each star represents a "conquest." I wonder just what you mean by "strategic points". (This same thing happened in Gravity's Rainbow by Thomas Pynchon.
2) My pretty purple walls I painted all by myself, along with my closet doors, and the matching white bedspread w/ purple and green flowers (the green brings in the carpet which is also green) and curtains that I helped my mom quilt and sew.	2) my neatness - every thing has to be co-ordinated. Also my love of color around me. It reflects my sunny outlook.	2. That you are very proud of your accomplishments. You have a pride that burns very bright.	Because you painted the walls & closet doors all by yourself, it gives a feeling of content. This also shows you like the color purple.	You're female. Women are the ones who worry about color coordination. I bet you even have a box of purple Kleenex.
3) My group of objects that stay together. A big candle that's a rainbow and the two plants that are planted in an A & W mug and a Stonyridge winery glass.	3) My dedication to these objects. They're my "friends." They show my love of life, of color, of health.	3. That, despite your taste for things that are fine, you also have a taste for simple and homey things. That you're the type of girl who'd wait at home late for hubby to come in. That even though you'd love to be showered with flowers, you wouldn't be disappointed with a kitten or a book.	I think you keep these 3 objects together because you either got them at the same time, or they look nice together.	You are sentimental. You attach emotional significance to inanimate objects.

was completed, that "students #1 and #2 described me to a T—especially #1, he really could see the significance of my things." She concluded further, "Personal environment can tell a lot about a person, as seen from the responses to me. Someone with pictures of tanks and machine guns obviously isn't too sensitive to life."

Following this exercise I ask students why a writer bothers to describe a character's room, house, or environment. I ask them to consider why the decor might be important in reflecting someone's character. Students recognize this technique as a way of *showing* or revealing personality without directly *telling* what that character is like.

Step 6. After students have connected setting to characterization, I assign the *telling* sentence "She is strange" for expansion. Although strangeness might be revealed in an infinite number of ways—actions, gestures, clothing, dialogue—I ask them to show this character's eccentricity exclusively through personal setting. In training students to expand their repertoire of descriptive techniques, I insist that they focus primarily on setting, to see what happens. This strategy is one they will find very useful as they interview various authorities for their I-Search papers. Here is one student's response to "She is strange."

As she opened the door to her room, my eyes began to ache from the bizarre white and black, checkerboard-type pattern painted on all four walls that seemed to begin swimming the minute I set my eyes upon it. In various places on the walls, she had put up posters resembling her walls, only none of them were black and white but were red and white, blue and orange, pink and purple. Her floor was made up of different tiles, all in bold colors—hot pink, sunshine yellow, and blood red. But the worst thing about her room were the four different-colored strobe lights placed in the four corners of the room, each flashing at different moments.

—Carrie Fox

Notice how the entire sketch revolves around the decor—the walls, floor, posters, and strobe lights. Without any mention of the character's personality, we are made to feel that the occupant in question is perhaps a bit out of the ordinary. As you can imagine, students have a good time creating these bizarre environments. In this focused assignment, everyone enjoys hearing more than a few read aloud. During class, then, I go beyond my usual ten-minute limit and read until we get tired of hearing them.

After sharing their writings, after some of the laughter has died out, I hand out the following passage from *The Ballad of the Sad Cafe* by Carson McCullers. With this, we begin to examine how real writers use personal environment to suggest character.

The large middle room, the parlor, was elaborate. The rosewood sofa, upholstered in green threadbare silk, was before the fireplace. Marble-topped tables, two Singer sewing machines, a big vase of pampas grass—everything was rich and grand. The

> most important piece of furniture in the parlor was a big,
> glass-doored cabinet in which was kept a number of treasures
> and curios. Miss Amelia had added two objects to this collection:
> one was an acorn from a water oak, the other a little velvet box
> holding two small, grayish stones. Sometimes when she had
> nothing to do, Miss Amelia would take out this velvet box and
> stand by the windows with the stones in the palm of her hand,
> looking down at them with a mixture of fascination, dubious
> respect and fear. They were the kidney stones of Miss Amelia
> herself, and had been taken from her by the doctor in Cheehaw
> some years ago.[9]

Students are amazed at McCullers's talent for creating an aura of strangeness. Since most of them have written about environments that include one bizarre item after another, they are struck by this author's using *one* unusual object in the midst of normalcy. The fun of McCullers's paragraph is that everything seems rather ordinary until she reveals the kidney stones in the velvet box. Students learn from this lesson that sometimes the mentioning of a few, selected items has more impact than describing everything in sight.

Notice the organization of the assignment. The students wrestle with the concept first, *before* they study a model from literature. This way their appreciation for style is deepened. Having tried to create a similar mood or environment themselves, they will now value more the expertise of a gifted writer. The daily sentence, then, can be used to practice techniques for developing characterization and to prepare students for their upcoming visits and interviews.

Below are two additional models I show students to demonstrate how professional writers use setting to portray character. The first, from *Slouching Towards Bethlehem* by Joan Didion, gives a sense of the typical up-and-coming young couple in San Bernadino, California.

> . . . he bought a dental practice in the west end of San
> Bernadino County, and the family settled there, in a modest
> house on the kind of street where there are always tricycles and
> revolving credit and dreams about bigger houses, better streets.
> That was 1957. By the summer of 1964 they had achieved the
> bigger house on the better street and the familiar accouter-
> ments of a family on its way up: the $30,000 a year, the three
> children for the Christmas card, the picture window, the family
> room, the newspaper photographs that showed "Mrs. Gordon
> Miller, Ontario Heart Fund Chairman. . . ."[10]

Here is another model, from *In Cold Blood,* in which Truman Capote describes the hotel hideout for two ex-convicts who have just committed a gruesome murder. The quality of the surroundings enhances the seediness of the characters.

---

9. Carson McCullers, *The Ballad of the Sad Cafe* (Boston: Houghton Mifflin, 1936; Bantam, 1971), p. 71.

10. Joan Didion, "Some Dreamers of the Golden Dream," *Slouching Towards Bethlehem* (New York: Farrar, Straus, and Giroux, Inc., 1968), pp. 8-9.

In Miami Beach, 335 Ocean Drive is the address of the Somerset Hotel, a small, square building painted more or less white, with many lavendar touches, among them a lavendar sign that reads, "VACANCY—LOWEST RATES—BEACH FACILITIES—ALWAYS A SEABREEZE." It is one of a row of little stucco-and-cement hotels lining a white, melancholy street. In December, 1959, the Somerset's "beach facilities" consisted of two beach umbrellas stuck in a strip of sand at the rear of the hotel. One umbrella, pink, had written upon it, "We Serve Valentine Ice-Cream." At noon on Christmas Day, a quartet of women lay under and around it, a transistor radio serenading them. The second umbrella, blue and bearing the command "Tan with Coppertone," sheltered Dick and Perry, who for five days had been living at the Somerset, in a double room renting for eighteen dollars weekly.[11]

Providing students with numerous models like the foregoing helps them appreciate the power of a rather simple technique. I also encourage students to find their own samples in outside reading; I offer extra credit for students bringing in excerpts they discover themselves in which writers use setting to portray character. In this way I have collected a rich file of examples that I can use year after year. Finally, I usually have students practice this technique a second or third time to make certain they've mastered the strategy. *Telling* sentences like "He is lazy" or "She is artistic" are simple enough to generate fascinating personal environments.

Focus on Costume

The chart I used earlier to have students evaluate their own possessions can be used in another way, too. In place of attention to personal items of decoration, we can ask students to focus on clothing or costume. Obviously the way people dress says much about their character. Instead of listing three favorite objects on the chart, the students list three items of clothing—which may include accessories—that they are currently wearing. In the same way that students have thought about the images their possessions convey to others, they now consider the impression their clothing makes. After class discussion at the close of the activity, I assign the usual *telling* sentence to see whether students can reveal character solely through dress and attire. Some suitable sentences are: "He is very sporty." "She is extremely shy." "He is a complete comic." Once again, after the students have made their own attempts, model paragraphs by professional writers serve as proof that the technique can be very forceful. Here are several such models. The first is from *The Big Sleep* by Raymond Chandler.

He was a gray man, all gray, except for his polished black shoes and two scarlet diamonds in his gray satin tie that looked like the diamonds on roulette layouts. His shirt was gray and his double-breasted suit of soft, beautifully cut flannel. Seeing Carmen he took a gray hat off and his hair underneath it was gray and as fine as if it had been sifted through gauze. His thick gray eyebrows had that indefinably sporty look.[12]

---

11. Truman Capote, *In Cold Blood* (New York: Random House, Inc., 1965), p. 199.
12. Raymond Chandler, *The Big Sleep* (New York: Aldred A. Knopf, Inc., 1939), p. 42.

This next model is from an article in *Rolling Stone Magazine*, describing the actor Sean Connery.

He is dressed casually, in light blue slacks, loafers and a pink knit shirt bearing the small but celebrated crest of the Sunningdale Golf Club. A thin gold chain around his neck sets off his clear brown eyes and deeply tanned features. His hair is long on the sides and frankly graying. He is, of course, not wearing his working toupee. A dapper mustache droops down over the corners of his mouth, and his occasional smile is craggy and rather magnificent. Yesterday, August 25th, Sean Connery turned fifty-three. He looks great.[13]

A third model in which clothing is mentioned to convey character is from Joe Schaeffer's story, "Rituals."

The pavement blisters in the noon sun and beads of white heat quiver off the concrete walks. A scattering of people—mechanics in shirts with Bob's Conoco, Sampson Ford, or John Deere stitched on the pockets, clerks from hardware and feed stores, bankers and insurance men in short-sleeved shirts and narrow ties, farmers in bib overalls, women in summer dresses and pant suits—move, squinting and exchanging how are yous, toward the sign saying "Try Dr. Pepper—Bea's Restaurant." In the window are posters advertising the Table Grove Merchants' softball schedule and the Lewiston County Fair.[14]

Focus on Mannerisms

Gestures and mannerisms are also a common part of character description. Encouraging students to examine closely the interesting facial expressions or unusual body language of their subjects adds to the quality of their descriptions. Here are some professional models that show the use of gesture and mannerism to develop character. The first is from an article by James Mills.

George Barrett is a tough cop. His eyes, cold as gun metal, can be looked at but not into. His jaw is hard and square as a brick, and his thin lips are kept moist by nervous darting passes of his tongue. When he laughs, only his face and voice laugh. Inside, George Barrett does not laugh.[15]

---

13. Kurt Loder, "Great Scot: Nobody Pushes Sean Connery Around," *Rolling Stone Magazine*, October 27, 1983, p. 17.

14. Joe Schaeffer, "Rituals," in *Writings from Amidst the Uproar* (an unpublished collection prepared by the Bay Area Writing Project summer fellows, 1977).

15. James Mills, "The Detective." Time, Inc., 1972. Appeared in a different form in *Life*, December 8, 1972.

This second excerpt is another from "Rituals."

> On summer nights June bugs fly in maddened, searching patterns in and out of street lights, and teenage boys, in cars and pickup trucks with wide mag wheels and flaming metallic paint jobs, circle Al's A&W, the engines panting and vibrating as the drivers accelerate and brake, accelerate and brake, the right hand loosely atop the steering wheel, the left shoulder lowered, the chin barely visible over the door, the eager eyes seeking, the car stereo blaring out the open windows. They circle once, twice, three times, then back into a dim stall to watch as others circle, accelerate, brake, and look. . . .
>
> They swerve recklessly off the warm asphalt pavement and into Tate's Texaco station, screeching to a halt near the side of the garage. Their drivers emerge smiling and walk in long, bowed strides toward a black, red-flamed Trans Am parked under the station lights. They kick gently at its tires and investigate its soft red interior. The owner inserts a tape and turns up the volume as the boys peer under the hood, touching its parts and commenting.[16]

Again, for more practice we can assign *telling* sentences and require that students develop the generalities into specifics, using one or more of the techniques we have studied: attention to setting, to costume, to mannerism and gesture. Sentences like these work well: "She is nervous." "He has complete confidence." "She is poised and graceful." Students also need to be shown that they need not isolate each category of description in separate paragraphs but might think about incorporating all three together, as in this selection by Rex Reed, describing the aging movie actress, Ava Gardner.

> She stands there, without benefit of a filter lens, against a room melting under the heat of lemony sofas and lavendar walls and cream-and-peppermint striped movie-star chairs, lost in the middle of that gilt-edge birthday-cake hotel of cupids and cupolas called the Regency. There is no script. No Minnelli to adjust the CinemaScope lens. Ice-blue rain beats against the windows and peppers Park Avenue below as Ava Gardner stalks her pink malted-milk cage like an elegant cheetah. She wears a baby-blue cashmere turtleneck sweater pushed up to her Ava elbows and a little plaid mini-skirt and enormous black horn-rimmed glasses and she is gloriously, divinely barefoot.[17]

Mock Interviews

After all their rehearsing in the practice *telling* sentences, the students are much better prepared to write up the results of their visits with the people they have chosen to interview for the I-Search paper. But there's one more important technique they usually need to practice first: observing during the

16. Schaeffer, "Rituals."
17. Rex Reed, "Ava: Life in the Afternoon," *Esquire*, May 1967, p. 102.

interview itself. Students are likely to be nervous doing their first interviews. Even more than being prepared with appropriate questions, they need to practice taking notes—mentally, if not in writing—about such things as setting, costume, and gesture that they notice even while they are asking and jotting down the person's answers to their questions.

For this purpose, I set up a mock interview during class in which students will ask questions of a fellow classmate, getting the information they need to write up a character description. Students select whom they would most like to interview and come to class the following day equipped with at least four interesting questions. At the conclusion of the interview, students will take home their notes and compose brief characterizations based on their dialogues with and observations about the interviewed classmate. Here is one student's characterization of Michael, a well-known, well-liked figure on campus.

A TYPICAL TEENAGER

Sliding comfortably into the desk at the front of the class and extending his blue-jean clad legs, Michael Doyle looked expectantly around the room. The silence was broken by the first of many questions to come as Mike was asked what his philosophy on life is. His head bobbed up excitedly and with a crooked grin he replied, "Enjoy it. We aren't here that long so we might as well enjoy it while we are here." A slight chuckle. "It sounds like a game. Let's have fun, guys." The classroom is instantly at ease. Laughter and giggling can be heard around the room and I myself wonder if this is an interview or a performance.

Questions fill the air and Mike (or Michael, as he prefers) answers them all without so much as a moment's hesitation. When asked what he enjoys doing, he answers, "Sports, going out with friends, and drawing (except in class)." Once again the class was filled with laughter and I decided that we were watching an actor on a stage rather than an interview. But an actor acts a part, and what part is Michael trying to act?

He has the typical teenage look of 501 jeans, Varsity Block jacket, and Adidas tennis shoes, but how can you call anyone a typical teenager when everyone is unique and different. Then came a question which revealed a little of Mike's true personality. He was asked who he was most influenced by and his answer was his mom. Then he was asked about his childhood. "I was born in Georgia and lived in Atlanta before moving to Calua (a small town outside of Memphis)." As Mike described the Southern atmosphere he was brought up in, I noticed that his humorous air was no longer there. He was serious and I saw that the actor was no longer acting, he was involved in the portrayal of his own life.

But the moment didn't last long as once again Mike became the actor and answered a question about how he felt about women. "I don't think women are inferior. I met one or two that were smarter than me, once." And once again the sly chuckle, and the classroom broke into laughter.

So perhaps Mike isn't a typical teenager, but who can be classified as typical?

—Jesse Brennan

This student's portrayal is successful because she really pays attention to the entire conditions of the interview. Not only does she deliver her own impressions, she allows those impressions to be based on the interactions of everyone. She has a keen ability to stand back from the interview itself and observe the entirety of the discussion. At the same time she incorporates costume, gesture, and dialogue to enhance her image of Michael.

The piece is not yet complete, for she leaves us with questions unresolved. Is Mike "acting" or just "typical"? For a finished piece, she would have to draw her conclusions more concisely. As a class exercise, however, she details the 25-minute interview realistically. Here is a student who is ready to do her interviews in the real world.

By hearing read aloud many of each other's portrayals, students acquire new ideas for turning question-and-answer sessions into narration. Since each writer's rendition is usually quite different, students enjoy comparing results; often they learn new stylistic techniques from each other.

Here is another student interview that is more complete in its interpretation of the "character." The class chose to interview Matt because of his outstanding intellect. Students were always amazed by the ease with which Matt could consistently understand obscure symbolism in literature, and by the outstanding responses he would write to difficult composition questions. Many were curious to discover the "real Matt."

WHO IS MATT?

"Are you nervous?" Miss Caplan asks as Matt seats himself at the table facing the class. Flashing a toothy grin, he shrugs an "I dunno" as he draws the chair up to the edge of the table. Eyes quickly glance up to him, then return to their papers. Pencils scribble furiously, noting his every move, attempting to capture him.

He sits, waiting for the first question, arms folded across his chest, legs extended underneath the table. Various questions are thrown at him from the participating classmates—"What's your idea of a fun evening? What kind of food, music, and books do you like?" His face remains molded into a knowing smirk as he contemplates his answers, carefully choosing his words. He responds to each inquisitor dutifully, supporting with examples, being sure to answer every aspect of the question.

Through this barrage of words, he remains slouched in his chair, occasionally scratching his right ear, and staring. He stares intently at the tiny black marks in the grain of the table before him, as if they were giving him some insight. He listens, laughs, and stares.

"What is your opinion of the nuclear arms issue, Matt?" With this question he straightens up, pulling his legs under him. He uncrosses his arms, one hand now stroking an imaginary beard. He looks up. "Well, I feel that total disarmament would be ineffective . . . in a way they (nuclear bombs) have been good to establish peace . . ." He continues on, his words more spontaneous, eyes darting about the room. He is now more at ease, both hands resting flat on the table, his ankles crossed underneath the chair.

For the first time during the interview he seems to be genuinely interested in answering. He also appears more self-condifent. It is during the more intellectual questions that more of his personality is reflected. During the other, superficial questions he tries to put up somewhat different characteristics. When asked about music, for instance, he at first responds with the outer image of liking rock, but as he continues talking more of his inner personality comes out with admitting he enjoys some classical music. Matt is basically a person with a lot of intelligence, but sometimes feels he must put out a somewhat superficial image in order to be accepted.

—Mish Denlinger

This writer, like the previous one, observes the entirety of the interview, not simply the responses to specific questions. Since the students have been trained to notice mannerism and gesture as a way to "show character," this writer focuses just as much attention on Matt's body language as on his responses to the questions. In fact, she ties together nicely the questions and Matt's physical reactions to them, so that her sketch becomes a piece on his *reaction* to being interviewed. She notices when his gestures indicate insecurity or reflect confidence; she senses at what moments he truly becomes involved and at what moments he seems threatened. At the end of the interview, she concludes that Matt's confidence expands when he is asked truly intellectual questions and shrinks when he feels he must "put out an image" in order to be accepted. This writer captures one dominant impression and spotlights it; here is another student ready to interview in the real world.

Focus on Sentence Style

I have found that this I-Search unit also lends itself to the study of improved sentence style. Since so much of the report will focus on close observation, I have frequently incorporated into this preparation period several assignments on improving sentence style, having students examine and imitate the smooth-running, descriptive patterns of professional storytellers and journalists. Earlier in this book, when I described variations for the daily sentence workouts, I spoke about the success I've experienced using the teaching methods of James Gray and Robert Benson in their book, *Sentence and Paragraph Modeling*. Gray bases his approach to sentence modeling on the work of Francis Christensen, who did serious studies of the prose style of the twentieth century. In his work, Christensen discovered that a common syntactic pattern, a frequent use of certain phrasal modifiers, characterizes the sentence styles of many modern writers. These phrasal modifiers—adjective, verb, and noun clusters, and absolutes—embellish the simple independent clauses, making the ideas more elaborate and vivid. Gray carefully describes how he teaches students to imitate these constructions, having them observe real-life subjects to inspire vivid prose. He sends his students around campus and the community to observe interesting scenes and activities; the assignment is to turn their observations into brief scenarios, using the various methods of modification he has introduced in class. Students end up composing longer, extended sentences that are rich in detail and that transform the students' writing styles immediately to a higher level of sophistication.

In my work with "showing, not telling," I immediately recognized a correlation between the "tellingness" of a simple, independent clause and the "showingness" of phrasal modifiers. By using Gray's approach, I could show students how to take simple abstractions and enrich them with colorful detail through the use of various forms of modification. For instance, take this sentence by Katherine Anne Porter:

The jockeys sat bowed and relaxed, their faces calm, moving a little at the waist with the movement of their horses.[18]

Students can distinguish the opening clause, "The jockeys sat bowed and relaxed," as a *telling* idea; they can see how the phrasal modifier (a present participial phrase), "moving a little at the waist with the movement of their horses," extends the original idea into a *showing* statement. In fact, a writer might continue adding phrases and clauses to enrich a simple idea even more. Take this sentence by Conrad Richter:

Asa deliberately busied himself about the post, filling the bin beneath the counter with navy beans and green coffee, leafing through the packet of letters in the drawer, making a long rite out of feeding the occupants of the picket corrals. . . .[19]

In this sentence, the opening clause indicates that the character is "busying himself," a *telling* idea. The author then adds three phrasal modifiers that *show* what is meant by "busying."

Taking Gray's suggestion, I have students imitate these particular patterns, asking them to invent interesting *telling* sentences that are enriched by one or more present participial phrases. Here is one student's model.

> **My mother stirred the spaghetti sauce, wiping the hair out of her eyes with her free hand, bending over now and then to smell the tangy aroma.**
>
> **—Joe Holstine**

This writer expands the scene of his mother's stirring the sauce, zooming in, as though he were the lens of a camera, to record the finer details of that

---

18. Katherine Anne Porter, "Old Mortality," *Pale Horse, Pale Rider* (New York: Harcourt Brace and Co., 1939), p. 49.

19. Conrad Richter, "Early Marriage," *Early Americana and Other Stories* (New York: Alfred A. Knopf, 1936), p. 296.

action. Students can immediately upgrade the quality of their sentence styles by imitating many different cumulative sentence forms. In particular, I spend time introducing them to the use of present and past participial phrases, adjective phrases, and absolutes. After plenty of practice with imitation, I send them out for twenty minutes on campus, asking them to record intriguing situations they observe. I ask that they incorporate several of the modification structures we've been studying. I also suggest they underline and label particular phrases and clauses they decide to use so that I can see they've applied the lessons in a conscientious manner.

Following are some student models that resulted from this assignment. Notice how in all pieces, the writing has a smooth-running, sophisticated style that is unusual and quite impressive for average high school students.

CUSTODIAN

The small golf-cart type vehicle came to a stop. A school custodian, elderly, skin tanned from the long hours of working outside, stepped off the cart. Reaching into the back of the utility vehicle, the man pulled out a broom, the painted handles worn from use, the bristles withered from age. Pulling a large dustpan from the wagon also, he proceeded to a corner of one building. Meticulously sweeping crevices, the custodian cleaned up, not leaving a gum wrapper or a week-old apple core behind. With the dustpan becoming laden with refuse, he went back to the utility wagon and dumped the trash into a tough, plastic receptacle. He placed the things back in the cart and, switching on the high-torque electric motor, rolled another twenty-five feet, continuing the same routine, almost systematically.

—Jim Cowart

THE SMOKING SECTION

A red line encloses thousands of squished cigarette butts and empty Marlboro packs upon an unpaved section of dirt. A brown wall bordering part of the smoking section reveals the words "Heavy Metal" and "Rock and Roll" sprayed in dark, black paint. Scattered trees have been added in an attempt to make the smoking section look more pleasant to other school members and staff. Sitting amongst all this are two girls, their bodies dressed in black leather jackets, tight faded blue jeans, and hiking boots. Pinned to the jacket collar of one of the girls are buttons with little sayings or names of rock groups on them. Both girls are holding cigarettes between their fingers and talking about the morning's events. Putting the cigarette between her lips, one of the girls takes in a deep drag, then twisting her lips to the side, she blows a cloud of smoke out over her shoulder. The girls continue talking, laughing, and puffing, until they soon realize their cigarettes are no more than an inch and a half long. Flicking their cigarette butts onto the dirt, both girls simultaneously get up and wander on their way, leaving only two round, smoking cigarette butts on the ground to add to the decor of many.

—Dina Tavares

P.E. CLASS

As the slow melodic music started, the girls jumped to their places, all except one. She languidly and listlessly pulled herself up, a white, sagging t-shirt hanging from her body, gray ankle sweats clinging to her legs, light-blue Nikes with dark blue stripes encompassing her feet. Her naturally brown hair was topped off with glaringly blonde hair, making her stand out among the rest of the bodies, who moved as one in the aerobics class.

She was always at least two moves behind, obviously bored by the dull, unlively music, laughing with her friend, frantically waving to people crouched behind the door. The music climbed up to an old, up-beat song and her face lit up with ecstatic craze as she put her own moves in, shining uniquely through the one mass of bodies stretching together. She played around, acting out John Travolta, pointed fingers moving in a criss-cross motion. She pulled at her friend, dragging her into a world all their own where they pointed and laughed at other people and played tag, oblivious to the pattern around them. She always had to be different, feet apart when theirs were together, swinging her right arm when they were swinging their left. The music died but she played on, still being different.

—Michelle Teves

COWBOYS

Three Sunolian guys casually sat on the brown-painted wall in front of the Counselor's office, cutting class without a care in the world. They were of the cowboy type from head to toe—a cap with "Copenhagen" or a rodeo logo printed across the forehead resting on their heads, eyes staring through tousled bangs beneath the low brim; they dressed in warm, plaid flannel shirts, dusty down vests, and faded blue jeans, worn thin at the knees and frayed at the bottom, covering scuffed cowboy boots of weathered brown leather, caked with mud and manure. With their hands in their pockets and a wad of chewing tobacco between cheek and gum, they carried on an interesting conversation, or so it seemed, occasionally stopping to spit tobacco juice through their teeth. Their conversation finally came to an end and they casually ambled on their way as an eagle-eyed administrator approached them, referrals in hand.

—Karla Fritts

When the time comes for students to compose their final I-Search reports, I ask students again to try incorporating the cumulative sentence style into parts of the narration; I ask them to see whether this style helps them add detail to their descriptions almost automatically. Many respond by saying the attention to sentence style has helped them weave more detail throughout the report.

Finally, since students are reading *The Right Stuff* as a model of new journalism, I ask them repeatedly to watch for any strategies Tom Wolfe uses that they might apply to their own I-Search papers. Even though I have presented certain techniques such as attention to personal environment, clothing, and mannerism, and attention to cumulative sentence style, I want students to begin isolating new and different investigative approaches *on their own;* I want them to recognize particularly effective reporting techniques that distinguish Tom Wolfe's style. As a final exam on the book, I ask students to write up an analysis of two particular writing techniques in *The Right Stuff* and show how they might apply those techniques in writing their own reports. Here is the exam question I give them:

Select two memorable passages from *The Right Stuff* and analyze the techniques Wolfe uses to do his reporting. You need *not* quote the passage, but *summarize* in your own words the main idea presented. Then, explain what strategies Wolfe uses that you find effective in reporting. During your analysis, you may find it useful to *quote* specific lines that demonstrate the technique you're describing. Finally, relate how you might adapt these particular techniques to your own I-Search paper.

Now, *RE-READ THE EXAM QUESTION.* I am asking for three things as you discuss *two* separate passages:
1. summary of the passage.
2. analysis of the techniques, using quoted lines.
3. application of the techniques to your own paper.

One student who plans to do her I-Search report on preparing for and taking the California driver's license test analyzes two techniques that Wolfe employs. Notice the careful way she applies the strategy to her specific situation.

 One passage I found memorable was near the end, when Yeager is flying the NF-104 and he goes up to 104,000 feet and he can't get the nose of the plane to tip downwards because of the aerodynamic pressure (pp. 357-362). Tom Wolfe writes the passage in sentences linked together with three dots: "He's weightless, coming over the top of the arc . . . 104,000 feet . . . It's absolutely silent . . . Twenty miles up . . ." He does this to show how Chuck Yeager is thinking. He's in space and millions of things are going through his mind and Tom Wolfe lets one get the feel of it by having these bits and pieces of thought flying around between three dots, like Chuck in space. Chuck is probably hyped up now and his adrenaline is pumping and he's thinking in fragments; Tom Wolfe shows this. My I-Search is on taking the driving test, and this strategy may be useful to me. I'll be driving for another

stranger who will be grading me and I'll think in fragments and use Tom Wolfe's technique. For example, "the blinker's off . . . the light is green . . . the car ahead of me is moving . . . press the gas pedal . . . not too fast . . . not too slow . . ." I think that it will show how I'm thinking at that moment, in bits and fragments. It will show what happens in my driving test without repetitiously using "I"—"I saw the green light. I saw the car ahead of me move. I pressed the gas pedal. I made sure I didn't speed, or go too slow." It breaks the monotony of starting all the sentences with "I."

The other passage I found memorable is when Pete Conrad is having his barium examination by the radiologist and after he's done he has to walk to a john two floors below the one he is presently on and he has to hold the balloon, which keeps the barium in place, and he has to hunch over and walk "with his tail in the breeze" in a public corridor (p. 76). Tom Wolfe has interviewed Pete Conrad but he doesn't describe it like an interview, he writes it out as if he could see Pete Conrad then. He doesn't write "and Pete Conrad said, 'My tail was in the breeze' as he walked down the corridor." He incorporates it into the third person form and shows what Pete Conrad has told him, without using direct quotes and quotation marks. I think this will come in handy for me when I interview people and they tell me how their driving tests went. For example, if a person told me he forgot to stop at a stop sign, instead of writing, "Jim said, 'and I realized I had passed it just as I passed it. That's what made me flunk,' I could write instead, "After realizing he had just passed a stop sign, Jim continued on, knowing he had flunked the test." This will become useful so I don't have to keeep on writing "He said" or "And she said." It also lends a certain continuity to the paper without the constant breaking in of quotes and quotation marks which tend to alienate the reader from the writer's work and who said what.

—Wendy Yee

Wendy is ready to apply the strategies she has discovered. Not only is it apparent that she understands Tom Wolfe's reporting techniques, she knows under exactly what circumstances she might apply them to her own style. Whether she actually uses them in her final report is unimportant; she has shown she can discover new options on her own and know how to use them.

After these tests have been graded, I share particularly effective models like Wendy's so that students can learn additional strategies of application from each other.

The Final I-Search Paper

All the while that we've been examining various ways to record interviews and visits, and while we've been spending classtime in close attention to sentence style and new reporting techniques, the students have been arranging their interviews and visiting their chosen places of interest for the final report. At the same time, they have checked out books from the library and have been reading outside information on their topics. Some have gone to the local library to read, on microfilm, past newspaper articles that add to their knowledge of certain contemporary issues. For instance, while investigating crime in a local neighborhood, one student researched all the evidence of crime that had been reported in the local newspapers around the area. Other students have sent away to private companies or individuals to obtain pamphlets and brochures that would enrich their knowledge of a particular occupation. One girl who wanted to become involved in cosmetic sales in the home wrote to both Avon and Mary Kay Cosmetics to ask for informational literature. In their final reports, students share such outside information by weaving in the relevant findings.

For the remainder of this chapter, I want to present three final I-Search papers. You should be aware that these samples were written by students with varying English skills. The first two writers had trained in honors English since their freshman year, while the third writer had moved up from an average English program to the honors section only that year, when his former teacher decided he was ready for more advanced work. As a result, this third student found he had to work diligently to keep up with his peers. Nonetheless, his paper is a valuable model. I hope to show that even though a student may not have accelerated skills, he is able to pursue his I-Search spiritedly and learn something refreshingly new about himself and about the world.

Notice how all three writers use the techniques and strategies we've been studying for strengthening narrative style. Each gives some attention to characterizations, including environment, costume, gesture, and mannerism; to recording events, using the cumulative sentence style where effective; and to incorporating outside reading and research, to add authenticity to their investigations and to help them draw conclusions about their findings.

In the first paper, a young woman shows her careful investigation of the world of veterinarians. Having felt a love for animals since she was a small child, this student decides to find out whether she has what it takes to become a dedicated animal doctor.

ANIMAL DOCTORS

[The cover page of this paper displayed six color photographs related to one of the three veterinarians the writer interviewed, a doctor at Wildlife Safari Land in Oregon. The paper began with a table of contents and ended with the requisite end notes and bibliography citing her outside reading.]

I think I could turn and live with animals, they're so placid and self-contained,
I stand and look at them long and long.
They do not sweat and whine about their condition,
They do not lie awake in the dark and weep for their sins,
They do not make me sick discussing their duty to God.
Not one is dissatisfied, not one is demented with the mania of owning things,
Not one kneels to another, nor to his kind that lived thousands of years ago,
Not one is respectable or unhappy over the whole earth.

Walt Whitman
Song of Myself

As long as I can remember, I have loved animals. One of my first childhood memories is chasing Simba, our tiger-striped manx cat, around the house. Throughout my young life I have owned a variety of pets including dogs, cats, rabbits, horses, hamsters, and even a duck. But it was not until high school that I became interested in pursuing a veterinary career. It was then that I realized I not only loved animals but I enjoyed science and medicine too! I had found a career into which I could fit in, now I have only to discover how to go about getting involved and which field I want to be a part of.

The veterinary field is a very large one and contains a variety of different types of careers. Different careers include Doctor of Veterinary Medicine (D.V.M.), Animal Health Technician, Medical Lab Assistant, Nutritionist, Animal Science Teacher, Feed Manufacturer, Animal Trainer, Pack Station Operator, Zoo Animal Keeper, and Blacksmith. In considering the amount of schooling necessary for these careers, it ranges from no schooling for an Animal Training career, Medical Lab Assistant career, or a Pack Station Operator career to two years of schooling (college) or other specialized training for a Zoo Animal Keeper career, Blacksmith career, or an Animal Technician career, to four or more years of college for an Animal Science Teaching career, Doctorate of Veterinary Medicine career, or Nutritionist career.

Both people and my sources of reading strongly suggest that you get involved in the career of your choice before wholeheartedly deciding to spend four college years working towards something you may discover later is just not right for you. In order to really enjoy a career you must understand and accept the pitfalls along with the joys and inspirations because the pitfalls do exist. It is often said among veterinarians that "Loving animals is not enough to get you through veterinary school or a veterinary career, you really have to love medicine and science too!"

DR. LYNN FAUGHT, Doctor of Veterinary Medicine

The dark, brown building loomed ominously before me. The wooden brown sign reading "Village Parkway Veterinary Hospital" seemed to reflect the afternoon sunlight almost as if it were a mirror. Gathering my wits and taking a deep breath, I entered the hospital. The smell of antiseptic greeted my nostrils as I stepped in. Finding myself in a small, brown panelled waiting room with cream colored vinyl seats and colorful animal posters, I paused to get my bearings. The waiting room was vacant and I glanced at my watch to assure myself that it was a little after 12:30 p.m. I remembered the pleasant voice on the phone and our arrangements to meet for an interview during her lunch break. But where was she now?

Then I heard a doorknob click and, turning, I saw an older woman enter through a side entrance. She flashed me a welcoming smile and her eyes gleamed at me from behind silver-rimmed glasses. She wore a white smock over a blue cotton blouse and blue jeans and I smiled at the Nike tennis shoes she wore. "Sorry to keep you waiting," she said. "I had a couple of things that had to be done." I nodded and told her I hadn't been waiting that long. "Have a seat," she added and I dropped thankfully into the soft vinyl chair opposite her.

"Tell me about yourself," I asked. "How did you become interested in a veterinary career and where did you get your education?"

"When I was a little girl, I used to have fantasies about the animals I was going to have when I grew up. My father was dead, we lived with my grandparents in the East, and although I was crazy about animals, I wasn't allowed to have many pets. I remember once they did give me a puppy. I was ecstatic—but three days later it died of distemper. And once I had a little black cat that had been injured, and we weren't able to housetrain it. Very soon, it disappeared; I found out later my grandmother had disposed of it.

"So I used to dream that when I grew up I would have a great big house with many, many dogs and cats, and they would all have their own rooms and belongings and whatever special foods they wanted, and we would all be so happy. I planned also to have a huge barn and pasture where old, worn-out, unwanted horses would live out their days in bliss. (I guess I had read *Black Beauty* a hundred times!) In my fantasy, I could take in every homeless animal I met, and it would grow fat and sleek and happy. Maybe my ideas about veterinarians formed vaguely then, all I know is that my mother and grandparents tried to discourage me at first. After all, this was in the 1950s—women veterinarians were still looked upon as freaks. 'Didn't I want to be a nurse instead?' they asked me. 'Or a teacher?'

"But I was a stubborn child, and once my mother saw how determined I was, she supported me. When I was in high school, she arranged for me to visit a local veterinarian regularly and watch him work. He also encouraged me. I was accepted at Cornell University and a year later was accepted at a veterinary college."

"Did any problems arise because you were a woman in a so-called man's career?" I continued.

"I had heard that in some of the lab courses, the male students grumbled about having a female lab partner, and there I was, the only girl in my class. I was apprehensive at first. But the boys were nice—I always had a lab partner. In fact, throughout my veterinary college years, it was like having thirty-nine brothers."

"How did you come by this job?" I asked.

"Most veterinarians take an internship or apprenticeship right after graduation and get some supervised experience, but I didn't so I was very nervous about taking in surgical cases. I didn't want to take on someone's pet and mess up. So for quite a long time I referred any surgical cases to other vets, but then we moved. I found new work here at the Village Parkway Veterinary Hospital and it was then that I began gaining experience with surgical cases."

"Is there something you wish you could change?" I continued.

"Yes, in my experience as a vet, I see a great deal of neglect of animals, and usually there's nothing you can do about it. I wish there was something I could do. Millions of animals each year suffer and even die from neglect."

"Is your career satisfying?" I questioned.

"To me, a practicing veterinarian of thirty years experience, each case pulses with excitement, truth, sincerity and the humor that is somehow always bound up with the treatment of animals. I don't think I could be happy doing anything but what I'm doing."

DR. DONALD GARDNER, Doctor of Veterinary Medicine

The white house I pulled to a stop in front of on Sunol Blvd. could have been any other home on the road except for the white sign hanging out front reading "Town and Country Veterinary Hospital." I climbed out of my car and walked up the brick walkway, through the landscaped front yard to the tall, oak door. I grabbed the golden door knocker and let if fall three times in rapid succession. I heard footsteps and then a dark haired man of about thirty, wearing brown slacks and a plaid shirt, opened the door. His brown eyes looked questioningly at me for a second, then with a reassuring smile, he opened the door wider and bade me to accompany him to his office. Following him down a short hallway, I entered his office—an ivory carpeted room, with blue sofas and chairs, complete with a desk and a wall containing some six different degrees and certificates of schooling. Sitting across from me behind the desk he said, "Fire away!" in a calm level voice, and fire I did.

"Tell me about yourself and how you became interested in becoming a veterinarian?" I asked.

"I never wanted to be anything but a veterinarian. My father was a veterinarian, my uncle, my grandfather—it never occurred to me that there was anything else worth becoming. When I was a kid, the high point of my life was helping my father in his clinic on Saturdays and holidays, sometimes all summer."

"Have you encountered any rare or dangerous cases in your veterinary practice?" I continued.

"So far, in the two and a half years I've been practicing, I haven't seen many rare, medically unusually cases, but there sure have been a lot of challenging ones. Dogs mostly—in the country they are always getting run over by mowing machines or hit by cars, and they all are brought in broken and mangled, with their bones sticking out. It makes you feel really good if you can succeed in putting them back together and make them well again."

"What have you learned that you wish you might have learned sooner?" I questioned.

"One thing I've learned is to always answer my clients' questions fully, no matter how difficult, or dumb, or in some cases—funny. Some weeks ago, for example, a lady brought in a six-week-old puppy for a checkup. It was the first puppy she had ever owned. I examined him, and he was a real healthy little pup. But in the course of the conversation the lady said, 'You know, Doctor, he does seem to have a problem that worries me.'

"'Well, what's that?' I asked.

"'He doesn't seem to know how to urinate,' she said hesitantly. 'As a male dog, he should lift his hind leg, but he only wants to pee squatting down like a female dog. I've been trying to teach him the right way. When I take him for walks, I tie a rope around one of his hind legs, and then lead him up to a tree and lift his leg with the rope so he's in the right position for a male dog to be peeing in. But he doesn't seem to be catching on! Do you think he's sick?'

"I'm happy to say that I was able to contain my laughter and keep a straight face. I told her that all pups urinate that way, and that when he was full grown and more mature he would lift his leg."

"What are some things you would suggest to a beginning veterinarian?" I asked.

"First-year-itis is the trouble with most young vets at the end of their first year of private veterinary practice. They come out of veterinary school wanting to lick the world and cure every disease. But those who go right into private practice find themselves swamped with heavy case loads before they are really ready. Handling emergency cases all by yourself is especially scary. The pressure builds up and then the young vets begin to give under the strain. If help is not soon given, the young vets lose their practices and lose interest in their career."

"Is your job satisfying?" I questioned.

"The people we deal with as veterinarians are usually under some degree of emotional strain. They have an involvement with their animal, or they wouldn't be seeing us in the first place. They may be farmers with a herd of milk cows they know intimately, or hog farmers with only a financial involvement with their hogs, or pet owners who think of themselves practically as parents of their pets. You have to remember their feelings at all times, even when you are having a bad day, and they are exasperating you with their unreasonable demands. In the long run, though, I find that most people who come to us with their animals are nice. And the satisfaction I get when I'm able to help the animals—well, I think I have the best job in the world for an animal lover!"

DR. MELODY ROELLKE, Doctor of Veterinary Medicine

My final interview was under surprising circumstances. I was in Oregon for a state soccer tournament when we visited Wildlife Safari Land, a wilderness preserve in which people drive through actual habitats where lions, tigers, cheetahs, elephants, rhinos, antelopes, monkeys, and birds of all kinds run free and uninhibited by cages or fences! At the end of our tour, an idea struck me and I rushed over to the Wildlife Safari Clinic and asked to see the veterinarian. I was lucky enough to find her in her office and agreeable to have me interview her. Dr. Melody Roellke sat before me in a black desk chair with framed pictures of animals surrounding her on the walls of her office. She was a woman of about twenty-five, with long, brown hair, brown eyes, and a dark complexion. Her white teeth gleamed at me from behind her smile.

"Tell me about yourself and how you became interested in being a veterinarian?" I asked.

"I was born and raised on a Willamette Valley farm in Lebanon, Oregon. I developed an early concern and love for animals and when I was fourteen I was lucky enough to get a job at the Portland Zoo. I was fascinated by the veterinarian and his dealings with exotic animals. It was then that I realized that I wanted to be a Zoo Veterinarian! I went to school and three years later I was hired to the post of Wildlife Safari Veterinarian over fifty other hopeful applicants!"

"What was your most satisfying moment?" I questioned.

"It had to have been treating Tanga, a 700-pound baby African elephant for a fractured tibia (lower bone in the leg). Tanga fractured his leg while jumping over a fallen tree and it took two tractors and a dump truck to get him back to the clinic and seventy pounds of plaster to cast his leg. But four months later, Tanga was back on the Wildlife Safari range, running and frolicking just as well as any of the other elephants."

"What rare or dangerous cases have you encountered?" I asked.

"I once treated a boa constrictor with a toothache. It was one of the strangest cases I have ever encountered! The constrictor, whose name was Bo-Bo, wouldn't eat and a ranger noticed it knocking its head up against a tree stump. I got out there as soon as I could and, failing to locate a throat obstruction or abscess, I looked at its teeth. Sure enough, there it was, a huge, rotten tooth! Five minutes later, with Bo-Bo under anesthesia, I extracted the tooth. When Bo-Bo woke up, he was right as rain! It was the oddest thing that ever happened to me!"

"Is your career satisfying?" I questioned.

"I wouldn't live any other way. The animals and the people here are the only family I know and I wouldn't give them up for anything!"

Some veterinarians take a roundabout route to arrive at their profession. Instead of studying a pre-veterinary course in college and then going straight into veterinary school, a few people start off in a different direction. Later realizing what they really want to do is go to veterinary school, they eventually wind up happy and busy in the type of veterinary practice that's right for them. I have already decided that a veterinary career is right for me. Before me lies a rough road, but I am willing to follow it to the end. I believe that if my love for animals will not carry me through, then my love for science and medicine will.

—Jesse Brennan

Jesse's I-Search report is successful because she seems to see herself in the doctors she interviews. She declares her early fondness for animals and finds that her subjects, too, shared that same childhood fascination. She seems to enjoy hearing the histories of their careers; it is as if she is discovering what her *own* future might be as she delights in the fascinating stories they have to tell. We are inclined, then, to believe her when she reaffirms her commitment to pursuing a veterinary career. Having researched her field options and the required schooling, and having seen real veterinarians at work, she is willing to take the plunge.

If I had one suggestion to offer Jesse, it would be to develop more her "love for science and medicine." Since she stresses the importance of enjoying the academics of veterinary schooling, both in her introduction and conclusion, she needs to prove to us that this would, as she puts it, "carry her through."

In the second report, which I have excerpted here because of its exceptional length (some 18 pages, or more than 4500 words), Bob Boughn observes the happenings at a "pyramid party" and researches the aftereffects of this crazed fad, which hit the local community like wildfire in the spring of 1980.

EASY MONEY

[First he sets the scene, and the tone, by taking us directly to one of the vaguely mysterious pyramid parties.]

April 16, 1980

As the investors drove the Ford station wagon with the faded paint job down the residential street of the suburb, they came along rows of cars parked along the roadside. There was a '68 Volkswagen bus with a dented side, a couple of Dodge vans, a few pickups, Cadillacs, and Chevys, and a 1980 black Corvette with its license papers taped to the window. They knew that the directions to tonight's meeting were correct. There was a tall man with a full beard standing outside, looking at the people in the cars as they drove by and waving as if to say, "Yes, this is the place." The driver went down the road and pulled around the corner to avoid parking in front of the house. They watched a carload of people pile out of a Granada and swarm to the house behind a large willow tree, acting as if they were trying to be incognito. One middle-aged lady in a business man's outfit was wearing dark glasses. The investors themselves parked and walked up to the house, feeling the bulge in their wallets and purses in anticipation of being convinced to become "involved." As they walked in, they saw 100 strange faces staring with a high intensity, all having one thing in common: the large chart set up in the back of the room, the pyramid, the key to $16,000. And all it took was a thousand.

When the majority of the people had arrived and entered the house, the meeting was underway. Doctors, lawyers, factory workers, and hustlers sat on couches and in chairs encircling the speaker, the chart, and the secretary sitting at a bridge table. The room was busy with a nervous chatter. There was a sharp knock at the door, causing the chatter to cease as the speaker jumped up, grabbing the chart and hiding it in another room. Someone near the door answered it. It was only a latecomer. As soon as he sat down, the nervous chatter returned to its normal level and people began to mill around. The investors sat quiet and still. They weren't really sure yet why they had come, but felt that it held the answer to their problems, the capitalistic dream. A friend (no, actually an acquaintance) of theirs, whom they had met by buying some furniture from once, came over one day and told them of this pyramid he was in. He brought over a chart and explained to them how it worked and convinced them to come to a pyramid party with him, and here they were. They still didn't quite understand how the chart worked and were a bit skeptical of the whole operation. But their friend was so self-assured, so involved, so enthusiastic and hyped up that he couldn't be *that* wrong. In fact everyone at the party was that enthusiastic, that hyped up. Not all of those people could be wrong. Their friend told them success stories of persons he knew who won $16, $32, even $64 thousand. "I know a good thing when I see it," they remember him saying. . . . The speaker now stood up in front of the large chart drawn on poster board and tried to get everyone to quiet down. He politely asked if anyone was from the police department, FBI, CIA, IRS, or any other government agency and if so, to make themselves known. All was still. The speaker then explained to the new investors how the pyramid worked. What they would do is invest $1000 into the pyramid, giving $500 to the person on the top and $500 to the person he/she signs up under. When the pyramid's bottom line of 32 spaces is filled up, the pyramid splits into four new pyramids. . . . After the explanation, there would be an endless amount of confusion from new investors and old ones who found something they didn't realize before. The speaker would have to be firm, confident, and at all times be glorifying the pyramid, since the only way for it to exist is to have a continual flow of new investors. An unconvinced potential investor is a threat to the entire system. It took quite a salesman's attitude to be a successful speaker. One would have to have a certain talent; some even considered it an art. . . .

[*He goes on to explain the actual exchange of money.*]

A new investor would bring up two sealed envelopes, both containing $500 each, and written on the outside the words "a gift." The secretary would take the envelopes and pull out a dish with pieces of paper with numbers of the vacant spaces on them. The investor would pick a number and his name would be written in the numbered space he picked, along with his phone number. The secretary would call the person whose name was above the new investor's spot up to receive his/her "gift." The new investor would then receive a "thank-you note" from the persons that his "gift" went to. After all the proceedings had taken place, there was warm, hearty applause and the next investor would be called up to fill the next spot on the chart. . . .

[*All this cash changing hands—was it noticed by local banks? The student interviewed a local bank manager to find out.*]

Banks were running low on $100 bills and West Coast Federal's branch in Castro Valley actually ran out of cash for a day. One would have to go into Hayward just to cash a check. "It was one of the strangest things I have ever encountered since I have been working here," says Larry, the branch manager. "About a month later, after the pyramid schemes had phased out, we had so much cash we couldn't get rid of it.". . .

[The writer also talked to the dreamers who rushed into these schemes.]

People pictured exotic trips to Hawaii and Europe, being able to buy a microwave oven, new carpeting, and other home improvements, or a new car. One lady dreamed of buying a Winnebago motor home and having a license plate spelling PYRAMID to show off to all those who didn't believe she would make it to the top. (By the way, she never did.) To most, it was a way to pay off all their bills and debts.

The only way to achieve those dreams would be to get to the top of the pyramid, and to get to the top of the pyramid meant to recruit more people. . . . Asking someone if they were on a pyramid became the first thing one would say to someone after saying hello.

[He describes the time-consuming, obsessive nature of the pyramids—the continuous need to recruit more investors—and how this interfered with people's daily working lives. He also describes the reservations and skepticism of those who refused to become involved. Then he turns to media treatment of the phenomenon.]

Articles were run in the newspapers telling how impossible it was for a pyramid to stay in circulation for very long. They would explain that after a series of splits, it would take the entire population of the world to keep them going. Local TV news stations ran special coverage on the "pyramid people" in hopes of raising their ratings by showing the lives of real people involved in another California fad. Channels 5 and 7 would show scenes of parties getting broken up by police raids, . . . Then some kind of statistician from a university would appear on the screen and say that one such pyramid could go around the world in *x* amount of days involving *x* million people, mentioning what the odds of winning were, and how high the risk of losing. The people who read these articles and saw the TV news were convinced that the pyramids didn't work. They told their friends and convinced them to also not get involved. The media made the public wary. . . .

[With good choice of detail, this writer conveys the illicit flavor of the parties.]

Customarily the party location would be changed every night to avoid busts and to confuse police. No one would know where the next meeting would be. They were held at ranch homes, barns, warehouses, and even a moving motor home. Some parties would have passwords, and if one wasn't at the last meeting and didn't know it, he didn't get in. To protect their identity if a chart was uncovered, people frequently used "code names" when signing on the chart. One could find Dirty Harry, Robert Redford, or Emperor

Norton on his pyramid. If two or more people "went in on" one spot, they would combine their names together to create a tongue-twisting jumble. Some even signed up their dog or cat on the chart. Parties were known to attract masqueraders with Lone Ranger masks or Halloween ghoul faces. Others tried to disguise the party itself. An Amway distributor who held a party set up his Amway products in case of a raid. If there was a raid, the chart would be hidden and it would look like an Amway party. His idea worked so well that one person who showed up, who didn't even know about the pyramid, really did think it was just an Amway party.

[The writer then leads us into the self-destructive nature of the whole scheme. He describes the problem of area saturation and people's frantic attempts to take their pyramids anywhere, even across the country, just to keep them going. He explains how greedy, obsessive investors created confusion by joining several pyramids at once, or creating their own, sometimes with new rules.]

About six weeks after a pyramid hit an area, it became saturated and the parties became slow and frustrating. One had to be one of the first on a list in an area in order to make it to the top. Timing was crucial. The pyramids came and went so quickly that some didn't even notice their presence. But for those who were still on their way to the top when their pyramid was no longer active, it was a bitter struggle to try to keep it alive. Parties were no longer fun; they were serious, deadly serious. . . . Fights broke out amongst dissatisfied investors. Threats were made and best friends now became enemies. It was a bitter scene.

[The writer includes notes from interviews he conducted with one-time participants in the scheme, after it has died away—most of them losers, most reluctant to discuss it at all. Then, curious about the "legal or not?" question, he interviewed police to inquire about the oft-cited raids on pyramid parties.]

I went to the Pleasanton police station and asked if they had made any arrests. They answered no and said they didn't even try to bust any parties. They told me to try the Livermore police station. At Livermore, they didn't know about any arrests made, either. The officer I talked to went around asking everyone if they knew anything about the pyramids. They made no arrests and, like Pleasanton, didn't even try to.

[Finally, he concludes his paper with an astute observation.]

Operations like the pyramids have been around since the 1930's. They seem to come and go in cycles, every two, five, or ten years, or whenever there is a halt in the nation's economy. Scams like the pyramids will always exist as long as people have the desire to become rich.

—Bob Boughn

[Included as an appendix was a handout from one of the parties, titled "Business List Concept Memorandum," explaining the details

of the scheme. Also included were photos and drawings of the party scene, labeled "Visions of Pyramid Madness."]

Bob does a masterful job of incorporating the three major requirements for I-Search—visits, interviews, and outside research. From his exhaustive descriptions of the pyramid scheme, parties, characters who bought in, and officials remotely connected (bank teller, local police), to his reporting of newspaper and television coverage, he shows his serious commitment to his search. The work he put into this paper will certainly stay with him long after he graduates from high school. Whenever he sets out to do research again, he will likely remember the satisfaction gained from being so personally involved; research in the future may seem less of a drudgery, more of a delight.

In the third report, Ross Woodard (the junior who was new to the accelerated English program) intended to track down and interview Bay Area rock musician Carlos Santana. Lead guitarist for the Latin-influenced band Santana, Carlos has been an idol to Ross for three years. Since Ross himself plays Latin rhythms on his conga drum, he was excited about interviewing one of the hottest musicians of the decade. However, when he learned that he would be unable to talk to Carlos, he had to change direction. Instead, he interviewed another member of the Santana band, a personable fellow who encouraged Ross to play improvisationally with the conga drum musicians who gather in Berkeley square—which Ross did as part of his search. Though this student may not share the advanced writing skills of his peers in honors English, he writes a report tremendously appealing and compelling; once again, we get the feeling that his experiences in I-Search will be long remembered.

THE RHYTHM HAS MY SOUL

"A perfect solo is the best of your imagination, feeling, sincerity and simplicity. Louis Armstrong once said that when he was going to take a solo, he would picture an orchard and pick the fruit that is most ripe."

Carlos Santana
Musician Magazine

About three years ago, I was record shopping and I bought an album by a group named Santana. I had heard one of the songs off the album on the radio and I really enjoyed the intensity of the percussion section. I had been playing drums two years prior to this, but I had never really listened to any Latin devices such as the conga and timbales. Enthused by this new and exciting sound, my Santana record collection began to multiply faster than a colony of rabbits. I soon owned twenty-one different Santana albums.

Being a drummer, I was utterly shocked by the complexity and speed of the Santana percussion section. I soon began the search for my own conga drum. After days of disappointment due to high prices and a low budget, I finally found one that satisfied me both musically and, most important, financially.

That night, I had been playing for about three hours straight when I noticed my conga head had little red stains on it. I was in hysterics! I thought someone had spilled red ink on it. To my surprise, I glanced down to find blood languidly trickling from the joints of my fingers.

My drumset, once the apple of my eye, lay dormant, collecting mounds of dust, while I gave my conga my most conscientious attention.

The conga, tall, sleek and slender, has become my everyday habit, hobby, and obsession. In the immortal words of Peter Gabriel, "The rhythm is below me, the rhythm of the beat, the rhythm is around me, the rhythm has control, the rhythm is inside me, the rhythm has my soul."

When the "I-Search" paper was first assigned, I desperately wanted an interview with Carlos Santana. As I soon found out, you can't always get what you want. Santana had been on tour in Europe for three months until a week ago. So instead of writing a big sob story on how I couldn't reach Carlos Santana, I changed my topic.

With three days left before the deadline, I had to move fast. I remembered a former student from Foothill telling me his cousin had played in the Santana band for several years.

I called him up and he gave me the phone number of a Mr. Pete Escovedo. "Pete Escovedo!!!," I exclaimed. "He is only the hottest timbale player ever to play with Santana!" What do you say to someone you have idolized for more than two years; someone who has mastered the craft I so obsessively love.

Pete Escovedo has played on five different Santana albums, including my favorite "Moonflower" in which he plays my most favorite solo ever.

Nervously, I sat down at my desk to compose a list of choicely selected questions. After all, one doesn't want to look like an ignorant orangutan while speaking with his idol.

My questions, all grammatically perfected, were all ready for answering. With my hands shaking, I dialed cautiously, awaiting the moment of truth.

"Hello, may I please speak with Mr. Escovedo?"

"This is him speaking."

When I heard those four words, I nearly passed out from a severe case of anxiety. I calmly proceeded to explain the purpose of my call and he told me he was flattered! Can you believe that! I was expecting him to be disturbed by my call and the guy is flattered! I was absolutely freaking out.

Right from the start of the interview he was cooperative and willing to answer not only the questions asked, but also many others that related to the original question.

He told me that taking a solo is like the writing in a good book. Organization and creativity are the keys whereas the conga is the lock, anticipating its own opening.

One of my questions dealt with his favorite Santana album. He told me that his favorite was "Santana III" which also just happens to be my favorite!

One of the more humorous segments of the interview was when I asked him how he got his nickname "Coke." He replied, "No comment," followed by a snickering chuckle.

When asked if he had a second chance to choose a different instrument, would he?, he said, "Percussion is the center of a song. I believe the most challenging instrument used for artistic expression is the basic drum. One must keep the tempo besides attempting creativity or else the song will become dissonant. So the answer to your question is no. I really enjoy the challenge that percussion presents."

Throughout the entire interview, "Coke" kept repeating the importance of the bass or root of a song. He said, "Beginners seem to forget about the root rhythm and therefore sound out of tune. Master the root rhythm before trying to solo upon it."

He told me to go to Berkeley and play with the guys in the square. He said they solely concentrate on the bass-root rhythm.

Coincidentally, the day before I got this interview, I went to the Berkeley square and played with the guys.

As I casually walked towards the group of conga palyers, my stomach began to feel like a blender. What if I wasn't good enough?

Tentatively setting up my conga, I watched the five Africanos play with joy and intensity. Once I started to play, I knew I could keep the pace! I was smothered with personal satisfaction.

After about five minutes of keeping a strong root rhythm, I began to solo. And as Louis Armstrong suggested, I went picking for that sweet old fruit. As I continued my blitzing solo (how modest can one be), the player next to me started smiling and said, "We got a new boy on the block."

Eyes glittering and ego expanding, I decided to stop while I was ahead.

There were two groups of percussionists that day, one of which was very professional and the other of which was concentrating less on solos and more on a steady flowing African rhythm.

I didn't even want to attempt playing with the pro's, due to my slight inferiority complex. I believe anybody would feel inferior to these guys! In simple form, they were jamming with a capital J. I brought a tape recorder along and came up with an array of interesting sounds, including rollerskates, crying baby, brawl between four-year-old brother and sister, unidentified flute soloist, one interview, and last but not least, some really cool conga playing.

On the other side of the tape, there is some incredible Pete "Coke" Escovedo soloing, besides the addition of myself.

For one year, I had never played with anybody but the Santana band on record. Although I had a lot of fun in Berkeley, I still enjoy the personal freedom of playing anything I want while I am at home listening to Santana. Notice the difference in style on side B as opposed to side A.

I prefer "Coke" Escovedo's ripping solos against the sweet harmony of the Santana band. I also prefer my solos with Santana records more than my solo with five other Conga players.

In conclusion, this assignment has opened my eyes to the world of rhythm. Before I spoke with "Coke" and the guys in Berkeley, I never was very interested in the bass-root rhythm. However, now I see how very important it really is. Courage to call Pete "Coke" Escovedo is courage I thought I never had, but the most incredible part of my research was actually sitting down with five African conga players and holding my own. When playing in my room, a mistake is only acknowledged by myself, but a mistake with five well inclined conga players would be absurdly embarrassing. Finally, I learned that no matter what it takes, I will always satisfy a personal goal. Although I never got hold of Carlos Santana himself, I redirected my path and achieved the next best thing, a former band member who plays the same instrument as myself!

—Ross Woodard

[The bibliography included several articles from music magazines, a list of albums that the interviewed Pete Escovedo plays on, and a newspaper article about the origin of African percussive music, as well as a note that the writer could find no books on Cuban or African music styles. He also submitted the tape he refers to in his paper.]

True, this student is not as conscientious as the other writers in incorporating all the required elements; he has only one real interview instead of three, and he does not go to great lengths describing the environment in Berkeley, submitting instead his tape recording of the event. Still, we cannot overlook the spiritedness of his search. I watched this student, weeks after the report had been turned in, roam confidently around campus telling anyone who would listen how he "met" Pete Escovedo and also played with professional conga drum musicians. I also witnessed him start his own rock band and perform several times before the entire student body.

It is easy to see why so many students come to enjoy this assignment; by giving them power, by telling them they have the *authority* to find out the things they care about in this world, *and* by showing them how to go about it, they come to see research writing as something relevant in their own lives instead of seeing it as a project teachers *make* them do in school.

4 Training in Revision Techniques

CHAPTER NINE
Using Response Groups
for Effective Criticism

Throughout this book, I have mentioned the effectiveness of having students rehearse their rough-draft compositions in front of a larger audience. When students have the opportunity of airing their ideas before finalizing them, they come to learn the importance of writing as a *process*—that writing is not necessarily complete the first time around. They also learn that in writing, what we *think* we have said and what we have *actually* communicated might not be in agreement. If students come to see that writing can change and improve with directed revision, and if they notice their own improvement often enough, they are likely to value the service that the response group offers. Also, students who are themselves composing paragraphs for the same assignments have a vested interest in reading their classmates' papers and giving advice; in so doing, they can learn how to improve their own papers. Once students come to trust the advantages of a response group, once they *expect* the opportunity of rehearsing in front of a live audience, they find they cannot live without their groups. If I fail to provide time for sharing, they beg me to reconsider. Of course, they will not always be provided with such attentive private audiences in their future years of writing, but they might learn how to become their own effective critics through having served as critics so regularly in the classroom environment.

As a rule, I don't organize response groups until students have had plenty of training in responding to *telling* sentences daily in front of the class. During our daily evaluation of their *showing* paragraphs, I provide the training ground for effective criticism. I steer students toward the proper ways of giving a fellow writer praise and guidance.

To help students respond effectively, I discuss some general guidelines with them; we explore different ways to say something positive about the writing, and ways to make specific suggestions for improvement. (A set of "Guidelines for Responding to Student Writing" is included in the Appendix.)

It isn't until I sense that the group knows the difference between general and specific, both in the actual text of a composition and in the way we give appropriate feedback, that I turn them loose in regular response groups. I generally place them into their groups when we are ready to compose our first major assignment—usually after six weeks of daily sentence practice and oral critiques. From here on in, they will meet in their groups whenever they begin work on another major assignment. The amount of time spent in the response groups will vary, depending on the nature and length of the assignment.

Basically, I direct students to help classmates improve their rough drafts by telling each other what works and what still needs development. When response group members tell a writer what parts of a piece *succeed*, they are giving the writer confidence to proceed with his or her ideas. By the time students move into response groups, they are better at giving *specific* feedback in both areas—what works and what doesn't. For instance, they have been trained to go beyond statements like "good introduction" or "good details" to indicate which specific details really work. Citing "wearing curlers in the supermarket" as a good detail shows the writer what parts of the piece of writing catch the reader's attention. As a result, it might occur to the writer to include more of this exactness in his or her writing. If a student tells his partner in response group that her introduction is effective because "it gets my attention when you re-create the family argument; I can picture how frustrating your father's interruptions on the phone really are," the writer will see the value of using scene re-creation as an option for introducing provocative ideas into essays.

At the same time, I ask students to spot underdeveloped ideas, underlining on their classmates' papers the generalities that need clarity and expansion. Student editors write "SHOW" in the margins to indicate that the writer should spend time developing the underlined abstractions. A student might find that response partners have underlined four *telling* sentences that need increased *showing*. The writer might then spend the next two days developing those four ideas exclusively, putting the rest of the essay aside for the time being. As a writer expands and reshapes her ideas, she comes back to the response group again and again to see whether or not her revisions are working. Students treat the underlined sentences in their drafts as if they were homework assignments just like the daily workouts for changing *telling* to *showing*. They write each underlined sentence at the top of separate sheets of paper, then expand each idea into whole paragraphs. In this way, they can give careful study to each abstract thought. (You will see this process at work in the following chapter.)

Paper of the Week

There is another approach that helps students learn to spot underdeveloped ideas. Every week I put a sample rough draft on the overhead projector—a paper from another class, or a paper from a previous year—and generate discussion on the merits and shortcomings of that particular piece, which we call the Paper of the Week. As students prepare their own compositions on major topics, they study anonymous pieces like these to learn ways of improving their own writing. First we collectively respond to what is favorable in the draft. With a wax pencil, I star those sections on the transparency and write a brief note in the margin next to them, jotting down the complimentary phrases the class has agreed upon. Alternatively, if there is insufficient room in the margins, or if we have lengthy comments, we compose a summary at the end of the paper, detailing the successes of the work. For below-average classes with students who need more training in how to respond to each other's writing, I hand out identical copies of the piece that appears on the overhead. Then, as I record our comments in wax pencil, they can write down the same phrases and notations on their own copies.

SHOW — If I had a lot of money I would most likly travl all around the world to meet diffrent people and to see what their agriculture is like. after I got back I would go out and by SHOW — a blown corvette and race on a drag strip and race for fun. then I would go out and by a drive SHOW — boat an race it to. and then I would go and by a greenhouse to SHOW — grow exotic plants.

Dear Writer,

Your ideas for spending money are very unusual. Not many people can say they know about agriculture and exotic plants, and at the same time, know about drag and speedboat racing. Your ideas make us want to learn more about you and your talents.

Next, I ask the class to decide which phrases need more *showing.* We underline those places and write "SHOW" in the margins, just as they will do on their own when set loose in their own response groups. It is important to note that sometimes a student editor might select an idea that does not really need more *showing;* sometimes in the impatience to help a writer, a student will underline *any* generality, just so he can believe he has helped. The value of these Paper of the Week sessions in heading off such overzealousness cannot be overemphasized. With the chance to practice spotting underdeveloped ideas regularly, students gradually become more secure in their role as critics. They come to learn which elements of a paper might need more elaboration and which might not. Sometimes, I'll present a paper that really needs no further elaboration, just to see if they're paying careful attention. Not every essay they read will need the same amount of revision. As I watch students begin critiquing each other's papers, I circulate around the room, sitting in on their discussions, making certain they're applying the training properly.

To demonstrate further how I use anonymous student models on the overhead projector, let's examine the workings of a typical training session. In a remedial class, for instance, I put a copy of the following paragraph up on the wall; students have identical Xeroxed copies at their desks. This model essay was written in response to the question, "What would you do with a lot of money?"

If I had a lot of money I would most likly travl all around the world to meet diffrent people and to see what their agriculture is like. after I got back I would go out and by a blown corvette and race on a drag strip and race for fun. then I would go out and by a drive boat an race it to. and then I would go and by a green house to grow exotic plants.

Obviously there are several mechanical errors in the model. However, I train students to overlook mistakes of this sort for the time being and focus instead on the strengths and weaknesses of the *ideas.* Later, as a class, we can edit the piece for proper spelling, punctuation, capitalization, and usage.

So, I ask the class to remark on the favorable aspects of the paper. (Remember that this model is one I present in the remedial classroom, so the quality of writing is representative of the competency level of the students.) In response to my question, students usually tell me that they enjoy the variety of things this writer would do with his money. Traveling around the world to observe the agriculture of foreign countries and buying a greenhouse in which to grow exotic plants are two very unusual and interesting plans for spending money. The writer seems interested in nature, in particular plant life, but at the same time enjoys the more material pleasures of owning a fancy sports car and speedboat. In one class, we composed the following note to the writer, placing it at the end of his paragraph.

> *Dear Writer,*
> *Your ideas for spending money are very unusual. Not many people can say they know about agriculture and exotic plants, and at the same time, know about drag and speedboat racing. Your ideas make us want to learn more about you and your talents.*

As I wrote this in wax pencil, students wrote the same remarks on their own copies.

Next we collectively decided which areas of the paper needed more *showing.* We ended up underlining each of the four sentences in his essay, deciding all were *telling* sentences that needed further elaboration:

> I would most likly travl all around the world to meet diffrent people and to see what their agriculture is like.
> I would go out and by a blown corvette and race on a drag strip . . .
> I would go out and by a drive boat an race it to.
> I would go and by a green house to grow exotic plants.

Everyone agreed that if the writer developed each of these four *telling* sentences in individual *showing* paragraphs, he would have a much better essay. If this writer were actually in the class, he would write each sentence at the top of a sheet of paper, treating each one as the assigned daily *telling* sentence for homework. He would develop each and bring his revisions back to his response group the following day; the group could then tell him whether or not he had made adequate progress. If four sentences seem too many for one night's homework, especially in the remedial classroom, you might decide to assign the revision work as two nights' homework instead. I often screen the group's suggestions for expansion in this way and tell individual writers how long they have to make their expansions. And, if I am in a classroom situation in which I struggle with students' doing any homework at all—I think most teachers know this problem—I provide in-class time for the students to revise their papers. In this way, I can guarantee that most students *will do* their revisions; I can oversee the process through to the end. For unmotivated students like these, it is essential that we provide the time for them to revise and refine, for they need the discipline and the practice probably more than any other sort of student. If they refuse to do homework, I'll see that they get the experience *in class.*

After students have responded to the content in the Paper of the Week, we go through the piece correcting errors in spelling, capitalization, punctuation, and usage. With regular practice, students become better at correcting such errors in their own writing, too. However, I *do not* ask that when remedial students are in response groups, they make major grammatical corrections. I cannot guarantee that every response partner will know the proper rules of mechanics and usage. Certainly some rules are manageable, like capitalizing the first words of sentences, or spelling *and* properly; but as a rule, I ask students to consult with me or another trusted adult to help them polish the final drafts of their major assignments. In more advanced classes, students can help each other make corrections in grammar and usage because they have more sophisticated skills. I always advise students, though, that they should have an adult outside the school environment read their final drafts to help spot mechanical mistakes. Certainly not all adults are able to correct perfectly a student's mechanics and syntax, but they *can* direct students to reconsider confusing passages. A student can always consult with me to ask *how* to remedy the problem in question.

In my remedial classes, this Paper of the Week ritual is extremely valuable in helping students progress as evaluators; not only does it help them become conscious of effective and noneffective prose, it helps them write better themselves. As they practice reminding others how to develop ideas, they naturally teach themselves the same principles.

The Paper of the Week approach is of course valuable in average and accelerated classes as well. In my advanced classes, we frequently examine *more* than one paper per week. As students take on new and more difficult assignments—the comparison/contrast papers, the argumentative essays, the I-Search reports—we study several student models at each different stage of the writing process. During the class exercise that prepares students to do interviews for their I-Search reports, for example, I am likely to project on overhead model student interviews like those you saw in chapter 8, where I describe the in-class interviews. Before students go home to summarize and write up their own interviews with their classmate, they analyze the strengths and weaknesses of a "typical" student's work. Besides suggesting strategies that students might use in their own writing, this whole-class evaluation continually models and reinforces the type of critique they should be giving each other in response groups.

CHAPTER TEN
Seeing the Effects of Revision

To demonstrate the effectiveness of using response groups for students at all ability levels, I'd like to show you a variety of essays as evidence that students can make dramatic improvement in their ability to develop ideas more thoroughly, and colorfully, through the revision process.

Following is a paper written by a below-average sophomore, an essay on "What makes me special." First you'll read his rough draft, then the notes from his response group and his homework revision efforts, showing the movement from rough to final composition. This was the first time I had these students try using response groups, so I directed them to underline only one *telling* sentence that needed more *showing*. The writers were to try composing an entire additional paragraph as they expanded the underlined generality in their draft into further description.

What makes me special? (rough draft)

The only thing that I can think of that makes me special is, that I am a pretty good shot with a gun. I know that I am because every time I shoot at something I hit it and <u>every time I go hunting I always come back with something.</u> You might not think this is anything special but it's the only thing I can think of right now. If I were in any competition I might win but then again I might lose. It all depends on how I feel that day.

Students in this writer's response group wrote the following note, summarizing the strengths of the paper.

Dear David,
You seem really good with a gun. You seem to know what
you're doing. If you come back with something every time you
go hunting, you must be very good. That's pretty special.

Students in the response group also underlined the words "every time I go hunting I always come back with something" as an idea that needed increased *showing*. For homework, this writer wrote that sentence at the top of a sheet of paper and expanded it as follows.

TELLING SENTENCE:
Every time I go hunting I always come back with something.

Every time I go hunting I always come back with something. For example, one time me and my grandfather went hunting somewhere over by Mt. Diablo. There was a huge buck about 50 to 100 yards away. My grandfather was about to shoot it and all of a sudden I shot it and it went down. We ran over to it and there was a big hole in its head where it was hit.

This writer brought in his revision to his response group the following day. They approved of his colorful addition, but suggested he show another example of "always coming back with something." They felt he needed additional stories to prove his claim of "every time." So, as a final paper, the writer turned in the following.

WHAT MAKES ME SPECIAL

The only thing that I can think of that makes me special is that I am a pretty good shot with a gun. I know that I am because every time I shoot at something I hit it and every time I go hunting I always come back with something. For example, one time me and my grandfather went hunting somewhere over by Mt. Diablo. There was a huge buck about 50 to a 100 feet away. My grandfather was about to shoot it and all of a sudden I shot it and it went down. We ran over to it and there was a big hole in its head where I had shot it. Another time me and my dad went phesant hunting up in the Searras for the weekend and I brought my 22 and my dad brought his shot gun. Everyone thought that my dad would shoot more of them because he had a bigger gun than me but he didn't. I brought back 5 of them and he only got 3. If I were in any competition I might win because I'm an even better shot at still targets than I am with moving targets.

—David Pipkin

Notice how the writer has strengthened his paper with the additional examples. Through his stories, we see just how talented he is with a gun. He even adds another detail to his conclusion. Instead of saying only, "If I were in any competition I might win but then again I might lose," as he did in his rough draft, he now says, "If I were in any competition I might win because I'm an even better shot at still targets than I am with moving targets." Of course, this last thought could be developed into another series of stories, developing his entire piece into a much more effective whole; but, at this stage, with his first attempt at revision, we can see much progress taking place even as it stands. We do not need to continue forcing expansion after expansion of the same paper; through regular training with revision he will, by the end of the year, begin making these additions on his own. His previous successes, his noticing of his own strengthened writing, will push him to develop his ideas more completely as time goes on.

We can't entirely ignore this writer's errors in mechanics, spelling, and usage. He writes the whole piece as one giant paragraph, misspells *pheasant* and *Sierras*, and says "me and my grandfather" and "me and my dad" rather than "my grandfather and I" and "my dad and I." During the early stages of working with revision, however, I would not lower this writer's grade. His improvement is remarkable, and I would lavish praise on him for his increased attention to detail. I would keep reminding him, though, throughout the year, to consult an adult for help with the final corrections, and to begin *applying* our weekly lessons in grammar and usage to his own composing. I would circle his errors and draw his attention to them, asking that he work on polishing his final drafts with closer consideration of proper mechanics. If, as the year progressed, I noticed continued laziness toward correcting these mechanical errors, I might lower his grade accordingly.

Now take a look at the work of two more students—their rough drafts as marked in peer response groups, and the ensuing work with revision. Notice the way response partners underlined *telling* sentences and made supportive comments. Also notice the improved quality of the final papers, written after each student has worked to change the underlined *telling* sentences to *showing* paragraphs. Often, students end up creating additional details that weren't necessarily called for in the first notes for revision—a natural outgrowth of thinking more specifically. These papers were written by remedial sophomores after four previous practices with improving rough-draft compositions.

Topic: Describe a memorable experience with a best friend.

Well I remember an old friend I had back when I was about 4 or 5 years old. We had just moved here from Walnut Creek into a housing tract called Vally trails. I went out to play one day and thats when I met him. We used to play over at his house Most of the time because he had a lot more neet stuff to play with than

What did
he have?

Show more
of the
fishing.

there was overe at <u>my house</u> like he had a play house out in his
back yard and we used to pretend it was a fort. <u>As we moved along
in age we used to love to go fishing with his dad or mine</u> and we'd
catch these little sun fish and think it was the catch of the day,
the biggest fish ever. But one day my friends father got a letter
from his bussiness saying they would have to move back east
some where so they moved and I don't think Ill ever see him agin
but we still keep in touch by phone and send pictures ever few
yers.

Good detail, nice job.
Eric,
This paper is very good. You have a lot of personal details that
make it easy to picture you and your friend. I liked the way
you described the fishing, the way you thought that it was the
"catch of the day" but it was really just a sunfish.

Suzanne

With this encouragement and two requests for more showing from his
response group, this writer set off to do his homework—two *showing*
paragraphs based on the underlined sentences.

Changing telling to showing, #1.

<u>My friend always seemed to have a lot more better thengs to play with
over at his house for some reason.</u> Maybe they were rich or somthing
but I didn't relly care I would just go over there and have the time of my
life. One of the best toys he had was this great big playhouse, painted
to look like a castle. I mean that never wore out we could pretend
somthing new every day. We could have played in that little house all
day every day and never got board but there were other neat things to
like he had this hudge racing set that seemed at the time to strech
through the whole liveing room and we would play with that for hours
to Well there were a lot more things we did but thoes were my favorits.

Changing telling to showing, #2.

<u>Well as we moved along in age we used to love to go fishing with either
his dad or mine.</u> We'd go to shadowclifs or Del Valea and it was great.
We'd leave at about 9 or 10 in the morning and get there at about 10:30
or 11 becaus when we were that young we didn't know that fish bite
more in the early morning hrs. so my dad told us the fish bite most
around lunchtime because I think he liked to sleep in in the morning.
So we'd get there and set up and sit there for hours looking at the dead
water, thinking every little movement in the water was a giant fish
waiting to be hooked. Im sure my dad was board to death the way he
would just kind of fall asleep all day and we may have nevere cought
anything but we loved it.

Now, the next step—the next homework assignment—is for the writer to
revise his rough draft, inserting the additional showing material he has created
and making other corrections. Here's the result.

A memorable experience with a best friend, final draft.

Well I remember an old friend I had back when I was about 4 or 5 years old. We had just moved here from Walnut Creek into a housing tract called Valley Trails. I went out to play one day and that's when I met him. We used to play over at his house most of the time because he seemed to have a lot more neat stuff to play with. Maybe they were rich or something but I didn't really care. I would just go over there and have the time of my life.

One of the best toys he had was this great big playhouse painted to look like a castle. I mean that never wore out. We could pretend something new every day. We could have played in that little house all day every day and never gotten bored. But there were other neat things to do too like this neat racing set that at the time seemed to stretch through the whole living room and we would play with that for hours. Well there were a lot more things to do but those were my favorites.

As we moved along in age we used to love to go fishing with our dads. We'd go to either Shadow Cliffs or Del Vale. It was great. We'd leave at about 9 or 10 in the morning and get there at about 10:30 or 11. Because when we were that young we didn't know that fish bite more in the early morning hours. So my dad told us that fish bite the most around lunch time because I think he liked to sleep in the morning. So we'd get there, set up our poles, and sit there looking at the dead, still water, thinking every little ripple in the water was a giant fish waiting to be hooked. I'm sure my dad was bored to death the way he would just sort of sit there and sleep, and though we may have never caught anything we had a great time.

But one day my friend's father got a letter from his business saying they would have to move back East somewhere. And when I got the news it was terrible. It seemed like the neighborhood got so quiet after he left. But we still keep in touch by phone and send pictures every few years.

—Eric Nordseth

The next writer took his paper through the same process: rough draft, getting suggestions from his response group, expanding two telling sentences, and incorporating his new material into a revised final draft.

Topic: If you could take off with a good friend, today, where would you go? What would you do?

If I had a choice of going somewhere with one of my friends I would go to a motorcycle park called Hollister. My friend would be Keith because we both like to ride bikes.

Show what this is like. I would have a lot of money for beer and food. Also for gas and oil for my bike. We would be there for about a week. <u>They let you camp out there during the 4 WD races.</u>

Sometimes they let you go night riding all over the park. The first day is when they tell you all about the rules and regulations.

Good! What's
this like ?

They have a lot of things you can do there. <u>They have a poker
run. The mudhole contest and racing on tracks.</u>

As you can see you can have a lot of fun out there doing the
races and the other events they have there.

Dave—
This sounds like "biker heaven!" I learned a lot from reading
your paper. This park sounds like an endless amusement
park. You gave many good details. I'm curious to learn more
about the camping facilities and the actual mud holes and
runs. Good paragraphing!

It is very important, especially in remedial classes, not to skip this step
where writers work on individual telling sentences. It gives them a chance to
really focus on single ideas before they must think about the paper as a whole
again. Here is this writer's work for the crucial second step:

Changing telling to showing, #1.

<u>They let you camp out there during the 4WD races.</u>

When you camp out there they let you go anywhere. There are
places to go right next to the mudhole and one of the race tracks.
You can also camp on the hill right above the mini track that has a
lot of obstickels for the trucks to race on. But for the people that
like to go near the showers there is another camp ground at the
other end of the park. The quiet people like it there better too
because you can't here the trucks so bad.

Changing telling to showing, #2.

<u>They have a poker run, the mud hole contest, and just racing around
on the tracks.</u>

They have a variety of contests to go in. One is the poker run.
The poker run is when they make up a race track that has different
pit stops for every truck intered. Say the poker hand is five card
stud, you would have 5 pit stops. Every time you stop at them you
get a card. When it is over you see if you got a good hand or not. It
is just like poker. If you had a bad hand you would fold and if you
have a good hand you would stay in the game. Also they have a
mud hole contest. The mud hole contest is when the people of the
park dig a big pit and fill it with water and dirt to make mud. They
start out with the smaller trucks to see who can get across it
without getting stuck. But when you get stuck you are baried up
halfway to the doors. After the small trucks they have the big 4
wheelers to try and get across. The big wheelers have a hard time
in it because they have big tires and they just get themselves
baried because they hit the hole to fast. And the other contest is
the race tracks. They have different tracks for different trucks. The
small trucks and jeeps have real sharp corners on the tracks. Also
they have small obstickels too. But the big trucks have longer
tracks. The big trucks have big mud holes and rivers to go
through.

After the response group approved his rewritten paragraphs, he carefully inserted them into his original draft:

Taking off with a best friend, final draft.

If I had a choice of going somewhere with one of my friends I would go to a motorcycle park called Hollister. My friend would be Keith because we both like to ride bikes.

I would have a lot of money for beer and food, also for gas and oil for my bike. We would stay there for about a week. When you camp out there they let you stay anywhere. There are places to go right next to the mud hole and one of the race tracks. You can also camp on the hill right above the mini track that has a lot of obstacles for the trucks to race on. But for the people that like to go near the showers there is another campground at the other end of the park. The quiet people like it there better too because you can't hear the trucks so bad.

Sometimes they let you go night riding all over the park. The first day is when they tell you all about the rules and regulations.

They have a variety of contests to go in. One is the poker run. The poker run is when they make up a race track that has different pit stops for every truck entered. You get a card at every stop. When it is over you see if you got a good hand. It is just like playing poker. If you have a good hand you would stay in the game and try to win.

Also they have a mud hole contest. The mud contest is when the people of the park dig a big pit and fill it with water and dirt to make it muddy. They start out with the smaller trucks to see who can get across it without getting stuck. But when you get stuck you are buried in mud halfway to the doors. After the small trucks they have the big 4 wheelers to try and get across. The big wheelers have a hard time in it because they have big tires and they just get themselves buried because they sink too fast.

And the other contest is the racing on the tracks. They have different tracks for different trucks. The small trucks and jeeps have real sharp corners on the tracks. Also they have small obstacles too. But the real big trucks have longer tracks. The big trucks have big mud holes and rivers to go through.

As you can see you can have a lot of fun out there doing the races and other events they have there.

—Dave Stickney

Sometimes student writers can make effective changes in their compositions by adding only one or two details to enrich an abstract idea. In other words, students might not always need to create whole paragraphs to take an idea further. Students have sometimes come to realize that not all *telling* sentences need to be belabored; a brief phrase, rich with details, could add sufficient impact and power. Following are some excerpts from average student papers. Notice how, when asked to change the underlined sentences from *telling* to *showing*, the writers improve their ideas considerably through a limited number of additional details.

In an earlier chapter, you saw how one seventh-grade student started with this description of a hide-and-seek game:

> **Leonardo was approaching her. He was <u>getting closer and closer</u>. She thought for sure she was going to be caught.**

When her response group suggested she show the telling sentence "He was getting closer and closer," she revised her paper by adding a series of simple but vivid details:

> **Leonardo was approaching her. She could hear him near the barn, his footsteps crunching the gravel. Next he was on the lawn, and the sounds of the wet grass scraping against his boots made a loud, squeaky noise. Next she could hear him breathing. She thought for sure she was going to be caught.**

A senior writer, assigned a character sketch, began by describing a photograph of Janis Joplin, a blues and rock singer in the late sixties. This was her opening sentence:

> **Sitting on the sofa, she looked exhausted.**

Having said so much for appearances, this student went on to suggest *why* Janis was so fatigued. A student editor thought it important for the writer to *show* the exhaustion, so she underlined that opening sentence. The writer revised it this way:

> **Her eyes told of her pain—deep, set back, reaching inside of herself. Dark caves formed where her cheeks were. Her mouth was a hardened straight line, down at the corners.**

As if this writer were the camera lens itself, she zooms in for a close-up, examining in detail the elements that make Janis appear weary in the photograph.

Another student, a junior, creates a mood at a rock concert as an introduction to his short story. He writes:

> **The auditorium was dimly lit.**

Students in his response group suggested that he develop the atmosphere more carefully, so they underlined that sentence as one that needed more showing. His revision:

> **The newcomers into the room paused for a moment at the door as their eyes adjusted to the difference in light. Each object and figure had a long, faint shadow.**

The reader is now made to feel the effects of an auditorium that is dimly lit; *showing* has effectively replaced *telling* in only two sentences.

Still, other writers enjoy spending considerable time with their expansions. Some students are such descriptive writers naturally that they enjoy the challenge of turning their underdeveloped ideas into something very vivid. Take the following example. For this assignment in a junior honors class, students explained the impact of an important decision they had made at some point in their lives. They were instructed to describe in details their alternatives, then show how they came to make a choice and how the outcome affected them.

This junior describes how she chose between going to a public or private school when her parents had to live abroad for one year. Choosing the private school meant leaving home for the first time. Here is the original opening paragraph to her essay, along with its revision.

> I was aboard the London-bound train now. In just eleven hours I would be five hundred miles away from home. Staring at my flowered overnight bag, I <u>frantically reflected upon the decision that I had made</u>. Inside I gasped, "Oh, God, did I make the right decision? Pull yourself together," I thought, "and just think the whole thing over logically; then you'll realize that your decision was wise." Swallowing hard and trying to keep the tears away, I remembered that first day at Brechin High School.

Both her response-group editors and I advised her to reflect more on the decision, since she didn't give an account of her actual deliberation. "Pull yourself together" does not show us her weakness, does not show what she's afraid she'll give in to. It only *tells* us that she's fighting something inside. Here is this writer's revision:

> I was aboard the London-bound train now. In just eleven hours I would be five hundred miles away from home. "Home." I caught myself repeating the word; how winsome and beautiful it suddenly sounded. Home, where stark white plasterboard walls were softened with woven baskets, dried flowers, and herbs that hung upside down from exposed rafters. I could smell the cardamom from my mother's kitchen, mingled with the pungent aroma of sweet pekoe tea that floated up from the shiny copper teapot. I could see a radiant and crackling fire, dancing to the music of Scott Joplin and the New Orleans Preservation Hall jazz band. I was so overcome by the remembrance of home that I jumped when the conductor opened the door to my compartment to check the ticket which was damp and crumpled in my hand. As he left, the compartment door slammed shut, and the crash of metal against metal echoed in my head. Shivering for a moment, I pulled my woolen sweater across my chest and buttoned it up.

> —Meg Caldwell

Now we *see* what is tearing her apart inside; we *feel* her dilemma more forcefully because she has taken the time to slow down and remember what it was she thought about as she considered her alternatives.

To illustrate further the positive effects that regular practice with revision can have on a student's progress, I'd like to share the compositions that two students wrote at the beginning of a year and compare them to pieces those same students wrote at the end of the year. In the first instance, we'll read the work of a remedial junior; then we'll examine the progress of an advanced junior. In both cases, I believe the dramatic change in competency grew out of this disciplined approach to writing regularly, practicing the art of being specific, responding to *others'* writing regularly, giving and receiving effective feedback, and repeatedly revising rough drafts into more developed wholes.

At the beginning of the year, a remedial junior writes the following paragraph in response to this essay question: "If you were stranded on a desert island, what record album would you take and why?"

> If I were out in the middle of a desert and could take one record it would be Molly Haitich [Hatchet] because all his albums have lots of meaning to all of them. It seems like I know where he's coming from. Molly Haitich is one of the finer recorders today. He is none [known] through the world. that's why if I get caught out in the desrt I will take Molly Haitich. the end

At the end of the year, when the same essay question was posed once again, the student changed his choice and wrote the following final draft. For this piece, he had the opportunity of meeting in a response group to receive suggestions on how to improve his composition. This final paper of the year shows dramatic progress in the writer's ability to develop his ideas and carry an idea through to the end.

> If I were stranded on a deserted island I would bring Black Sabbath by Ozzie Ozborne. The album is well done the lyrics give me food for thought. I would never get tired of this album.
>
> They have a wide variety of instruments not just guitars. This enables them to get a lot of different effects in their music. Some of it's low and mellow. They usually tape their albums live so that you can hear the audience and their responses. It allows you to be part of that time and place away from the lonely deserted surf and sand.
>
> Black Sabbath will bring back a flood of fine memories of special friends and special places.
>
> I would remember the warm summer nights down on Main Street, drinking a Lowenbrau, sitting on the fender of a friend's car, playing tunes loud so that all can enjoy them. I could hear my friends yelling back and forth across the way about the girls going by and the parties we're going to.
>
> The Black Sabbath album will give me plenty to think about while I'm lying on the beach enjoying the hot sun and cool tropical water. Perhaps I can solve some of my problems since as the album says in Black Sabbath "no one answers when you ask why/just say you're on your own" and "all people do is fill you full of lies you can see through." I could do as they say in "Spiral Architect" and look into myself to try to find a solution to the problems of the world. I could figure out why and what I'm working for. Who I could trust. What I could believe in.
>
> —Rick Chimenti

In my advanced junior classes, I traditionally measure writing growth by giving timed writing exams at the start and close of the year. Timed exams give me the opportunity to find out what all the students can do in the same pressured situation. Students know in advance that they will not receive grades for these pre- and post-exams, but will in the end receive commentary on their growth over a year's time. I give essay topics that reflect two different modes of writing—narrative and argumentative. In this way I can judge the effects of my training program on both personal and analytical forms of writing. Following are the timed-test writings of one junior, each written in 45 minutes. The student, Jim Cowart, didn't seem much interested in English and often belittled his own efforts at composition. He kept claiming that he didn't know how to write. Nonetheless, his progress over the year is clear. Notice that in both his narrative and his argumentative papers, he has learned by the end of the year to give more attention to specifics. Notice also his improvement in writing summary conclusions; his ability to derive meaning from the examples he gives has increased considerably.

SEPTEMBER PRE-TEST, NARRATIVE:
Describe a memorable childhood experience.

The first death I experienced was that of my grandfather. I never knew what death was like until then. Since no close relatives of mine ever died, it was a very different experience.

We sometimes take knowing people for granted, and it's not until something drastic happens to them, like a serious injury or death, that we totally appreciate the relative or friend.

I knew my grandfather well and loved him very much. I stayed with my grandparents many summers and learned from my grandfather how to do and work on many things. I didn't think about him dying, at least not in the near future. But when it happened one thing I felt was sadness.

I was also upset with myself for not gaining more knowledge of this very intelligent man.

After his death I wished I could've seen him at least once more, which is something I think everyone wishes, but a person can't. I'm trying to know my friends and relatives even better, so if one of them passes on, it will be a great loss, but it won't be as if I forgot to ask them something.

MAY POST-TEST, NARRATIVE:
Describe an experience from which you learned a lesson.

As the hot summer morning sun broke through my shutters, I awoke, hearing the screams of children playing outside. Flopping the few sheets on my bed off me I kicked my legs over to the side of my bed and sat up, still half asleep. Getting to my feet, I looked for something to wear. Clothes were strewn on a tall wooden rocker, leaning back under the weight, and piled on my already cluttered desk. Noticing the screams from outside again, I went to the shutters and, lifting the bar that controlled the many little shutter pieces, I was blasted with sunlight. Pupils having readjusted, I looked down upon the street and saw all my friends playing ball.

I wanted to be down there too! So looking again for a shirt, I pulled one off my desk. "Is this clean?" I thought to myself, holding it up. I examined it and finally smelled it.—Passing the final test, I slipped it over my head and picking up some toughskin jeans on the floor, slipped those on.

After shoveling down a bowl of Count Chocula's Booberries, while watching "Bambi Meets King Kong" in cartoon, I ran outside and started playing.

Fifteen minutes later I heard "JIM SCOT" (my mother calls me Jim Scot when she's mad) from our house.

Leaving the game, I went to see my mother.

"How many times have I told you to clean your room before going out? Just for this, I want you to stay in your room for the rest of the day."

"But . . ." It was no use. For the rest of the day I would watch my friends play through my window.

Staying in my room for the whole day was the worst. I mean it, I had nothing to do, I never wanted to do it again. From then on, and even to this day I have tried to make my room somewhat organized before I go out, to keep my mother happy.

SEPTEMBER PRE-TEST, ARGUMENTATIVE:
We would all be idle if we could. Agree or disagree, using examples to support your viewpoint.

I believe the world's people would not be idle even if they could. They are social people that earn money to live and for personal enjoyment or entertainment.

The large majority of people in the civilized world wouldn't enjoy not doing anything or not working. If they didn't do anything they would eventually become extremely bored and would want something to occupy their time.

Most people have hobbies they do or sports activities they are engaged in because these things make their life prosperous and enjoyable. If they didn't do these activities their life would be slow and dull.

If the world's people had a choice to live idle, do nothing, not working, or the choice to be active, live like they are presently, I am certain the choice would be to be active.

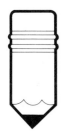

MAY POST-TEST, ARGUMENTATIVE:
Happiness occurs more in the struggle to achieve what we want than in the final acquisition of what we want. Agree or disagree, using examples to support your viewpoint.

Happiness occurs more in the struggle or striving to achieve happiness, rather than in the final resting state. As a person works on a project (which was a dream of his), he puts in countless hours of work—in the enjoyable sense—and, as he works, imagines the finished product, thus bringing happiness. As his goal is completed, he is fulfilled, but he cannot get more happiness from it like he did while he was working on it. The finished product becomes like a picture on the wall.

I see happiness occurring in the striving for something, rather than in the finished state, when it comes to possessions. I knew a guy who worked for days, pulling weeds, mowing lawns, and doing backbreaking work under the hot summer sun and all the time telling us about this go-cart he was going to buy with the money he had earned. As he would tell us about this go-cart, his eyes would sparkle, and for a person who didn't ever do much work, he seemed not to be bothered by the sweaty work. Once he got the cart, everyone else was envious. He would speed around the streets with a big grin on his face. Then after a while the cart began to sit in his garage more and more—he was bored with it.

The thought of buying the cart made him happy, so as he worked to buy the cart, because he knew that all the work would lead to the cart, he was happy. Getting the cart was a climax and from there it went downhill, not bringing as much enjoyment.

That is why I think people never totally complete a project because the completion will be anti-climactic.

Training in *showing* writing has taught this student to support his general ideas with examples and details, not just in narrative prose but also in the analytical style of an argumentative essay. Even though we cannot call these essays *polished* drafts of writing—for each piece would certainly have been much tighter with time allowed for revisions and response group discussions—nonetheless the quality of the writing and the overall development of ideas in the post-test papers is far richer than the attempts made at the start of the year. Even the students themselves can see the improvement. As one girl put it, describing her growth over a year, "My earlier writing seems to be a skeleton of my later writing's richer style."

AFTERWORD
Making the Training Ideas Work for You

Recently I conducted a weekend course on the teaching of composition at the University of Anchorage in Alaska. During my three days of instruction, I shared with teachers this four-part training program, taking them through the daily sentence expansions, the follow-up oral evaluations, the response-group strategies, and sample curriculum units in which I showed them how I use shorter exercises and drills to work toward longer pieces of writing. Teachers wrote themselves, trying out some of the preparatory assignments which lead to writing a comparison/contrast essay or an I-Search investigative report. In this way, teachers had the opportunity of really testing the logic of my approach to teaching writing and deciding for themselves whether or not this training system felt workable for their particular classroom situations, in their particular courses.

During our last hour together, when I had opened the session for questioning, I was completely amazed by a request from three high school teachers: they asked me if I wouldn't mind outlining on the board my lesson plans for one year in my junior English classes; they wanted to see *all* the units I devised and how I incorporated them into the rest of my language arts curriculum. At first I thought they were teasing me, trying to get a good laugh out of me at the end of a long and industrious workshop. But there was no giggling and chuckling when I gazed at them with disbelief; they meant it. Hearing this final request, I realized they had missed a vital point of my workshop, of my very program.

Don't get me wrong. In one way, I couldn't have been more flattered. They had become so enthralled with the program, they wanted as much as they could get before I returned to the "Lower 48," out of their range of contact. However, they failed to realize that what I had given them was a *framework*, a structure for teaching writing that allowed them the freedom to experiment with their own ideas. In order for my program to become theirs, they would have to try inventing their own units of study, deciding whether or not they could use the built-in discipline of my "showing, not telling" approach as a foundation for expanding their own favorite writing units.

It has taken me a number of years to shape the curriculum units I have presented in this book, and each year I am likely to change them again, modifying them to undo problems that arose in previous semesters. However, once I had created a *structure* for myself, one that emphasizes giving students time to experiment while still pushing for final products, one that moves from open creativity to formal organization, I felt I had developed a program that encompasses the best of both worlds. What teacher doesn't want to encourage creativity and individuality? Yet what teacher doesn't also feel the need to enforce logic and order? It seems to me that the variety of writing experiences that can take place within this four-part structure is infinite; at the same time, the built-in discipline of the system encourages students to *do* something with their creative dabblings. We do not compose "showing, not telling" paragraphs only for the sake of marveling at the best approaches; students continually learn developmental techniques from each other, and furthermore are required to expand, *regularly*, their short experimentations into finished pieces of prose.

But, in order to develop my detailed composition units, I had to watch my students as they moved through the stages from free writing to finished writing. I had to devise ways for them to go *beyond* vague intrigue and move toward definite resolution. As I researched the sorts of writing assignments my students would be likely to encounter in college, I planned units that would move them in stages from the brainstorming of ideas to the certain expression of those ideas. Before I could invent such preparatory sequences as writing short comparisons on "Saturday is different from Sunday," and "My mother is different from my father," to help students get ready for a major comparison-/contrast essay, I had to sit down and write a comparison/contrast essay *myself*, watching and monitoring my own writing process so that I might become a better organizer of instruction. The shaping of the curriculum units in this book grew not only out of my students' struggles with various complicated topics, but also out of my own problems in writing as I tried out the exact assignments I would be giving them. As I discovered ways to overcome blocks, I built in new steps or preparatory procedures that might prevent students from becoming tangled in the overwhelming process. As a colleague of mine in the Bay Area Writing Project says, "Would we want our children to learn piano from someone who never played himself?" Teachers of writing *must* write themselves, and it is because I believe in this practice so fervently that I have been able to create these thorough units of instruction. Just as I knew that my improvement as a young dancer depended on the combination of improvisation and applied instruction, and just as I knew that student writers needed the same mix of creative exploration and discipline, so I knew that my own *teaching* could mature through the blend of frequent experimentation within the workings of a secure disciplined foundation. If you, as a teacher, simply take everything that I do with my students and try reproducing it exactly in your own classroom setting, you might become rapidly disillusioned. Perhaps you won't receive the winning pieces of prose I have presented here as typical models. You might even give up the program or the unit entirely as "something that works for her, but *not* for me." My guess is that if you do not try some personal experimenting on your own, you cannot possibly reproduce what I do in my classroom. I *sell* my ideas to students with my enthusiasm—an enthusiasm that comes from personal involvement with the invention of my assignments. If an assignment doesn't work, and many times one has not, I become challenged to *make* it work because it is my own.

This idea of personal enthusiasm brings me to another point. Enthusiasm is something that came easily to me when I started my teaching career. Most young, aspiring teachers have that quality—they want to change the course of education. When I learned I could not be as effective as I had hoped, when the everyday hassles of teaching 150 students a day set in, I lost a considerable amount of that inspiration. Rather than devising my own units of study, I sought out textbooks to do the teaching for me. It was far easier going over a lesson in a grammar book, teaching a particular rule of language, and testing for competency with those rules at the end of a week. It was easier, after all the grading of papers, all the discipline problems, all the varying degrees of language ability, *not* to have to think up my own ideas.

But, I was one of the lucky ones. I found a way to get out of my slump. My involvement with the University of California, Berkeley, Bay Area Writing Project gave me a chance to rediscover what I *was* doing that was succeeding; it gave me the opportunity to hear of other teachers' successes, too. Through the process of trying out for myself the ideas of other teachers, and through their testing of my ideas, I came away from that summer course *renewed*, not for the time being, but for what seems to be forever. For you see, this project is ever-changing itself. It offers teachers a place to come and share discoveries, share their experimentations, to help all of us continue to refine our teaching. None of us believes that we will find *the* successful approach once and for all; we simply know that we are perhaps keeping each other headed in the right direction.

Those familiar with conducting experimental/control group research projects are acquainted with the term *Hawthorne effect*. If a subject in an experiment knows he is receiving special treatment, if he is aware of being singled out, he is likely to perform better in the end, is apt to score better in the final tallying. This phenomenon of heightened performance in response to special treatment may also be true of teachers who have received special attention for their efforts in the classroom. For the past seven years, my involvement with the Bay Area Writing Project as a teacher consultant has given me a new sense of professionalism, a sense that *I* am being treated specially as an innovative instructor in the teaching of composition. Ironically, it is this very organization that has encouraged me to become innovative and experimental. I have become a better teacher because I have been chosen to be a participant in a national experiment, one in which we are trying to see whether or not teachers teaching each other successful classroom methods can improve the quality of writing instruction throughout the country. As a teacher consultant, I must test my beliefs and share them with an audience who will be in a position to test their philosophies against my own, to see if we might together improve the quality of composition instruction through our sharing. As a result of this opportunity, I have been reminded once again of the important interplay between presenter and audience. As I have worked to make my own ideas clear to an educated group of listeners, I have first had to make my ideas clear to myself. I have had to turn theory into practice, had to know the research to authenticate my position. As a result, my beliefs have taken on a new importance, and my professionalism has been enhanced. In short, what I say "matters."

As I go out to do in-service presentations, I am constantly required to think on my feet. Participants in Bay Area Writing Project programs often challenge my position with thought-provoking questions, sometimes even severe attacks. This kind of confrontation forces me to evaluate my theories on the spot; yet, this kind of testing is the best way I know to grow. At one point in my career as a consultant, I was sure that my four-part training program was foolproof, inviting relatively little challenge. But, I soon found that as I closed the door on one problem, I opened a door to another. My teacher-audience taught me that. I soon realized how crucial it was for me to return to the classroom to rethink and retest my original ideas. I am still defining, then, what I believe to be the writing process and how it should be taught.

For example, in the past I have focused my teaching primarily on students' improving their use of specific details. But, in having them practice regularly the art of being specific, it seems I have diminished the importance of the topic sentence, the generality that explains the meaning of the examples. I believe that emphasizing *showing* has been an appropriate and important step in enhancing students' ability to explain to themselves—and to the world—what they mean. Students need to consider where their general impressions and ideas come from; in effect, they need to slow down their thinking and look at the world more closely. However, up to now I have not spent a great deal of time having them *abstract* once they've elaborated their ideas.

When I realized how difficult it was for my students to make judgments, analyze material, and draw conclusions from a body of facts, I knew that training them to *show* in their writing was not enough. That is, I need to ask students to interpret their examples *after* they have elaborated them, ask them to invent altered *telling* sentences after they have created *showing* paragraphs. This way I will be better developing their critical thinking capacity and their ability to interpret a set of facts pertinently and concisely. Take the *telling* sentence, "Camping is a rewarding experience." After elaborating such an idea, a student might write as a new conclusion, "Camping teaches self-reliance," certainly a more effective and more specific *telling* sentence than the original. In a paper I presented earlier, student Wendy Yee arrived at a final generalization, "Teaching causes teachers to become Jekylls and Hydes," a critical point of her short piece. The careful development of her ideas led her to that generalization, but it's one she might have missed, because the assignment did not *ask* her to draw any conclusions.

What students need, then, in addition to frequent practice in elaboration and development, is frequent practice in drawing conclusions and making general points. I have described a few of these reverse exercises at the end of chapter 5, "Variations for the Daily Workout." This is just one example of the way my teaching changes directions as I explore different aspects of the writing process.

I hope I have shown that the joy in being a teacher of writing is actually in being a *student* of writing, a student of learning. If teachers or consultants or researchers knew everything once and for all, we wouldn't be so actively seeking ways of improving composition instruction. It is because I share with my students the struggle of my *own* learning while they learn, because I tell them that they teach *me* how to do it better the next time, that they see the importance of our shared goal. It is not only important that *they* succeed, but that I succeed, too. My students always feel that they are being treated specially, and indeed they *are;* they are as important to my growth as I am to theirs. By being a perpetual student, I infuse the joy of learning into the students I greet everyday. Here, then, is one of the secrets of being an effective teacher—believing for ourselves that learning never stops.

And so, in closing, I hereby give you permission to consider yourselves a part of an important experiment. I ask you to take the ideas, the *framework* explained in this book, and try experimenting on your own. Assign the *telling* sentences for homework, practice teaching students how to evaluate writing, and allow yourself the time to become familiar with these two basic practices alone. Notice what kinds of responses you get; save the exemplary models and study them. Begin recognizing *when* it is that your students begin to show progress and growth in being able to move from the general to the specific. Notice how long it takes at different grade levels and for varying student abilities. Learn from what happens in your particular setting. When you feel more secure in knowing what results you're after and in knowing what students really can accomplish, try assigning one of the composition units, let's say the comparison/contrast assignment. After taking the class through the various stages, after reading their final projects, decide for yourself what worked and what did not. Compare what happened in your situation to what I said happened in mine. If they aren't the same results, take that as a challenge. Try to adjust the entire series of exercises to work for you. Decide how you would improve the unit next year, then *write it down* somewhere. When you really make the unit your own, you might want to write to me and share how you managed to change the procedures and reap improved results. Remember, we are in this together; I can learn from your trials and successes as much as you can learn from mine.

Try creating your own composition unit—say a unit on the short story or the cause/effect essay—in which you build your own series of *telling* sentences and accompanying directed instructions to facilitate the completion of a particular full-length assignment. See if the use of warm-ups helps prepare your students for their final performances. See if your own strategies for developing ideas, the ones *you* use in your own writings, might not be useful for your students as well. Center a lesson around something *you* employ in your own writing process, rather than consulting a textbook. See what happens. After reading an enormously powerful article in, let's say, *The Atlantic Monthly*, try having your students write a similar theme, using the published piece as your teaching guide. In short, take something *you really like* and try infusing some of your enthusiasm for it into your student writers.

Writing, in the long run, is a developmental process that takes years to come to know and to feel secure in. That's the joy of it. As we grow and change, so does our writing change—constantly. As long as we accept change as the exciting part of a student's learning and as the exciting part of our own teaching, we will keep the idea of experimentation, and therefore the Hawthorne effect, alive and well in our classrooms, and we will serve our students well.

REFERENCES

Baker, Sheridan, and Dwight Stevenson. *Practices in Exposition: Supplementary Exercises for the Practical Stylist.* 5th edition. New York: Harper & Row, Publishers, Inc., 1981.

Britten, Norman A. *A Writing Apprenticeship.* 4th edition. New York: Holt, Rinehart and Winston, 1977.

Capote, Truman. *In Cold Blood.* New York: Random House, Inc., 1965.

Chandler, Raymond. *The Big Sleep.* New York: Alfred A. Knopf, Inc., 1939.

Clemens, Samuel Langhorne [Mark Twain]. *The Autobiography of Mark Twain,* ed. Charles Neider. New York: Harper & Row, Publishers, Inc., 1959.

———. *Life on the Mississippi.* 1883. Signet Classics. New York: The New American Library, 1961.

Didion, Joan. *Slouching Towards Bethlehem.* New York: Farrar, Straus, and Giroux, Inc., 1968.

Doctorow, E. L. *The Book of Daniel.* New York: Random House, Signet Edition, 1971.

Fitzgerald, F. Scott. *The Great Gatsby.* New York: Charles Scribner's Sons, 1953.

Friday, Nancy. *My Mother, Myself.* New York: Dell Publishing, Inc., 1977.

Gray, James. "Teaching the New Rhetoric." Unpublished article, Bay Area Writing Project, University of California, Berkeley, 1969.

Gray, James, and Robert Benson. *Sentence and Paragraph Modeling.* Berkeley, Calif.: Bay Area Writing Project, 1982.

Hemingway, Ernest. *The Sun Also Rises.* New York: Charles Scribner's Sons, 1954.

Loder, Kurt. "Great Scot: Nobody Pushes Sean Connery Around." *Rolling Stone Magazine,* October 27, 1983.

MacKillop, James, and Donna Woolfolk Cross. *Speaking of Words: A Language Reader.* New York: Holt, Rinehart and Winston, 1978.

Macrorie, Ken. *Searching Writing.* Rochelle Park, N.J.: Hayden Book Company, 1980.

McCullers, Carson. *The Ballad of the Sad Cafe.* Boston: Houghton Mifflin, 1936. Bantam, 1971.

Mills, James. "The Detective." Time, Inc., 1972. Appeared in a somewhat different form in *Life,* December 8, 1972.

Porter, Katherine Anne. *Pale Horse, Pale Rider.* New York: Harcourt Brace and Co., 1939.

Reed, Rex. "Ava: Life in the Afternoon." *Esquire*, May 1967.

Richter, Conrad. *Early Americana and Other Stories*. New York: Alfred A Knopf, 1936.

Schaeffer, Joe. "Rituals." *Writings from Amidst the Uproar*. Unpublished collection prepared by the Bay Area Writing Project summer fellows, University of California, Berkeley, 1977.

Simon, Sydney B., Leland W. Howe, and Howard Kirschenbaum. *Values Clarification: A Handbook of Practical Strategies for Teachers and Students*. New York: Hart, 1972.

Wolfe, Tom. *The Right Stuff*. New York: Farrar, Straus, and Giroux, Inc., 1979.

Wolfe, Tom, and E. W. Johnson. *The New Journalism*. New York: Harper & Row, Publishers, Inc., 1973.

APPENDIX
Reproducible Teaching Aids

This appendix includes a variety of material designed to help you implement the ideas I have presented in *Writers in Training*. These pages are blackline masters that you may reproduce for use in your classroom; they can be used to make either handouts or transparencies for overhead projection, as you prefer.

The first item (pages 168–70) is a list of guidelines I have been developing to help teachers and students respond constructively to student writing. Students need training in spotting weaknesses and in making suggestions that will genuinely help the writer understand what is good about the paper and what still needs work. My guidelines, while originally written with teachers in mind, can easily be adapted to give your students direction in responding to a piece of writing. (The section on grammar and usage will probably be the least useful to students as response-group editors.) I have left room for you to write down additional ideas that you and your students discover as you evaluate daily writings.

The remainder of the appendix consists of pages you can use to generate class discussion and written work. These are organized to parallel the exercises I describe in chapters 3-10 of the text. Some of the pages are worksheets or explanatory handouts related to specific writing units; however, the majority of the pages present models of student writing from my classes, with an occasional model by a professional writer. These models demonstrate both strengths and weaknesses in different forms of *showing* writing; they also give students new ideas, new techniques, new approaches to try in their own composing. The questions accompanying the models can help you guide students into making specific responses as they evaluate a paper. You may want to add questions of your own to those I have provided; these questions are simply guidelines for talking about writing.

As you become familiar with the types of models I use in teaching writing, I encourage you to begin collecting similar models of your own, both from books you read and from your students' papers, to embellish the program and make it *yours*.

Guidelines for Responding to Student Writing 168

THE DAILY WORKOUTS (WRITING AND EVALUATING WRITING)

Introducing "showing, not telling"
MODEL 1   "The Bus Stop" 171
MODEL 2   "The pizza tasted good." 172

Effective/noneffective writing models

MODEL 3 "My room was a mess." 173

MODEL 4 "Those girls are snobs." 174

MODEL 5 "She was depressed." 175

MODEL 6 "The relationship changed." 176

MODEL 7 "The room was romantic." 177

Undoing clichés

MODEL 8 "A chill ran down my spine." 178

MODEL 9 "She really put her foot in her mouth." 179

Encouraging brevity

MODEL 10 "He was the picture of health." 180

MODEL 11 "The student who cheats abases himself." 181

MODEL 12 Showing through single sentences (five examples) 182

Modeling paragraphs

MODEL 13 Modeling a paragraph from *The Great Gatsby* 183

MODEL 14 Modeling a paragraph from *The Sun Also Rises* 184

Imitating other styles

MODEL 15 "The Splendid Spider" (Miss Muffet à la Fitzgerald) 185

MODEL 16 "The Spider Also Scares" (Miss Muffet à la Hemingway) 186

MODEL 17 "Catch 'er in the Web" (Miss Muffet à la Salinger) 187

Making generalizations

MODEL 18 Creating Telling Sentences (Mark Twain, Nancy Friday) 188

THE COMPARISON/CONTRAST ESSAY

Parallel sequence

MODEL 19 "Saturday is different from Sunday." 189

MODEL 20 "My mother is different from my father." 190

MODEL 21 "My geography teacher is different from my English teacher." 191

MODEL 22 "My Spanish teacher is different from my geometry teacher." 192

MODEL 23 "My dog B.J. is different from my dog Pal." 193

Integrated comparison

MODEL 24 "Sooty Albatross" (Norman Britten) 194

MODEL 25 "Frosted Mini-Wheats" and "Tennis" 195

MODEL 26 "My French teacher is different from my U.S. history teacher." 196

Combining parallel sequence and integrated comparison

MODEL 27 "Lady-Chick" 197

MODEL 28 "Rug-Carpet" 198

MODEL 29 "Curiosity-Nosiness" 199

Contrasting illusion/reality

MODEL 30 "The Mississippi" (Mark Twain) 201

MODEL 31 "What a Nightmare, or How to Live with a *Mini* Muscle Car" 202

THE ARGUMENTATIVE ESSAY

Exploring the issue
WORKSHEET   Parent-teen Dialogue 204
WORKSHEET   Practicing Concession 205
MODEL 32   "Rock Music" and "My Room" 206

Fallacies in argument
HANDOUT   Red Herring and Begging the Question 207
HANDOUT   Faulty Cause/Effect and *Argumentum ad Hominem* 208
HANDOUT   The False Dilemma and Glory/Guilt by Association 209
WORKSHEET   Spotting Fallacies 210

Final essays for analysis
MODEL 33   "The Truth about Dirt Bikes" 211
MODEL 34   "The Battle of the Room" 213
MODEL 35   "Mommy's Baby" 214

THE I-SEARCH REPORT

Ways of revealing character
WORKSHEET   Personal Setting (Simon et al) 216
MODEL 36   Personal Setting (McCullers, Didion, Capote) 217
MODEL 37   Costume (Chandler, Loder, Schaeffer) 219
MODEL 38   Mannerism (Mills, Schaeffer) 220
MODEL 39   Combining Setting, Costume, Mannerism (Rex Reed) 221
MODEL 40   "Who Is Matt?" 222
MODEL 41   "Custodian" and "Smoking Section" 223
MODEL 42   "P.E. Class" and "Cowboys" 224

Final report for analysis
MODEL 43   "Animal Doctors" 225

TRAINING IN REVISION TECHNIQUES

Revising with response groups (remedial)
MODEL 44   "What Makes Me Special" 230
MODEL 45   "A Memorable Experience" 231
MODEL 46   "Taking Off with a Best Friend" 234

Improving details in rough drafts
MODEL 47   "Hide-and-Seek" 237
MODEL 48   "She Looked Exhausted" and "The Auditorium" 238
MODEL 49   "Leaving Home" 239

Guidelines for Responding to Student Writing

SAY SOMETHING POSITIVE:

1. Underline words, phrases, or sentences that stand out. If possible, tell the writer *why* the underlined area is effective. Instead of simply noting "good detail" or "good verb," tell the writer why that detail or verb enhances the meaning of her main idea.

   Example: Describing guilt as "a black velvet curtain falling in front of you" lets me feel the suddenness of your anxiety.

2. Write a narrative commentary in which you reflect back to the writer the idea that he set out to explain or prove; show him you understand (or think you understand) what he is trying to convey. I find this a useful approach whenever I am struggling to find anything favorable to say. This response at least lets the writer know that he has been *listened to;* it can help him feel *some* success in his first effort.

   Example: You're trying to show the tension between two angry people. It's important to you to build suspense around what happens.

3. Have a running dialogue with the writer, reacting to things she says as she says them.

   Examples: I agree with your argument completely here!

   I'm so glad you mentioned this; I was hoping you'd explain your mother's reaction.

4. Refer to progress the writer has made since the beginning of the course or writing unit. Highlight his improvements.

   Examples: You've learned how to divide into paragraphs now. Good for you!

   You're working harder on giving details. Your writing is becoming more interesting to read.

5. _____

   _____

6. _____

   _____

7. _____

   _____

8. _____

   _____

   Writers in Training © 1984 Dale Seymour Publications

Guidelines for Responding to Student Writing

SUGGEST IDEAS FOR IMPROVEMENT:

1. Underline a vague or general idea and ask for increased *showing;* if possible, accompany the suggestion with a question. That is, instead of noting only "Show more," try giving the writer some specific ideas about what to show.

   Example: What kind of fun did you have at the park? What activities did you do?

2. Suggest cutting out a weak beginning. Sometimes writers use the process of writing just to get started, to uncover ideas buried beneath the surface of cognition. Often they don't see that the first few sentences or beginning paragraphs of the paper aren't as interesting or powerful as something stated later on. Suggest eliminating these first few sentences or paragraphs.

   Example: This first part isn't as strong as what comes later. What would happen if you started your story (or essay) *here?*

3. Suggest better organization. Sometimes writers include powerful ideas, descriptions, or arguments early on in a paper, then find that the rest of the writing drags; frequently writers are more energized as they begin to compose and lose their fervor as the project becomes more arduous. Writers need to be reminded that saving some of their best ideas or best arguments for last will keep the forcefulness of their ideas fresh in the reader's mind. Suggest some rearrangement as needed.

   Example: Which argument (or description) do you think is most powerful? What effect would it have if you presented this one last?

4. Look toward the end of a paper for the emergence of a new or better idea. Often writers discover new thoughts as they write, but don't recognize them on their own. Point out these new ideas with suggestions for making better use of them.

   Examples: I notice here that you're onto something new: [then I describe what I think this idea is]. Could this fact be useful in proving your point?

   I see a whole new thesis emerging. Do you want to consider changing your main idea? Is this idea a more accurate expression of your feelings?

5. _____

   _____

6. _____

   _____

7. _____

   _____

8. _____

   _____

Guidelines for Responding to Student Writing

BE SELECTIVE ABOUT CORRECTING GRAMMAR AND USAGE:

1. Isolate recurring errors in grammar and usage; instead of marking up the entire paper, notice repeated mistakes. Circle them and write a note indicating the pattern of error.

   Examples: You're leaving out the apostrophes with possessive nouns. What is the rule for possessives?

   You're uncertain where to start new paragraphs. Do you need help?

2. Once a grammatical rule has been covered in class and a student misuses the rule, point out the error immediately. It's important to get on top of the problem right away so that the student sees the connection between the grammar study and the use of those rules in written work. *When a student's paper is filled with repeated errors, I opt for isolating those errors that reflect misuse of the rules we've already studied.*

3. Ask students to keep individual lists of the repeated errors they have made (and are likely to make again). Then, for instance, if "proofreading for spelling" is on a writer's list, she knows that for all future papers she must give special attention to spelling. When students turn in their final drafts, have them list on the title page the errors that have been pointed out in previous papers. This way, as you evaluate the paper, you can hold the writer accountable for certain rules.

4. _____
   _____

5. _____
   _____

6. _____
   _____

Writers in Training © 1984 Dale Seymour Publications

THE BUS STOP

> Each morning I ride the bus to school. I wait along with the other people who ride my bus. Sometimes the bus is late and we get angry. Some guys start fights and stuff just to have something to do. I'm always glad when the bus finally comes.

> A bus arrived. It discharged its passengers, closed its doors with a hiss and disappeared over the crest of a hill. Not one of the people waiting at the bus stop had attempted to board. One woman wore a sweater that was too small, a long skirt, white sweater socks, and house slippers. One man was in his undershirt. Another man wore shoes with the toes cut out, a soiled blue serge jacket and brown pants. There was something wrong with these people. They made faces. A mouth smiled at nothing and unsmiled, smiled and unsmiled. A head shook in vehement denial. Most of them carried brown paper bags rolled tight against their stomachs.*
>
> *E. L. Doctorow, *The Book of Daniel* (New York: Random House, Signet Edition, 1971), p. 15.

Both paragraphs describe a bus stop. What is the difference between the two descriptions? Underline the *showing* details in both paragraphs.

TELLING SENTENCE:
The pizza tasted good.

As I stared at the pizza set on the table, the colorful combination of cheese, meat, and spices suggested a pleasurable taste ahead. The aroma of the hot, bubbling mass made my mouth begin to water. As I took a bite of the crispy pizza, I savored the taste for a brief moment. My tongue curled around the mellow, warm cheese; my taste buds thoroughly relished the tangy Italian sauce, and as a result, made my saliva glands work faster. When I bit into the reddish-brown pepperoni, I was amazed at the spiciness. All these different sensations combined into one pleasurable experience.

I felt a little apprehensive that morning. I wasn't sure if, after so many years of separation, my brother and I could spend an entire day with one another and enjoy it. Pulling on my jeans, I tried to think of a few conversational topics that would interest us both, just in case conversation came to a standstill. I wondered if he could be thinking of the same thing. "Funny," I thought, "maybe I have no reason to worry; maybe we will have too much to talk about—maybe."

After just a few minutes on the Berkeley campus, I realized that all of my worrying and topic planning was unnecessary. Courtney and I had so much to share, so many years to catch up on, and of course, he was certainly expounding helpful, fascinating, or just plain factual information about Berkeley. He even took me to his favorite Mediterranean Cafe. Together we sipped their rich and aromatic coffee blend as he told me about the many hours he had spent there, reading the morning paper or engrossed in some outlandish novel. Of course Courtney was excited. He couldn't wait to give me a grand tour of "his" alma mater. He wondered if "his" old pepper tree was still as majestic as ever, and if "his" studying area in the Botanical Gardens was still as beautiful as he remembered. The campus came alive with Courtney's nostalgic memories of his old chemistry lab in the Life Sciences Building, or the old Greek Theatre where he enjoyed Shakespeare, Bach, and Sophocles.

By lunch, I knew that Courtney and I would never be at a loss for words. More importantly, I knew that there was a strong bond between the two of us—something that even time could not erase—love. Together we sat Indian-style on the grass just below the Campanile. The stringy pizza we had purchased for lunch brought childish grins to our faces, and through the warm silence, we both knew that pizza had never tasted so good.

Both paragraphs describe the taste of pizza. What is the difference between the two approaches? Is one approach more successful than the other?

Writers in Training © 1984 Dale Seymour Publications

TELLING SENTENCE
My room was a mess.

RESPONSE A

> My room was so cluttered, full of junk. My mother wanted to kill me. You had to step over everything and it made it hard to walk. She told me that I was a slob and that I didn't take care of my things. But I told her I didn't have time to clean. Everything was thrown and scattered around the room and it was completely a disaster!

RESPONSE B

> To enter the room, I was forced to squeeze in the small door opening, nearly getting stuck because heaps of dirty clothes obstructed the path of the door. Once inside, I had to concentrate fully on every step so that my shoes wouldn't become tangled in the laundry and cause me to fall. Steps later, after freeing my leg from a malicious pair of blue corduroy pants, I noticed that under the spot vacated by those pants was a matted piece of green shag carpet, the only piece of carpet not being smothered by clothing in the entire room. The next thing to attack me was a Pink Floyd poster only partially pinned to the wall. The feeling of my head coming into contact with a foreign object made me whirl about in apprehension, swinging my elbow out and knocking it with force against a drawer jutting out from the half-empty clothes chest. Howling in pain, I flung myself on the bed, long parted with its sheets, and wondered if I wouldn't be safer waiting in another room.

1. Both paragraphs show a messy room. Which paragraph is more successful in its showing?
2. If you were a response partner to the writer of response A, where would you indicate good showing? Underline those places. Do the same thing for the writer of response B.

TELLING SENTENCE:
Those girls are snobs.

RESPONSE A

> Those girls are so stuck-up! Whenever I'm around they act like they don't even know me. They ignore me. It really hurts my feelings because they think they're so special and I'm not. They never include me in anything they do and they treat me like I don't exist.

RESPONSE B

> While two girls slowly strutted themselves past me, I heard a soft sound much like the hiss of air being let out of a tire. Their eyes slowly shifted around following my every move. It took a second, but it finally hit me like a pie in the face that they were talking about me. One of the girls raised her finger and darted it towards me. As she did this they quickly exchanged glances and the sound of giggling now replaced the whispering. I rolled my eyes in their direction, catching their amused expressions. With my glance they lifted their hands, flung their hair back over their shoulders, straightened their posture, lifted their noses, and pompously walked off.

1. Both paragraphs show girls with a snobbish attitude. Which paragraph is more successful in its showing?
2. If you were a response partner to the writer of response A, where would you indicate good showing? Underline those places. Do the same thing for the writer of response B.

TELLING SENTENCE:
She was depressed.

RESPONSE A

> No matter how hard she tried, she could not fall asleep. She was
> still thinking about the test she had taken that day. It seemed to her
> that she had studied hours to pass the test and still she had gotten a
> bad grade. The rest of the day she had walked around feeling gloomy
> and upset. At the end of the day she went running and for that time
> she forgot, but later her gloominess returned. Now it was midnight
> and still she could not sleep. What a gloomy day it had been.

Underline the effective showing details. Can you find any places
where the writer *tells* instead of *shows?*

RESPONSE B

> As she stood there looking at herself in the mirror, her image
> was blurred from the continuous stream of tears that were falling
> down her face. She inhaled, then exhaled with a large sigh. "Maybe
> some music might cheer me up," she thought. She trudged over to
> the stereo and switched it on. A sweet mellow love song was playing.
> She angrily flipped it off and threw herself face first onto her bed.
> Lying there she grabbed her pillow and wept once again.

Underline the effective showing details. What could the writer of
response A learn from this writer?

TELLING SENTENCE:
The relationship changed.

RESPONSE A

> Her eyes were like those of a young puppy's moistened around the corners. Her mouth formed a careless line down at the edges. The facial color was no longer glowing with health but now wan. The flowing blonde hair seemed to sag like the limbs of the weeping willow. The once square shoulders now drooped like a basset hound's ears.

Underline the effective showing details. Do these details show the changing of a relationship, or do they show something else?

RESPONSE B

> The girl ran across the grass, clutching a worn football in her hands. Close behind her ran a boy, desperately trying to catch the girl. With one giant leap the boy grasped her shoulders, bringing them to the ground in a tangled maze of limbs. Their laughter filled the yard as they both tried to get up.
>
> Slowly the laughter faded, and the yard became quiet. They looked at each other with questioning eyes. Softly the boy placed a hand on the girl's shoulder and slowly leaned over to place a gentle kiss on the girl's lips.

Underline the effective showing details. What is the difference between response A and response B?

Writers in Training © 1984 Dale Seymour Publications

TELLING SENTENCE:

The room was romantic.

RESPONSE A

> The couple looked lovingly into each other's eyes as they sat on the sofa. They had waited all day to be together. He had thought of her all day at work, and she had thought all about him, too. They were going to be married soon. At last they were together and could share their evening together.

Which details show that the room was romantic. Underline them.
Suggest one improvement the writer might make.

RESPONSE B

> The sun, rising over the lake, created a rosy glow in the living room as it shone through the window, and the unseasoned wood in the fire gave the room a musky smell as Christy sat down on the couch. She snuggled closer to her husband, that word was going to take some getting used to, and took a sip of coffee. A honeymoon to her family's cabin in the Sierras was a wonderful idea, and now as she fell deeper into the couch and her daydreams, she could hear the ticking of the cuckoo clock on the wall, her grandfather's gift to her mother and father on their wedding day. So many memories, so much of a future.

Which details show that the room was romantic? Underline them. How is the room used to show a romantic mood? What is the difference between response A and response B?

TELLING SENTENCE—CLICHÉ:
A chill ran down my spine.

> Watching the Creature Feature, I saw the monster's distorted head and immediately threw my hands to my face and screamed in terror. I shivered violently and noticed the beat of my heart racing to an incredibly high pulse. A gust of cold air rushed through my body, causing me to pry my hands from my face to try to warm my upper arms. Doing this, I noticed goosebumps covering my entire body. The hair on the back of my neck became perpendicular to my skin.
>
> Finally, I overcame my fear and took a breath of relief which caused me to shiver again with another little convulsion. But that was the last of it, and the last of the movie. I turned it off immediately.

Which details show sudden terror? Underline them.

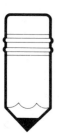

WRITING ASSIGNMENT
Try showing a similar cliché: **I was paralyzed with fear.**

TELLING SENTENCE—CLICHÉ:
She really put her foot in her mouth this time.

Cindy glared at the boy walking out of the office doors. She leaned on the switchboard that her friend, Nancy, was operating. "I think that Pete Dawkins is a stuck-up jerk! He walks like the coolest thing since Richard Gere." Cindy said this loud enough so that the people standing nearby could hear. They looked at her angrily.

Nancy looked up and asked, "What's wrong with him?" Cindy studied her fingernails and said, "He's just like Barbara; she thinks she's hot, too!" This was again overheard by the people standing nearby and they walked away shaking their heads in disgust. Nancy looked at her coldly as she fingered the microphone of the school P.A. system. "Listen, can we change the subject? You're always talking about other people." Cindy gave a loud sigh and removed a piece of lint from her blouse.

"OK," she sighed again and looked up at the ceiling. "You know what Mr. Horton gave me on that term paper?" Nancy rolled her eyes. They came to rest on the microphone. She giggled. "Well?" Cindy asked. "He gave me a D! He only gives good grades to those cheerleaders."

There was a soft click as Nancy switched on the loudspeaker. "Besides that, have you ever seen anyone as weird as Horton? Polyester suits! He's just a big, fat . . ." Her words stopped abruptly, eyes becoming large with fear, head cocked stupidly to one side as she listened to her own voice echo across the campus.

This writer tells a story and then shows the cliché at the end. How do the details leading up to the ending contribute to the conclusion? Underline what you consider to be the best details.

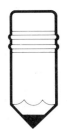

WRITING ASSIGNMENT
Try showing this cliché: **He was the picture of health.**

TELLING SENTENCE—CLICHÉ:
He was the picture of health.

> He leaned his muscular body against the racquetball court door. He casually removed his wrist weights and wiped the beads of sweat from his sharp-featured face. A group of interested females feasted their eyes on the athlete, bent over to remove his ankle weights.
>
> I let a nonchalant glance last a bit longer than what is considered "safe." I pretended that his wonderfully thick legs weren't headed in my direction although I couldn't help but notice the large, toned set of biceps connected to the pair of hands resting on my table.
>
> I stopped tying knots in my tennis shoes and found no reason to deny his proposal of our having lunch together. He tilted his tanned face toward the waitress and ordered two raw-egg coolers sprinkled with wheat germ, and a "Bran Muffin, Baked Liver, and Brussels Sprout Delight for two." As I searched for strength to stand, I sputtered, "Make it one—I've gotta run!!"

What technique does this writer use to show "the picture of health"? Underline the details that emphasize his healthiness.

> He was off again to the racquetball courts, running full-speed, leaving the Nautilus room far behind. Dodging through the corridors, leaping over sofas, and sliding down banisters, he soon found himself at the entrance to Court Thirteen.

This *showing* paragraph is much shorter than the first. Does it still show "the picture of health"? How important is it to tell a story in order to show our ideas? Are lots of showing details always better than fewer showing details? Underline the best details in this short paragraph.

discussed in "Variations," page 41

TELLING SENTENCE:
The student who cheats abases himself.

The girl managed to pry her desperate eyes away from her friend's paper and glanced up at the teacher. Her eyes met the piercing glare of the teacher's eyes and her heart skipped a beat. Her worst fears were made true as the teacher began to slowly rise from her desk. The student felt the red rising in her cheeks.

The teacher began to slowly walk towards her. As she approached the student, their eyes met again for an instant and the student saw the furious look. She knew she was about to be made an example of. Without a word, the teacher snatched up her paper and shrieked, "You were cheating!" Her classmates, who had been quietly working up until then, oblivious to what was going on, simultaneously jumped three feet out of their seats. The girl felt her stomach drop. Now she not only had to face the teacher's glare but also the laughter-filled eyes of her peers. She felt their staring eyes boring into her and could not raise her own eyes from the worn carpeting in front of her desk.

What technique does this writer use to show abasement? Underline the details that show shame.

"This is what happens when you cheat!!" She spoke sternly, staring at me with accusing eyes. I shifted in my seat but couldn't seem to find a comfortable position. I could feel my face burning, exuding guilt. Wiping my sweaty palms on my jeans, my hands suddenly seemed like foreign objects, and I couldn't find a place to put them. The stares of the other students bored holes into me as they exchanged hushed whispers. Throbbing heartbeats swelled my throat, making me unable to speak.

This paragraph is shorter than the first. Does it manage to show shame as well? How does the opening line save the writer from having to create a whole story, as the first writer above did? Underline the best details in this paragraph.

SHOWING THROUGH SINGLE SENTENCES

TELLING SENTENCE:
The jocks think they're cool.

A small group of boys clad in shorts and tank tops stand inside the shady entrance of the cafeteria, puffing up their chests to full capacity as they proudly recall last Saturday's drunken exploits.

TELLING SENTENCE:
Mother Nature absorbed us.

A bluejay, flapping its wings frantically, comes to a sudden stop on a sturdy tree branch, squawking wildly, demanding attention, and without hesitation flies to another tree twenty feet away, still shrieking.

TELLING SENTENCE:
The children were having fun.

Tumbling off the couch, letting out banshee-like screams, the small children fell to an imaginary death at the foot of the torn and tattered "cliff."

TELLING SENTENCE:
I was annoyed.

The blue Ford pickup came bouncing down the winding dirt road, grinding to a halt beside me, the dust rising and writhing up into the air, curling its way into my eyes and making them itch.

TELLING SENTENCE:
The soldier was impressive.

He was a stocky, barrel-chested man in his thirties with thick muscular forearms, a jagged scar running along his forehead, a Purple Heart and Vietnam Service Ribbon emblazoned on his chest.

Can a writer show an idea satisfactorily in only a single sentence?
Underline the effective details in each sentence above.

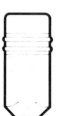

WRITING ASSIGNMENT
Try showing this idea in a single sentence:
She was embarrassed.

Writers in Training © 1984 Dale Seymour Publications

FROM *THE GREAT GATSBY*

We walked through a high hallway into a bright, rosy-colored space, fragilely bound into the house by French windows at either end. The windows were ajar and gleaming white against the fresh grass outside that seemed to grow a little way into the house. A breeze blew through the room, blew curtains in at one end and out the other like pale flags, twisting them up toward the frosted wedding-cake of the ceiling, and then rippled over the wine-colored rug, making a shadow on it as wind does on the sea.

The only completely stationary object in the room was an enormous couch on which two young women were buoyed up as though upon an anchored balloon. They were both in white, and their dresses were rippling and fluttering as if they had just been blown back in after a short flight around the house. I must have stood for a few minutes listening to the whip and snap of the curtains and the groan of a picture on the wall. Then there was a boom as Tom Buchanan shut the rear windows and the caught wind died out about the room, and the curtains and the rugs and the two young women ballooned slowly to the floor.*

*F. Scott Fitzgerald, *The Great Gatsby* (New York: Charles Scribner's Sons, 1953), p. 36.

FOOTBALL GAME

I jogged through the tunnel onto the bright green football field, boxed in on both sides by the stadium seating. The seats were filled and overflowing with noise from the fans that seemed to be spilling onto the field. A violent wind whipped through the stadium, blowing empty popcorn boxes out of the stands and onto the field like autumn leaves blowing from the trees, lofting them up toward the powder blue of the afternoon sky, and then letting them settle on the green plastic of the astro-turf, like feathers floating to the earth.

The only lifeless object in the stadium was a player dressed in blue, slouched on the rusty bench like a sack of potatoes. His oversized blue jersey bagged and flapped in the wind as if it were many sizes too large. I must have sat for a few minutes, listening to the whistle of the wind and the grunts of the players on the field. Then there was a screech of brakes as the motionless player was set in the back of the ambulance, and the doors slammed shut on the field, and the whistle of the wind slowly died to a hush, and the grunts of the players were just an echo and the lifeless body winced in the ambulance bed.

In the student's imitation of Fitzgerald, what descriptions or actions echo the author's style?

FROM *THE SUN ALSO RISES*

I wondered if there was anything else I might pray for, and I thought I would like to have some money, so I prayed that I would make a lot of money, and then I started to think how I would make it, and thinking of making money reminded me of the count, and I started wondering about where he was, and regretting I hadn't seen him since that night in Montmarte, and about something funny Brett told me about him, and as all the time I was kneeling with my forehead on the wood in front of me, and was thinking of myself as praying, I was a little ashamed, and regretted that I was such a rotten Catholic, but realized there was nothing I could do about it, at least for a while, and maybe never, but that anyway it was a grand religion, and I only wished I felt religious and maybe I would the next time; and then I was out in the hot sun on the steps of the cathedral, and the forefingers and the thumb of my right hand were still damp, and I felt them dry in the sun.*

*Ernest Hemingway, *The Sun Also Rises* (New York: Charles Scribner's Sons, 1954), p. 97.

A WISH

I struggled with my decision of what I would wish for, and I decided that I might wish for an 8-track player, so I wished that I would get an 8-track player, and then I was pondering over what 8-track tapes I needed to buy, and thinking of buying 8-tracks made me think of Styx, and I wondered when they'd have their next concert in our area, and regretting I missed their last concert in Oakland, and about Erin telling me how excellent they were, and as all the time I was leaning over the table with my face glowing because of the candles on my cake, and was thinking of myself as wishing, I was a little embarrassed and regretted that I took so long to blow out the candles, but realized it was too late to do anything about it now, at least for the moment, so I despairingly watched my ice cream cake, unknown to me that it was an ice cream cake, steadily flow onto my mom's lace tablecloth, but that anyway it was a luscious cake, or shall I say milkshake, and I only hoped that I could have blown out the last candle before it sunk into the lump of ice cream and maybe I might still get my wish if it meant not having good luck; and then I began ladeling up as much of my cake as was possible into the numerous bowls, and the candles flowed into the bowls with the ice cream, so I took them out and I licked the ice cream off of them.

In what ways is the student's imitation like the original? Why did Hemingway compile the entire reverie in a single sentence?

Writers in Training © 1984 Dale Seymour Publications

THE SPLENDID SPIDER

In my younger and more vulnerable years, my mother gave me some advice that I've been turning over in my mind ever since.

"Whenever you feel like complaining about your curds and whey," she told me, "just remember that all the people in this world haven't had the advantages that you've had."

She didn't say any more, but we've always been unusually communicative in a reserved way, and I understood that she meant a great deal more than that. In consequence, I'm inclined to eat only curds and whey, a habit that has opened up many curious natures to me and also made me the victim of not a few stomachaches.

One morning, I resolved to eat my accustomed breakfast outdoors. I walked through the large porch into a bright green-colored garden, fragilely bound into a circular shape by a white picket fence constructing the entire circumference. The flowers were dew-kissed and glistening against the fresh grass outside that seemed to grow a little way up the porch. A breeze blew through the garden, blew leaves on one tree and on another like light flags, rustling them together, enclosing all empty spaces and then moving them apart, making a tree shadow once again upon the ground.

The only completely stationary object in the garden was a small tuffet on which my cousin, nicknamed Miss Muffet, was sitting, eating *her* breakfast of the "delicious" curds and whey. She was wearing white and her dress was rippling and fluttering as if she had been hung outside to dry. I must have stood for a few moments listening to her slurping and smacking of the cereal and the clinking of the spoon against the bowl. Then there was a scream as my cousin saw a spider and watched it creep towards her, causing her relaxed breakfast to be interrupted.

At any rate, Miss Muffet's lips fluttered, she nodded at me almost imperceptibly, and then quickly tipped her head back again—the spider had obviously sped up and given her something of a fright.

I looked again at my cousin, who continued to scream in a high-pitched voice. It was the kind of voice that the ear tries to shut out, as if each burst is an arrangement of three out-of-tune pianos with a back-up set of pots and pans. Her face was frightened and alive with bright things in it, bright eyes and a brightly flushed complexion, but there was terror in her voice as she turned and ran into the house.

This student writes "Little Miss Muffet" in the style of *The Great Gatsby*. How does she give us the sense of Fitzgerald's style?

THE SPIDER ALSO SCARES

In the morning it was bright, and they were sprinkling the streets of the town, and we all had breakfast in a cafe. Across the street we witnessed a scene which we found amusing. We were all a little tight.

A three-legged stool, called a tuffet, was occupied by a girl. The girl who had sat down, her name was Miss Muffet, found toward the end of last summer that her figure was going, and her attitude toward food changed from one of careless choice and decision to the absolute determination that she should have curds and whey. She began eating.

After a while we heard a shriek from across the way and then we saw the girl running down the street. A spider had come along and frightened her. We continued talking and drinking.

"Oh, Justin," Bridget said, "she could have had such a damned good breakfast this morning."

"Yes," I said. "Isn't it pretty to think so?"

Here the student writes "Little Miss Muffet" in the style of *The Sun Also Rises*. How does she give us the sense of Hemingway's style?

CATCH 'ER IN THE WEB

If you really want to hear about it, the first thing you'll probably want to know is where I met her, and what I was doing when I saw the whole thing, and where it all happened, but I don't feel like going into it, if you want to know the truth. That kills me. You try and tell someone a simple story and all and they have to know the whole crummy background before they're even interested.

Well anyway, where I want to start telling is that day in the park. I was walking by when I saw this girl sitting on a stool-thing eating her breakfast. I asked her name and she said Miss Muffet. At first I thought she was being smart. I hate it when people feel like messing around and give you a phony name like that and all. I can't get too mad though cuz it's something I'd do. Anyway her name really was Miss Muffet and there she was eating her breakfast in the middle of the park. I can't believe she'd really sit there and do that. I mean, you'd have to be a damn moron to sit and eat breakfast where everyone can watch you. But there she was, munching away on the most god awful stuff you ever saw. It was all watery and lumpy at the same time and it damn near makes me puke now just to think about it. I asked her what it was and she said curds and whey. I *knew* that wasn't a lie cuz something that looked that bad would have to have a name like that.

Well anyway, she just kept on eating and I kept sitting on the end of the bench across from her thinking what I'd do today. I'm still sitting there and all when this damn spider crawls right up my leg. That kills me. Spiders think they can walk anywhere anytime they want to. They don't care what you're doing or anything, they just crawl right up and stare at you. Well, I took the damn thing and dropped it on the ground. I didn't see where it went.

Then I knew where it went. I heard the loudest scream coming from that dopey girl that I ever heard. She goes and drops her crummy bowl all over the ground and runs off cuz of that stupid spider. That *really* kills me. Girls are always so scared of spiders and all. They just look at them and you'd think they were shot twenty times in the head or something. Girls. They kill me.

Here the student writes "Little Miss Muffet" in the style of *The Catcher in the Rye*. How does she give us the sense of Salinger's style?

CREATING TELLING SENTENCES

The house was a double log one, with a spacious floor (roofed in) connecting it with the kitchen. In the summer the table was set in the middle of that shady and breezy floor, and the sumptuous meals—well, it makes me cry to think of them. Fried chicken, roast pig; wild and tame turkeys, ducks and geese; venison just killed; squirrels, rabbits, pheasants, partridges, prairie chickens; biscuits, hot batter cakes, hot buckwheat cakes, hot "wheat bread," hot rolls, hot corn pone; fresh corn boiled on the ear, succotash, butter-beans, string-beans, tomatoes, peas, Irish potatoes, sweet potatoes; buttermilk, sweet milk, "clabber"; watermelons, muskmelons, cantaloupes— all fresh from the garden; apple pie, peach pie, pumpkin pie, apple dumplings, peach cobbler—I can't remember the rest. The way that the things were cooked was perhaps the main splendor—particularly a certain few of the dishes. For instance, the corn bread, the hot biscuits and wheat bread and the fried chicken.[1]

1. Samuel L. Clemens, *The Autobiography of Mark Twain,* ed. Charles Neider (New York: Harper and Row Publishers, Inc., 1959), p. 4.

What do all these showing details tell us? What *telling* sentence would express everything in the paragraph?

TELLING SENTENCE: _____

When I was nine I went to a private summer camp, a beautiful plantation home on an island, hung with Spanish moss. . . . [My best friend there] was Topsy and she came from Atlanta. We slept together, we ate together, we jumped hand-in-hand off the diving board on the big oak pier together, and we made a pact to do everything together, especially to be best friends forever. One day a mother arrived and left her little girl at the big house. She was put into our room. Topsy and I eyed her during lunch, conspicuously leaving her out with our giggles, as we left out everyone from our secret world. By supper time I was the one on the outside. They whispered when they looked at me, sharing secrets you would think they'd shared for years. Their friendship was born on the strength of my exclusion. That night I lay in my bed and sang "Onward Christian Soldiers" to myself to keep from crying. My head ached, trying to know what I had done.[2]

2. Nancy Friday, *My Mother, Myself* (New York: Dell Publishing, Inc, 1977), p. 202.

What do all these showing details tell us? What *telling* sentence would express everything in the paragraph?

TELLING SENTENCE: _____

TELLING SENTENCE:
Saturday is different from Sunday.

> Without the help of an alarm clock, at 8:30 sharp Saturday morning, I wake up brimmed with energy and ready to take on any activity that floats my way. The sun is pouring bars of golden liquid in my window and the blue jays are singing merrily at the top of their musical voices. Anticipating a whole day to do whatever I want, I eagerly throw on my clothes and spring down the stairs. After a light breakfast I grab my old familiar cut-offs and my favorite beach towel, jump in the convertible, and with a delightful screech of the wheels, fly off to spend a beautiful day running and laughing in the sun.
>
> My mother is shaking me and saying, "It's past 11:00. Get up; there's work to do." With a deep groan I open my bloodshot eyes and am immediately blinded by the terrible glare of the sun beaming hot and stuffy directly on me. Very slowly I claw my way out of bed, and in a drained, limp state of semi-consciousness, stumble sheepishly down the stairs. My family, faces cheerful and repulsive, is having breakfast. Just the aroma of eggs turns my stomach, making me feel queasy. Instead, I trudge to the cabinet, fumble with a bottle of aspirin, and with a glass of warm water sloppily gulp three down. Then, still hung over and depressed, I sit down and stare straight ahead, thinking about the agony of mowing the lawn.

1. This piece was written in two paragraphs using parallel sequence. What do both paragraphs have in common? List the common characteristics.

2. How does the writer show the difference between Saturday and Sunday? List contrasting pairs of words or phrases that change the mood. Example: the sun—"bars of golden liquid" on Saturday, "terrible glare" on Sunday.

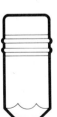
WRITING ASSIGNMENT
Try showing the following, using parallel sequence:
My mother is different from my father.

discussed in "Comparison/Contrast," page 58

TELLING SENTENCE:
My mother is different from my father.

My mom was sitting hunched over in front of her sewing machine, working on a dress or something. She worked steadily and silently, paying no attention to anything around her. Needles, patterns, and scissors lay on the sewing machine within her reach.

My dad stood by his work bench holding a piece of a carburetor up to the light. Whistling almost constantly, he walked to and fro, collecting tools as he needed them. Scattered all over the bench were tools and parts already used.

In what ways are these two paragraphs parallel?

TELLING SENTENCE:
My mother is different from my father.

Even though my eyes were on the road, I could tell she was smiling. She knew that she shouldn't smile and laugh when I tell a dirty joke, but she had thought it was funny. My mom and I drove in silence for a while, thinking about the joke; then I asked her a question and the conversation flowed once again. We talked unhesitatingly about my friends, school, or anything else that might be weighing down our thoughts. We talked as friends.

The heavy silence was broken as I reached over and clicked on the radio as I drove, my father sitting in the passenger seat of our Volkswagen bug. Even though the radio played, there was still the uncomfortable silence one feels when he thinks he should say something but he can't think of anything to say. First he would talk, asking a question or commenting on something, then I would answer. Then another stretch of silence would engulf us—drown us. We talked in uncontrolled, unpredictable spurts as if desperate just to break the strangling void between us.

In what ways are these two paragraphs parallel?

WRITING ASSIGNMENT
Invent your own telling sentence in this form:
_____ **is different from** _____.
You may use people, animals, or other items. Elaborate your sentence in two *showing* paragraphs, using parallel sequence.

Writers in Training © 1984 Dale Seymour Publications

TELLING SENTENCE:
My geography teacher is different from my English teacher.

Uttering phony excuses, my geography teacher straggles into class five minutes late with a newspaper stuffed under one arm. Dragging a chair up to his desk scattered with papers, coffee cups, and last Sunday's comics, he slouches into his seat and paws through the disaster on his desk for the day's assignment. Crying "Eureka, I found 'em," he yanks some papers from the depths of the mess, volunteers someone to hand them out, puts his feet up on his desk, and settles down to read the newspaper for the rest of the period.

My English teacher is in class early, sitting stiffly in her chair with the day's assignment already in hand. The moment the tardy bell sounds, she sharply states "Class has begun," causing everyone to stop talking and focus their complete attention on her. Rising formally from her seat behind her immaculate desk, complete with a stapler, Scotch tape, a ruler, paper clips, erasers, pencils, and pens, she personally distributes the assignments. Once done, with an ominous glance at the class, she stiffly sits back down to grade papers with her unmerciful red pen.

In what ways does this writer use parallel sequence? List the parallels in the two paragraphs.

TELLING SENTENCE:
My Spanish teacher is different from my geometry teacher.

As my Spanish teacher handed out progress reports, I prayed that she would somehow miraculously skip over me this time. But to my disappointment, there she stood a few moments later, with that wide-toothed grin of hers that resembles that of the Cheshire cat. She seemed to thrive on the chance of ruining someone's weekend by sentencing them to bring home those belittling "snitch" notices. And I swear her eyes seemed to light up with an almost triumphant excitement as we all grumpily signed our reports at the bottom as instructed.

Funny though, because my geometry teacher had seemed genuinely sorry about the progress reports he gave out. Just handing them out seemed to put him into a somber mood, as if he had somehow failed in educating us. As each new report would surface, he would call us up individually and explain to us why we were getting a report and what we could do to raise our grade. He seemed to understand our point of view about our almost certain punishment to come from our panicky parents, worrying that they were raising terrible juvenile delinquent children who got progress reports. So he would always include a good comment about our strong points. He seemed to hate giving progress reports almost as much as we hated to get them.

In what ways does this writer use parallel sequence? List the parallels in the two paragraphs.

Writers in Training © 1984 Dale Seymour Publications

TELLING SENTENCE:

My dog B.J. is different from my dog Pal.

> My dog B.J., a year-old black labrador, upon command comes running through the house, tennis ball in mouth, and running over like a bulldozer on new asphalt. I lie there with her pink tongue licking me like a child does a lollipop. It's really disgusting. I look into the living room and see her dog bowl and food scattered all over the brown, plush carpet. She runs down the hall and comes galloping back with one of my new black pumps in her mouth, the heel all deformed and raggedy. She drops it and runs to play.
>
> Pal, a sedate seven-year-old Doberman pinscher/German shepherd mix, comes clicking across the ceramic tile to see me. He sniffs my hand and nudges his muzzle against me as a sign to pet him. He picks up the ball that B.J. dropped and carries it back to his dog bowl, the food neat and still in place.
>
> B.J. comes trampling inside from the garden and carrying a small bush that my mother had just planted. She drops it on the linoleum and looks at me with her mud-streaked tongue hanging out, and grabs ahold of Pal's tail, chewing. Pal looks at me with his big brown eyes and if he could talk I know he'd tell me, "This is so degrading."

In what ways does this writer use parallel sequence? List the parallels that are set up in the paper.

discussed in "Comparison/Contrast," page 61

SOOTY ALBATROSS

There are two species of Sooty Albatrosses (Brown and Antarctic), both of which are quite similar in appearance. They both have dark plumage, a long, wedge-shaped tail, and long wings that are very narrow. On the underside of its body, however, the Antarctic Sooty Albatross has paler plumage than the Brown Albatross, and it flies less gracefully. On their bills, both species have a groove called a *sulcus,* which divides the lower segment of the bill; but, the sulcus of the Brown Albatross is yellow or orange, whereas the narrower sulcus of the Antarctic species is blue. For nests, both species build up a low cone of earth, hollowed out on top.*

*Norman A. Britten, *A Writing Apprenticeship,* 4th ed. (New York: Holt, Rinehart and Winston, 1977), p. 149.

---

1. How is this paragraph different from the ones that use parallel sequence?

2. Why do you suppose the writer chose *not* to use parallel sequence?

3. What are the transitional words and phrases that signal similarity and contrast? Underline them.

WRITING ASSIGNMENT

Try imitating this paragraph, writing about two contrasting items of your own choice. You may use some of the same words as the paragraph above.

Example: There are two kinds of chocolate bars (Hershey's and Nestle's), both of which are similar in taste.

FROSTED MINI-WHEATS

There are two flavors of Frosted Mini-Wheats (brown-sugar and cinnamon), both of which are quite equal in nutritional supplements. They both are made from 100% whole wheat, have frosting on one side only, and cost the same amount of money. On the frosted side of the wheat biscuit, however, the sugar coated Mini-Wheat has a smoother and lighter texture than that of the cinnamon frosted wheat biscuit, and it has a sweeter taste. On the uncoated side of the Mini-Wheats, both biscuits have hundreds of criss-crossed wheat fibers; but the fibers on the cinnamon coated biscuit are darker, whereas the smaller fibered, brown sugar coated Mini-Wheat is lighter in color. For breakfast, both flavors of Frosted Mini-Wheats give one a good supply of daily nutritional needs.

TENNIS

There are two ways of playing tennis (singles and doubles), both of which are played using similar techniques. They are both played on a regular tennis court, scored the same way, and require the same amount of skill. When playing singles, however, one needs to cover more area of the court due to the fact there's only one player. In the serving procedures, both the singles and the doubles players must serve the ball into the same area; but the doubles players stand one at the net and one at the baseline while serving, whereas the singles player stands alone at the baseline. In order to be good, both types of tennis require a lot of practice and dedication.

Here are two student imitations of the "Sooty Albatross" paragraph. Does each imitation integrate the similarities and differences smoothly?

Could either of these have been written effectively using two paragraphs in parallel sequence?

discussed in "Comparison/Contrast," page 63

TELLING SENTENCE:
My French teacher is different from my U.S. history teacher.

> My French teacher and my U.S. history teacher are both working Foothill High School teachers. They are both polite, considerate, and helpful when they are not teachers; between classes or after school has ended, they ask about students' problems and encourage students to continue to get good grades. But when they are confronted by uncooperative students in class, they act differently. My U.S. history teacher becomes rude, loud, and mean as her jaws clench and her face turns ugly from loudly berating the class. My French teacher becomes quietly distressed, calm, and patiently waits for cooperation as her lips silently purse and her eyes stare at the ceiling. Teaching causes teachers to become Jekylls and Hydes.

1. What do the two teachers have in common?

2. How are they different?

3. What is the writer's conclusion about the two teachers?

4. Which is a better telling sentence: "My French teacher is different from my U.S. history teacher" or "Teaching causes teachers to become Jekylls and Hydes"? Why?

5. What is the value of a specific telling sentence?

Writers in Training © 1984 Dale Seymour Publications

LADY—CHICK

A lady and a chick, while both representing the female sex, have many contrasting attributes. In fact, it is not likely that one would find them together. A lady, for instance, might be found in a shaded parlor reading Shakespeare or on the verandah sipping a cool drink. A lady is respected and admired, from afar by men, and in loving friendship by women. Even her physical appearance bespeaks refinement. Her hair may be pulled neatly back from her face, revealing well-scrubbed skin and clear, bright eyes. She presents a soft, smooth voice at all times, no matter what may ruffle the serenity of the moment. At times, however, a refined laugh may escape from rosy lips showing pearly white teeth.

A chick represents a different group of the female sex. She has the normal attributes of a woman, but what she does with them is the deciding difference between her and a lady. The chick might be seen on a hot Saturday afternoon slinking down the street, poured into tight jeans that have seen better days. Slogans like "I'll try anything once" or "So many men, so little time" adorn the front of her shrink-to-fit T-shirt. She, too, may be admired by men, though in contrast with the lady, *not* from afar. The chick's appearance, like the lady's, is representative of her personal attitudes and values. She may look out on the world through frizzy, unkempt bangs her eyes ringed with last week's eye makeup. Whereas the highest compliment to a lady may be a whispered word from the most eligible bachelor in town, a chick receives her compliments from total strangers in roaring cars who wolf-whistle as they screech by.

After a long day of socially acceptable activities, visits, trips to the library, cooking lessons, the lady comes home. About the same time, the chick flops down on her waterbed after a long guitar-playing session in the park. Now they both like to think a bit. If one could hear their thoughts at this moment, one may understand one very important similarity. The lady's secret wish is to be blatantly whistled at and the chick thinks how nice it would be to just once be called a lady.

1. When does this writer make use of parallel sequence? List the characteristics that are parallel.

2. When does the writer make use of integrated comparison?

3. What is ironic about the writer's conclusion?

RUG—CARPET

As I drove up to the unfamiliar landscape of the early twentieth century house, I had a feeling that this was not going to be one of my best days. As I was told by my boss, the key to the house was in the mailbox. I walked up to the ominous door and turned the key. The door opened and two decades of stale air blasted up my nostrils. I fought my way into the house, past the wall of air, to see the one sight I had hoped not to see. I had been sent by my boss to put new carpet in the ancient house. The sight before me was the rug that had been put in the house when it was built. Before I put the new carpet in, I had to remove the old rug.

I set to my work, beginning to pull out the old rug. The rug was holey and was almost ready to fall apart from the amount of dust and grime built up over the years. I pulled up the rug at one of the corners, only to be cut by one of the rusty staples around the edges. I knew there had been a dog living in the house because the smell of old urine made me gag as it was released in the air with each tug. There was mold growing on the bottom of the rug from water that had been spilled a long time before. I finally succeeded in pulling out the ancient rug and gladly took it out of the house.

I dragged the new carpet from my truck into the house and cut it to the size I needed. The carpet had just been received from the manufacturer, so it had that certain freshness that comes with newly woven yarn. The smell of the carpet was like that of a load of newly washed clothes. The clean carpet was now ready to be put into the house. I stapled down the edges of the stiff material with ease. The handling and installation of this new stock was a breeze compared to the pulling up of the old smelly rug. I stood back to look at my masterpiece which had turned the old dump of a house into an honorable mansion.

The carpet was so new and clean it outclassed the old rug. It was like comparing a royal cloak to the ragged jacket of a beggar. In time, the new carpet will become an old rug, because one cannot stop time from taking its toll, not even on new carpet.

1. When does the writer make use of parallel sequence? List the characteristics that are parallel.

2. When does the writer use integrated comparison? What is his point?

3. What is ironic about the writer's conclusion?

                                        Writers in Training © 1984 Dale Seymour Publications

CURIOSITY—NOSINESS

The mirrored door of the medicine chest is ajar and the drawer beside the bathroom sink isn't securely closed. A hand towel is crumpled into a damp heap on the counter and the hot water is slowly dripping, wasted, down the sink. The party brought many people through the bathroom; some wanted to "freshen up," some to throw up, and most merely to relieve themselves. Alone in the bathroom, behind a locked door, there were two kinds of guests—the curious and the nosy.

The worried person searching for another roll of toilet paper and the pre-teen hunting for mouthwash or toothpaste were curious, out of necessity. The first person didn't look to see if the spare roll was Charmin or bargain brand. He didn't care. The twelve-year-old eating toothpaste out of the tube was only concerned with getting the smell of Budweiser off his breath. He didn't even notice whether or not the cap was off the tube. Curiosity left the little smudgy fingerprints on the mirror and checked the scale after eating all those Ruffles loaded with onion dip. And it was only a curious little guest who went in the shower to figure out how to work the faucet and to find out if one could see out of the glass shower door.

The nosybody peeked into the bathtub to see if the harried hostess had skipped over a bathtub ring. Like comparison shoppers, nosies sniffed the towels for the "Downey fresh smell" and fussed over the soap, trying to guess whether it was the remains of a bar of Safeguard or expensive perfumed guest soap. They read labels on prescriptions in the medicine chest and formed opinions on their host's heart condition and whether or not their hostess was on Valium. Nosiness "borrowed" lipstick and mascara and noticed if the towels didn't match.

Throughout the night, this bathroom door had opened to the symphony of rumbling water pipes and guests had emerged feeling a trifle better, make-up repaired, bladder emptied, or stomach as the case may be, or hands washed for dinner. Once they left that bathroom, the curious forgot the taste of the Crest and the nosy no longer cared if the towels were Downey fresh. Back in the midst of the party, people ate, drank and were merry once more. Only behind the closed bathroom door did curiosity and nosiness define themselves into terms so clear.

Simple and basic interests such as understanding an unfamiliar faucet mechanism or the need for finding more toilet paper motivate a curious person to peek around a strange bathroom. The driving force that makes a nosy person snoop is the satisfaction he gets from being included, in a perverse sort of way, in somebody

(continued)

else's business—somebody else's bathroom. Knowing the deepest, darkest secrets of his host's medicine chest makes the nosy person feel important—part of the family almost—when he finds they use the same brand of shampoo as he, or makes him feel superior when he finds they need to rely on tranquilizers to get through their lives.

Think about the structure of this comparison.

1. Are the actions of the different people—nosy and curious—set up in parallel form?

2. What *is* parallel about this piece of writing?

3. How can a common setting be used as a form of parallel sequencing?

4. Where does the writer use integrated comparison?

5. What is the point she makes through her integration?

Writers in Training © 1984 Dale Seymour Publications

THE MISSISSIPPI

Now when I had mastered the language of this water [as a pilot], and had come to know every trifling feature that bordered the great river as familiarly as I knew the letters of the alphabet, I had made a valuable acquisition. But I had lost something, too. I had lost something which could never be restored to me while I lived. All the grace, the beauty, the poetry had gone out of the majestic river! I still keep in mind a certain wonderful sunset which I witnessed when steamboating was new to me. A broad expanse of the river was turned to blood; in the middle distance the red hue brightened into gold, through which a solitary log came floating, black and conspicuous; in one place a long, slanting mark lay sparkling upon the water; in another the surface was broken by boiling, tumbling rings, that were as many-tinted as an opal; where the ruddy flush was faintest, was a smooth spot that was covered with graceful circles and radiating lines, ever so delicately traced; the shore on our left was densely wooded, and the somber shadow that fell from this forest was broken on one place by a long, ruffled trail that shone like silver; and high above the forest wall a clean-stemmed dead tree waved a single leafy bough that glowed like a flame in the unobstructed splendor that was flowing from the sun. There were graceful curves, reflected images, woody heights, soft distances; and over the whole scene, far and near, the dissolving lights drifted steadily, enriching it every passing moment with new marvels of coloring.

I stood like one bewitched. I drank it in, in a speechless rapture. The world was new to me, and I had never seen anything like this at home. But as I have said, a day came when I began to cease from noting the glories and the charms which the moon and the sun and the twilight wrought upon the river's face; another day came when I ceased altogether to note them. Then, if that sunset scene had been repeated, I should have looked upon it without rapture, and should have commented upon it, inwardly, after this fashion: This sun means that we are going to have wind tomorrow; that floating log means that the river is rising, small thanks to it; that slanting mark on the water refers to a bluff reef which is going to kill somebody's steamboat one of these nights, if it keeps on stretching out like that; those tumbling "boils" show a dissolving bar and a changing channel there; the lines and circles in the slick water over yonder are a warning that that troublesome place is shoaling up dangerously; that silver streak in the shadow of the forest is the "break" from a new snag, and he has located himself in the very best place he could have found to fish for steamboats; that tall dead tree, with a single living branch, is not going to last long, and then how is a body ever going to get through this blind place at night without the friendly old landmark?

No, the romance and beauty were all gone from the river. All the value any feature of it had for me now was the amount of usefulness it could furnish toward compassing the safe piloting of a steamboat. . . . *

*Samuel L. Clemens [Mark Twain], *Life on the Mississippi,* 1883.

1. Underline the parts that show parallel sequence.

2. When does the author use integrated comparison?

3. What is the point he makes through his integration?

WHAT A NIGHTMARE
(OR HOW TO LIVE WITH A *MINI* MUSCLE CAR)

And ever since that day . . . Oh, hi. I was just telling these people about my new car; you see it? Over there, behind that green station wagon. No, not the Cadillac, the other one. Yeah, that little Volkswagen that looks like an Army surplus mini tank. Why would I own a car like *that,* you say? Well, why don't you just pull up a chair with these nice people and I'll start my story from the beginning.

When I was little I had always dreamt about owning my own car. Maybe a sleek, bullet-like sports car or a large powerful *muscle car* with enough brute force to blow the gates off Fort Knox. But until last July I had never had the chance to own my very own dream machine. Nor had I made up my mind as to what kind of car I would most like to buy.

I have always daydreamed about the most perfect and extravagant car I could ever own. One would fall head over heels if he would ever purchase the car about which I had so fondly fantasized. I would begin with one of the two most sought after muscle cars in history, a Mustang Mach I or a '57 Chevy. Into one of these I would drop a 454 Chevy engine with titanium valves and pistons. I would then place upon this massively mountainous mound of majestic metal an aluminum Edelbrock intake manifold. As its counterpart in crime I would add a Holley four-barrel carburetor. As no great undertaking should end, I would slap on a pair of Hooker headers to top off my fantastic, featherlight, fireball of a power-pac. As a finishing touch I would place in this awesome auto an all-aluminum Hurst four speed "Lightning Rod" transmission. I dreamt about this car day and night, making mental images of it in my mind.

It finally arrived—the day I would be able to buy my own car and turn it into a mean street machine. It was a hot summer day in July. My father, who is a mechanic at Shamrock Ford, came home from work and said that they took a car in on a trade at the shop and that he could buy it for a low price. My eyes got as big as balloon tires. Without hesitation, I said, "Yes, I want it; how much?" I didn't even know what kind of car it was; I was too caught up in just buying it. The phrase that was to follow dropped in my heart like a lead weight. It was as if my life had ended and the world was as lifeless as a black velvet coat in a darkened closet. My father said, "Now hold on a minute; let me tell you about it first. For one, it's a '72 Volkswagen Super Beetle with a few dents, ripped seats, a bad radio, and it needs a new generator. I can buy it for $55 and we can use the generator out of our other Volkswagen to replace the burnt out one. Now what do you want to do?" After I thought about what I could do with it for a while, I gave him my answer. I told him I would buy it, fix it up, and possibly sell it for enough to buy the car of my dreams.

(continued)

When he brought it home the next week, I couldn't believe my eyes. It was hideous! It was a faded red color with crash marks in the back and the left front fender. It looks like someone threw rocks at it from a bridge while the car was going 60 mph, if it could go that fast. The interior was, if possible, in even worse shape. The back seat, of which half was missing, was torn beyond recognition. The front seats looked as if they had just exploded. Well, if one would take the Hefty bags off them, he could try his best to recognize them as such. After seeing this, my hopes and dreams were shattered forever.

I've had this "car" now for about three months, and when I look back on its former appearance, all I can do is laugh. If one could see a picture of it now as compared to then, he would have to wipe his eyes and look again. It now boasts a fine running, clean engine, new mags and tires, new upholstery, and as of this week, a desert camouflage paint job. I put in a stereo a few days ago but it is an old one. It still works great, but my speakers are shot and as soon as the stereo is replaced I might consider this my new dream car. I figure by the time I receive my license next month, this car will be exactly the way I want it to be. I guess you could call this a sort of riches to rags to riches type of story!

Hey guys, wake up! Damn, they fell asleep during the best part; I was just about to tell them about my dream *house.*

1. List or mark the sections of this paper where the descriptions are parallel.

2. Does the writer use integrated comparison? Where?

3. What is the point the writer is making?

PARENT-TEEN DIALOGUE

My controversial issue: _____

_____

_____

_____

_____

_____

_____

One-liner my parents always say: _____

_____

_____

THE ARGUMENT

Teenager (your partner): _____

_____

_____

Parent (you): _____

_____

_____

_____

Teenager: _____

_____

_____

Parent: _____

_____

_____

Teenager: _____

_____

_____

Parent: _____

_____

_____

_____

(Continue your argument on another sheet of paper until you feel you have covered everything.)

 Writers in Training © 1984 Dale Seymour Publications

PRACTICING CONCESSION

Review all the points of your argument with your parents. Then:
1. Summarize the concessions you are willing to make.
2. Counter with your own arguments.
3. Take a stand—propose a course of action.

Create a single paragraph covering all of the above. Use one of the following rhetorical patterns:

It is true that . . . however . . . therefore . . .

Certainly . . . but . . . in short . . .

Admittedly . . . on the other hand . . . so

Of course . . . nevertheless . . . as a result . . .

Obviously . . . on the contrary . . . finally . . .

Write your paragraph below.

_____

_____

_____

_____

_____

_____

_____

_____

_____

_____

_____

_____

_____

_____

_____

_____

_____

_____

_____

_____

_____

_____

ROCK MUSIC

It is true that some rock music contains lyrics that are both provocative and rebellious. In fact, one form of rock music, punk rock, concentrates purely on antisocial subjects as a basis for its songs. However, rock music itself is not enough to make a teenager rebel against society. Even though some lyrics contain hints of social rebellion and moral decline, the average teenager does not take this seriously and concentrates more on the musical value of the songs rather than the inner meaning of the lyrics. In conclusion, I feel that even though lyrically rock music shows hints of anarchy and social rebellion, it is *not* a threat to society.

1. What does the writer concede?

2. What does the writer argue?

3. What is the writer's point, or what is his stand?

MY ROOM

It is true that, when using my room, my brother does sometimes clean up after himself. There have been times when he has used it every day for a week and kept it clean by putting things back in order. On the other hand, there are times when he has left my room in a total mess. I have walked into my room to find records and books spread all over the bed and I have had to clean it up myself. I think that if he uses my room freely, he should have to clean it up and leave it just the way he found it. Therefore, although he is able to keep my room clean most of the time when he uses it, I think he should be able to keep it clean *every* time he uses it or should not be permitted to make himself "at home."

1. What does the writer concede?

2. What does the writer argue?

3. What is the writer's point, or his stand?

Writers in Training © 1984 Dale Seymour Publications

RED HERRING

This is the term used to describe an irrelevant issue that is introduced to distract the reader (or listener) away from the matter at hand. It's also known as ignoring the question, or dodging the question, or "What does that have to do with the price of beans?" It's very common in arguments between teens and parents.

It is very tempting to try bolstering our position by alluding to another issue that is more easily argued. We might do this by bringing up a "worse case" that makes our own position look good by comparison.

For example: When her parents complained that she never makes her bed, one girl argued, "Well look, Jane Bradley next door is in juvenile hall every week; I'm not doing anything so terrible; why are you on my case?" Jane Bradley's behavior is a red herring.

Here is another red herring: "*So* I've been forgetting to do my chores. I drove Jesse to his piano lesson, didn't I? And I started dinner the night you worked late. And I picked up Dad's clothes at the cleaners. I was even nice to Aunt Gloria when she came over, even though you *know* how much she bugs me. You don't appreciate anything I do!" True or not, it's still dodging the issue of the chores the girl hasn't been doing.

BEGGING THE QUESTION

This means reasoning in a circle. Instead of giving real evidence to support a particular point, the arguer makes a statement that assumes *as already proved* the very issue he or she is supposed to be proving.

For example: If someone claims that "All high school students should be required to learn how to operate a computer because we live in a computer age," the speaker is evading the issue—or begging the question—by assuming as true that the term "computer age" means that everyone needs to know how to operate a computer to be a part of, or to survive in, these times. Do you see how that goes in a circle? Instead, the arguer should give specific reasons *why* knowing how to operate a computer would perhaps make life in an advanced technological society easier or more comprehendable.

discussed in "The Argumentative Essay," page 87

FAULTY CAUSE AND EFFECT *(POST HOC ERGO PROPTER HOC)*

The commonly used Latin name for this fallacy means "after this, therefore because of this." This form of illogical thinking occurs when we suggest that just because one thing happened *before* something else, it caused that thing to happen.

For example: A father might blame his son's low grades on the teenager's recent car purchase. "Ever since you bought that car, your grades have dropped. Therefore, you may not use the car until your grades change." This father is using faulty cause and effect reasoning. There needs to be actual evidence to support his claim, even though the claim may *appear* logical. Is the son going for drives in the car during the time he used to spend doing his homework? If so, then *the car* is not the cause of the lower grades; *not doing homework* is the real cause.

ARGUMENTUM AD HOMINEM

Another Latin term, this means literally "argument to the man." A person who uses argumentum ad hominem distracts the reader from the issue by attacking the *people* involved in the issue instead of discussing the issue itself.

For example: A student, instead of arguing fairly for the need to have a longer lunch hour at school, directs her attention to the newly appointed principal and sputters, "We can't have a longer lunch on this campus because our principal is opposed to excessive socializing. Everyone knows he is the strictest disciplinarian in the city!" Instead of sticking to the matter under discussion—that the lunch period is too short—this student moves into an attack on the principal. That's *argumentum ad hominem.*

Writers in Training © 1984 Dale Seymour Publications

EITHER/OR—THE FALSE DILEMMA

This form of fallacious thinking occurs when we present *only two* options as the possible result of a controversial issue—assuming (wrongly) that there are *only* two sides to an issue.

For example: A student claims that "those who do not attend the Friday night football games have no school spirit." This student is suggesting that school spirit is defined in limited terms: *either* a person attends all school sports functions *or* that person is a traitor to the school's best interests. This student has created a false dilemma; are there other good reasons, besides no school spirit, that students might not go to the games? If the student is trying to convince more members of the student body to attend the weekly games, he needs to find other reasons.

GLORY OR GUILT BY ASSOCIATION

This is a transfer technique by which we attempt to associate our own issue with other strongly positive or negative concepts to make the reader (or listener) accept our ideas.

For example: A student suggests that "liking punk rock music is the same as condoning drug use." This student implies that all punk rock music enthusiasts indulge in drugs; he is associating a strongly negative concept (drug use) with a form of music he does not like. In effect, he is asking his audience to reject the avant-garde sound, not for its own qualities, but for its "guilt by association" with the drug scene—an association that is not necessarily valid.

When "*glory* by association" is used, the arguer tries to associate his or her issue with the positive feelings about something else that most people approve of or respect.

For example: A teenager tells his parents that "owning a motorcycle is as American as apple pie and Chevrolet." He's trying to get them to believe that motorcycles are an upright and wholesome American tradition. The "all-American" associations in fact have nothing to do with the issue of owning a motor bike, but the teenager is trying to equate owning a bike with patriotism—a positive association with his issue—or "glory by association."

SPOTTING FALLACIES

Here are some arguments from a girl who has a running battle with her father over the amount of time she spends on the telephone. What's wrong with these arguments? Can you name the fallacies?

1. He says he doesn't understand why I have to spend hours on the phone each night. Well, I spend hours because that's how long it takes me and my friends to say what we have to say.

2. He doesn't want me talking quietly on the phone, bothering no one, yet it's perfectly all right for my brother to play his stereo, blaring at top volume throughout the house, disturbing everyone and making it impossible to think.

3. People my age *need* the telephone. How can it be wrong to spend hours on the phone listening to a depressed friend talk out her troubles—like the people who work at telephone-based crisis centers, offering a sympathetic ear, listening, helping to save someone's sanity, or even her life.

4. Just because my father is a cold fish who doesn't have any friends to talk to, he thinks no one else needs friends, either.

5. Two weeks ago when this guy I like called, my father made me hang up after ten minutes. He hasn't ever called back and now he's taking out someone else. No one asks me out because my father's strict phone policy is driving them all away.

6. Instead of allowing me to be a happy, well-adjusted teenager who knows how to relate to people, how to share my innermost thoughts, he's going to turn me into an isolated psycho, withdrawn into a private and lonely world.

Writers in Training © 1984 Dale Seymour Publications

THE TRUTH ABOUT DIRT BIKES

It is a known fact that off-road motorcycle riding, because dirt bikes use high-performance two-stroke engines, pollutes the air. Also, dirt bikes can tear up the land and can be dangerous to ride. However, dirt bikes are less polluting than almost any other type of vehicle, are fairly easy on the environment, and are not as hazardous as one would think. Therefore, dirt bike riding should not be banned.

Unhealthy polluted air is a big problem in America, and measures should be taken by the government to regulate air quality. However, banning dirt bikes is the wrong way to go about cleaning the atmosphere. Motorcycles in general, according to the government, account for only a fraction of a percent of all the pollution in the air, and dirt bikes are just a very small fraction of all motorcycles. Clearly, the pollution emitted by dirt bikes is extremely limited. A better and more efficient method of controlling car exhaust, jet plane exhaust, or any other kind of gaseous waste generated by transportation or industry would do more to cleanse the air than taking all the motorcycles in the world and submerging them to the bottom of the Atlantic Ocean.

A major concern of environmentalists everywhere is the effects of savage ORV's (off-road vehicles) ripping up tender grasses, mangling bushes and young trees, and killing scores of small animals. To an extent, ORV's do damage the landscape, sometimes severely. However, dirt bikes are certainly not the only type of off-road vehicle; so are four-wheel drive trucks and jeeps. These metal monsters, weighing thousands of pounds, dig up and destroy anything that happens to get in the way of their massive, churning wheels. Comparatively, a dirt bike weighs just over one hundred pounds and has just one small tire delivering power to the ground. It would take a dozen screaming motorcycles all day to do the destruction of one four-wheel drive doing doughnuts for twenty minutes. Also, because dirt bike riders are less protected from menacing thorn bushes, ominous cactus, and jagged rock, dirt bikers tend to stay more on established trails, leaving nature unmolested.

To a mother, letting her son own a dirt bike is like letting him drive a car without brakes. "Why don't you do something safe, like go skiing or play football!" she might shriek at her misguided son. Actually, dirt bike riding is safer than either of these sports, and not surprisingly, one doesn't see mothers fainting when their sons buy a football or ski boots. In southern California, where dirt bikes are more popular, some high schools got together and started school-sponsored motorcross teams. Complete with a coach and league meets, motorcycle racing became a major school sport. After a few years, some interesting facts emerged from this experiment. Year to year there were more injuries from playing football than racing motorcycles.

(continued)

One reason dirt bike riding is relatively safe is because of the vast expansion and improvement in motorcycle safety equipment. New, sophisticated helmets are able to take poundings that would have reduced helmets of a few years ago to a small pile of carbon and fiberglass soot. Thick leather boots, plastic and leather padded pants, padded nylon jerseys, and space-age plastic goggles and mouth protectors are all part of most dirt bikers' wardrobes. Crashing now sure isn't as painful as it used to be.

Because of the lack of knowledge and bad image associated with motorcycles, public opinion toward dirt bikes is unfavorable. With environmental groups pushing the government to stop off-road vehicle recreation and to enforce regulations to eliminate air pollution, the government is considering a ban on dirt bikes. This unnecessary ban would be a great injustice to dirt bike riders everywhere. The needless ban would be a great crime, depriving many people of the pleasures, thrills, and experiences of off-road bike riding.

1. What concessions did this writer make in his argument? Underline them. Are they thorough?

2. What does the writer argue in response to each concession? List his arguments.

3. Are his arguments logical? Do you spot any fallacies?

4. Does the writer convince you that there are good reasons ("pleasures" and "thrills") for defending off-road bike riding? What did the writer neglect to do?

Writers in Training © 1984 Dale Seymour Publications

THE BATTLE OF THE ROOM

I'm sure many a teenager taking up space in the households of today has heard at one time or another those famous words, "Clean up your room." These words (usually coming from a distraught mother) are unfortunately common in my household, with battles occurring after each usage. This typical argument between me and my mother is not one of casual remarks and small disagreements. But, rather one where both parties end in complete rage with doors slamming behind them. The central conflict, obvious mainly to me, is my mother's infatuation with a clean, well-organized room, and my insistence upon a right to keep my room the way I want it, whether it be tidy or in this case "lived-in."

My mother has always been an exceptionally neat, organized person. While I, on the other hand, am sloppy, completely unorganized, and downright messy.

At times when I feel like Felix Unger is vacuuming around my feet, I can realize that it is Mom's house and people do visit. Therefore, dusting the rims of lamps, vacuuming underneath couches, and organizing the sock drawers of her and my brother, really doesn't faze me. But when she lays down her views and demands about my room is when I become most argumentative.

I have been warned time and time again that without organization like clothes hung up in order, drawers all categorized, and dresser clutter free, I just won't make it in life and many losses will occur. Yes, it is true there have been times when a matching shoe was nowhere to be found, or a favorite brush was somehow misplaced. But, more times than not I have found my friendly pair of jeans resting on a chair, rather than stashed away in some closet. Or maybe my nighttime mouthpiece [retainer] thrown freely on a nightstand, instead of sealed up in its container, up high on an organized shelf. These things seem much easier to find when they are out in the open, instead of packed and pushed out of sight.

During the course of our discussions on my four-walled adventure, Mom always brings up the fact that living in this so-called "garbage pit" shows what kind of irresponsible person I really am. If this is to be true, then does she also mean that I am too irresponsible to hold down a job, maintain a car, and be voting in our upcoming elections, in which I will be considered a legal adult?

As it looks right now, Mom and I will be fighting over this issue until I move out or at least go away to college. Because of that, I am even more determined to stand up for my rights for my section of the house. If only she could realize that through the messiness of my room, my true personality emerges and I am allowed to express myself fully.

1. What concessions does this writer make in her argument? Underline them. Are they thorough?

2. List her arguments that follow each concession.

3. Are her arguments logical? Can you spot any fallacies?

4. Does the writer convince you that she needs to be allowed to keep her room messy in order to express herself fully?

discussed in "The Argumentative Essay," page 99

MOMMY'S BABY

It's ten after six. I've just driven home from work, and I'm thinking about having a taco before I start my homework. I jump out of the car with a smile on my face and walk through the door—to find my brother standing there, dressed in the pair of plaid bermuda shorts I had bought myself last week, my pink Izod shirt—which has a big brown stain in the middle of it that I have never seen before—and my new topsiders that I paid sixty dollars for last week. My mother is standing just behind my brother in the kitchen. My face goes cold white; the little jerk is doing it again; he's destroying my things. "MOM!" I holler desperately. "Tell him to take those off before he wrecks them all."

She stands there with a blank face. "Bennett, take the clothes off," she says without much emphasis. All he does is shrug and walk into the living room to turn on the TV.

I scream again, "Mom, make him take them off, NOW!"

She replies, "John, don't make this into a big deal again. I don't want to hear about it now." Then she walks away.

"MOM, MAKE—"

"No more!" she interrupts. I walk back to my room, my feet dragging as I go. I feel as though I have been mugged, completely defeated.

My mother buys my brother and me ample amounts of clothing. When we see something we want, or tell her there is something we need, she usually gets it for us, just so long as we don't get carried away. In the past year or so I have compiled a nice amount of clothing. I carefully select each item before my mother purchases it for me. My brother, on the other hand, chooses "fad" clothing and other sorts of clothes which don't last long. I also spend much of my own hard earned money on my clothes. It is for these reasons that I object to my brother wearing my clothing, and wearing it continuously after I have asked him to stop.

At least every other day I find my brother is wearing part of my wardrobe, whether it be a shirt, shorts, socks, and so on. It bothers me. I ask him over and over to stop stealing the clothing out of my closet, but he reacts to these requests as though he were deaf. Since direct confrontation doesn't work, I call in the law. My mother is then requested to command Bennett to quit infiltrating my closet, take off what he is wearing of mine, and return it to its place of origin, my bedroom floor. This usually doesn't work; Bennett shrugs her commands off and continues on with what he is doing. But, this is as far as my mother takes it. When she sees Bennett purposely disobeying her, she doesn't get worked up about it; she tells me to get out of her hair, as though it's no big deal that my brother is destroying my personal property.

It is not as though I am a selfish person. Bennett doesn't have much money, mostly because he is too lazy and unmotivated to do anything for which he will be paid, so I usually pick up the tab for lunches, movies, and other things we do together that cost money. This doesn't bother me much, though, because he usually *asks* me if I will lend him the money. When it comes to my clothes, he usually *doesn't* ask if he can use something; he just takes them as though they were his.

(continued)

Writers in Training © 1984 Dale Seymour Publications

I realize that my parents can't run out and get everything my brother and I want, and I don't expect them to. Raising three children is expensive. My father's income is limited. My mother works hard earning money for the "extra" things we own and do. I know they can't afford to get us duplicates of every item of clothing; therefore, to have certain items, we must share. I feel a person should share his things freely and unselfishly. I would like to think of myself as one of those people.

On the other hand, I feel when a person buys an item with his own money, it should be solely his to keep, which means that person has the right to regulate that item's use, and the lending of that item. Bennett obviously doesn't feel the same way as I. He feels he has the right to wear my clothes and use my things as if they were his own. Items *I* worked for, spent hours trying to earn, my brother uses just as if they were his own. I don't think an item which is earned should be community property.

My parents, who provide us with many of the things we have, don't make Bennett stop taking the clothes that I pay for. It is true that the money I have made thus far has afforded me many nice and desirable things. Bennett should feel he has the right to use some of my things simply because he is my brother, but as the owner of the property, I feel he should first have to ask to use the item before he uses it.

Sharing a person's property is one of the things that makes life enjoyable. When only one person has something to share, though, it turns into charity work. My brother uses my stuff unregulated by my parents, although I plead with them to stop Bennett's stealing of my clothes. I am not asking that my parents stop my brother from borrowing my things; I just want them to make my brother *ask* me if he can use an item before he takes it; therefore, the final decision of the lending of my property is mine.

In resolving this problem I am willing to compromise, but I am not willing to back down on what I feel strongly for. I feel Bennett should be made, by my parents, to ask me first before borrowing an item. This will give me the respect that I feel is rightfully mine as the owner of the property. I don't feel it is an unreasonable request for me to want to know what clothing he has of mine and what he plans to do with it. If this were to happen, I would be more than happy to allow my brother the use of my things. It would put an end to many of my mother's headaches, caused by continuous fighting over the issue, and do away with unnecessary hardships felt by us all.

1. What is the effect of starting an argumentative essay with a story or typical scene rather than beginning immediately with the "It is true that—however—therefore" form?

2. Underline the writer's concessions. Are they thorough?

3. List his arguments countering each concession. Are they logical?

4. Has the writer convinced you that his parents ought to enforce his request?

5. Does the title of this essay strengthen or weaken his arguments? Why?

Items in my room at home.	What I think these items say about me to others.	What these items **do** say about me to others. #1	What these items **do** say about me to others. #2	What these items **do** say about me to others. #3

Chart from Sydney B. Simon, Leland W. Howe, and Howard Kirschenbaum, *Values Clarification: A Handbook of Practical Strategies for Teachers and Students* (New York: Hart, 1972), pp. 331–32.

PERSONAL SETTING

The large middle room, the parlor, was elaborate. The rosewood sofa, upholstered in green threadbare silk, was before the fireplace. Marble-topped tables, two Singer sewing machines, a big vase of pampas grass—everything was rich and grand. The most important piece of furniture in the parlor was a big, glass-doored cabinet in which was kept a number of treasures and curios. Miss Amelia had added two objects to this collection; one was an acorn from a water oak, the other a little velvet box holding two small, grayish stones. Sometimes when she had nothing to do, Miss Amelia would take out this velvet box and stand by the windows with the stones in the palm of her hand, looking down at them with a mixture of fascination, dubious respect and fear. They were the kidney stones of Miss Amelia herself, and had been taken from her by the doctor in Cheehaw some years ago.

Carson McCullers in *The Ballad of the Sad Cafe*
(Boston: Houghton Mifflin, 1936; Bantam, 1971)

A *telling* sentence for this paragraph could be "She was strange."
What details in the setting show the character's strangeness? Can a single item be enough to show strangeness?

. . . he bought a dental practice in the west end of San Bernadino County, and the family settled there, in a modest house on the kind of street where there are always tricycles and revolving credit and dreams about bigger houses, better streets. That was 1957. By the summer of 1964 they had achieved the bigger house on the better street and the familiar accouterments of a family on its way up: the $30,000 a year, the three children for the Christmas card, the picture window, the family room, the newspaper photographs that showed "Mrs. Gordon Miller, Ontario Heart Fund Chairman. . . ."

Joan Didion in *Slouching Towards Bethlehem*
(New York: Farrar, Straus, and Giroux, Inc., 1968)

Create a *telling* sentence that summarizes the personality of the characters in this family.

TELLING SENTENCE: _____

(continued)

In Miami Beach, 335 Ocean Drive is the address of the Somerset Hotel, a small, square building painted more or less white, with many lavendar touches, among them a lavendar sign that reads, "VACANCY—LOWEST RATES—BEACH FACILITIES—ALWAYS A SEABREEZE." It is one of a row of little stucco-and-cement hotels lining a white, melancholy street. In December, 1959, the Somerset's "beach facilities" consisted of two beach umbrellas stuck in a strip of sand at the rear of the hotel. One umbrella, pink, had written upon it, "We Serve Valentine Ice-Cream." At noon on Christmas Day, a quartet of women lay under and around it, a transistor radio serenading them. The second umbrella, blue and bearing the command "Tan with Coppertone," sheltered Dick and Perry, who for five days had been living at the Somerset, in a double room renting for eighteen dollars weekly.

Truman Capote in In Cold Blood
(New York: Random House, Inc., 1965)

Create a *telling* sentence that summarizes the personality of these two characters (Dick and Perry).

TELLING SENTENCE: _____

Writers in Training © 1984 Dale Seymour Publications

COSTUME

> He was a gray man, all gray, except for his polished black shoes and two scarlet diamonds in his gray satin tie that looked like the diamonds on roulette layouts. His shirt was gray and his double-breasted suit of soft, beautifully cut flannel. Seeing Carmen he took a gray hat off and his hair underneath it was gray and as fine as if it had been sifted through gauze. His thick gray eyebrows had that indefinably sporty look.
>
> Raymond Chandler in *The Big Sleep*
> *(New York: Alfred A. Knopf, Inc., 1939)*

Create a *telling* sentence that summarizes the personality of this character.

TELLING SENTENCE: _____

> He is dressed casually, in light blue slacks, loafers and a pink knit shirt bearing the small but celebrated crest of the Sunningdale Golf Club. A thin gold chain around his neck sets off his clear brown eyes and deeply tanned features. His hair is long on the sides and frankly graying. He is, of course, not wearing his working toupee. A dapper mustache droops down over the corners of his mouth, and his occasional smile is craggy and rather magnificent. Yesterday, August 25th, Sean Connery turned fifty-three. He looks great.
>
> Kurt Loder in "Great Scot:
> Nobody Pushes Sean Connery Around,"
> *Rolling Stone Magazine,* Oct. 27, 1983

Create a *telling* sentence that summarizes the personality of this character.

TELLING SENTENCE: _____

> The pavement blisters in the noon sun and beads of white heat quiver off the concrete walks. A scattering of people—mechanics in shirts with Bob's Conoco, Sampson Ford, or John Deere stitched on the pockets, clerks from hardware and feed stores, bankers and insurance men in short-sleeved shirts and narrow ties, farmers in bib overalls, women in summer dresses and pant suits—move, squinting and exchanging how are yous, toward the sign saying "Try Dr. Pepper—Bea's Restaurant." In the window are posters advertising the Table Grove Merchants' softball schedule and the Lewiston County Fair.
>
> Joe Schaeffer in "Rituals,"
> *Writings from Amidst the Uproar*
> (Bay Area Writing Project, 1977)

Create a *telling* sentence that summarizes the personality of these characters.

TELLING SENTENCE: _____

MANNERISM

> George Barrett is a tough cop. His eyes, cold as gun metal, can be looked at but not into. His jaw is hard and square as a brick, and his thin lips are kept moist by nervous darting passes of his tongue. When he laughs, only his face and voice laugh. Inside, George Barrett does not laugh.
>
> James Mills in "The Detective"
> (Time, Inc., 1972)

Create a telling sentence that summarizes the personality of this character.

TELLING SENTENCE: _____

> On summer nights June bugs fly in maddened, searching patterns in and out of street lights, and teenage boys, in cars and pickup trucks with wide mag wheels and flaming metallic paint jobs, circle Al's A&W, the engines panting and vibrating as the drivers accelerate and brake, accelerate and brake, the right hand loosely atop the steering wheel, the left shoulder lowered, the chin barely visible over the door, the eager eyes seeking, the car stereo blaring out the open windows. They circle once, twice, three times, then back into a dim stall to watch as others circle, accelerate, brake, and look. . . .
>
> They swerve recklessly off the warm asphalt pavement and into Tate's Texaco station, screeching to a halt near the side of the garage. Their drivers emerge smiling and walk in long, bowed strides toward a black, red-flamed Trans Am parked under the station lights. They kick gently at its tires and investigate its soft red interior. The owner inserts a tape and turns up the volume as the boys peer under the hood, touching its parts and commenting.
>
> Joe Schaeffer in "Rituals"
> *Writings from Amidst the Uproar*
> (Bay Area Writing Project, 1977)

Create a telling sentence that summarizes the personalities of these characters.

TELLING SENTENCE: _____

COMBINING SETTING,
COSTUME, AND MANNERISM

She stands there, without benefit of a filter lens, against a room melting under the heat of lemony sofas and lavendar walls and cream-and-peppermint striped movie-star chairs, lost in the middle of that gilt-edge birthday-cake hotel of cupids and cupolas called the Regency. There is no script. No Minnelli to adjust the CinemaScope lens. Ice-blue rain beats against the windows and peppers Park Avenue below as Ava Gardner stalks her pink malted-milk cage like an elegant cheetah. She wears a baby-blue cashmere turtleneck sweater pushed up to her Ava elbows and a little plaid mini-skirt and enormous black horn-rimmed glasses and she is gloriously, divinely barefoot.

Rex Reed in "Ava: Life in the Afternoon"
Esquire, May 1967

---

1. List the details that show character through setting.

2. List the details that show character through costume.

3. List the details that show character through mannerism.

4. Create a telling sentence that summarizes Ava's personality.

TELLING SENTENCE: _____

WRITING ASSIGNMENT
Spend 25 minutes observing an interesting scene—children at play, students at lunch, saleswomen in a department store. Describe what you see, using setting, costume, and mannerisms to reveal character. When you have finished, create a telling sentence that summarizes the personality of your character or characters.

WHO IS MATT?

"Are you nervous?" Miss Caplan asks as Matt seats himself at the table facing the class. Flashing a toothy grin, he shrugs an "I dunno" as he draws the chair up to the edge of the table. Eyes quickly glance up to him, then return to their papers. Pencils scribble furiously, noting his every move, attempting to capture him.

He sits, waiting for the first question, arms folded across his chest, legs extended underneath the table. Various questions are thrown at him from the participating classmates—"What's your idea of a fun evening? What kind of food, music, and books do you like?" His face remains molded into a knowing smirk as he contemplates his answers, carefully choosing his words. He responds to each inquisitor dutifully, supporting with examples, being sure to answer every aspect of the question.

Through this barrage of words, he remains slouched in his chair, occasionally scratching his right ear, and staring. He stares intently at the tiny black marks in the grain of the table before him, as if they were giving him some insight. He listens, laughs, and stares.

"What is your opinion of the nuclear arms issue, Matt?" With this question he straightens up, pulling his legs under him. He uncrosses his arms, one hand now stroking an imaginary beard. He looks up. "Well, I feel that total disarmament would be ineffective . . . in a way they (nuclear bombs) have been good to establish peace . . ." He continues on, his words more spontaneous, eyes darting about the room. He is now more at ease, both hands resting flat on the table, his ankles crossed underneath the chair.

For the first time during the interview he seems to be genuinely interested in answering. He also appears more self-condifent. It is during the more intellectual questions that more of his personality is reflected. During the other, superficial questions he tries to put up somewhat different characteristics. When asked about music, for instance, he at first responds with the outer image of liking rock, but as he continues talking more of his inner personality comes out with admitting he enjoys some classical music. Matt is basically a person with a lot of intelligence, but sometimes feels he must put out a somewhat superficial image in order to be accepted.

1. As this writer recreates the in-class interview, does she focus more on costume, on setting, or on mannerism and gesture?

2. Why do you think she chose this showing technique? How does this strategy help her get her point across?

3. What is the writer's point? Invent a telling sentence that summarizes Matt's character.

   TELLING SENTENCE: _____

Writers in Training © 1984 Dale Seymour Publications

CUSTODIAN

The small golf-cart type vehicle came to a stop. A school custodian, elderly, skin tanned from the long hours of working outside, stepped off the cart. Reaching into the back of the utility vehicle, the man pulled out a broom, the painted handles worn from use, the bristles withered from age. Pulling a large dustpan from the wagon also, he proceeded to a corner of one building. Meticulously sweeping crevices, the custodian cleaned up, not leaving a gum wrapper or a week-old apple core behind. With the dustpan becoming laden with refuse, he went back to the utility wagon and dumped the trash into a tough, plastic receptacle. He placed the things back in the cart and, switching on the high-torque electric motor, rolled another twenty-five feet, continuing the same routine, almost systematically.

THE SMOKING SECTION

A red line encloses thousands of squished cigarette butts and empty Marlboro packs upon an unpaved section of dirt. A brown wall bordering part of the smoking section reveals the words "Heavy Metal" and "Rock and Roll" sprayed in dark, black paint. Scattered trees have been added in an attempt to make the smoking section look more pleasant to other school members and staff. Sitting amongst all this are two girls, their bodies dressed in black leather jackets, tight faded blue jeans, and hiking boots. Pinned to the jacket collar of one of the girls are buttons with little sayings or names of rock groups on them. Both girls are holding cigarettes between their fingers and talking about the morning's events. Putting the cigarette between her lips, one of the girls takes in a deep drag, then twisting her lips to the side, she blows a cloud of smoke out over her shoulder. The girls continue talking, laughing, and puffing, until they soon realize their cigarettes are no more than an inch and a half long. Flicking their cigarette butts onto the dirt, both girls simultaneously get up and wander on their way, leaving only two round, smoking cigarette butts on the ground to add to the decor of many.

1. Underline the sections of each paragraph that you feel do the most effective showing.

2. What kinds of details did the writers focus on to recreate the scenes and define the characters?

P.E. CLASS

As the slow melodic music started, the girls jumped to their places, all except one. She languidly and listlessly pulled herself up, a white, sagging t-shirt hanging from her body, gray ankle sweats clinging to her legs, light-blue Nikes with dark blue stripes encompassing her feet. Her naturally brown hair was topped off with glaringly blonde hair, making her stand out among the rest of the bodies, who moved as one in the aerobics class.

She was always at least two moves behind, obviously bored by the dull, unlively music, laughing with her friend, frantically waving to people crouched behind the door. The music climbed up to an old, up-beat song and her face lit up with ecstatic craze as she put her own moves in, shining uniquely through the one mass of bodies stretching together. She played around, acting out John Travolta, pointed fingers moving in a criss-cross motion. She pulled at her friend, dragging her into a world all their own where they pointed and laughed at other people and played tag, oblivious to the pattern around them. She always had to be different, feet apart when theirs were together, swinging her right arm when they were swinging their left. The music died but she played on, still being different.

COWBOYS

Three Sunolian guys casually sat on the brown-painted wall in front of the Counselor's office, cutting class without a care in the world. They were of the cowboy type from head to toe—a cap with "Copenhagen" or a rodeo logo printed across the forehead resting on their heads, eyes staring through tousled bangs beneath the low brim; they dressed in warm, plaid flannel shirts, dusty down vests, and faded blue jeans, worn thin at the knees and frayed at the bottom, covering scuffed cowboy boots of weathered brown leather, caked with mud and manure. With their hands in their pockets and a wad of chewing tobacco between cheek and gum, they carried on an interesting conversation, or so it seemed, occasionally stopping to spit tobacco juice through their teeth. Their conversation finally came to an end and they casually ambled on their way as an eagle-eyed administrator approached them, referrals in hand.

1. Underline the sections of each paragraph that you feel do the most effective showing.

2. What kinds of details did the writers focus on to recreate the scenes and define the characters?

Writers in Training © 1984 Dale Seymour Publications

ANIMAL DOCTORS

[The cover page of this paper displayed six color photographs related to one of the three veterinarians the writer interviewed, a doctor at Wildlife Safari Land in Oregon. The paper began with a table of contents and ended with the requisite end notes and bibliography citing her outside reading.]

I think I could turn and live with animals, they're so placid and self-contained,
I stand and look at them long and long.
They do not sweat and whine about their condition,
They do not lie awake in the dark and weep for their sins,
They do not make me sick discussing their duty to God.
Not one is dissatisfied, not one is demented with the mania of owning things,
Not one kneels to another, nor to his kind that lived thousands of years ago,
Not one is respectable or unhappy over the whole earth.

Walt Whitman
Song of Myself

As long as I can remember, I have loved animals. One of my first childhood memories is chasing Simba, our tiger-striped manx cat, around the house. Throughout my young life I have owned a variety of pets including dogs, cats, rabbits, horses, hamsters, and even a duck. But it was not until high school that I became interested in pursuing a veterinary career. It was then that I realized I not only loved animals but I enjoyed science and medicine too! I had found a career into which I could fit in, now I have only to discover how to go about getting involved and which field I want to be a part of.

The veterinary field is a very large one and contains a variety of different types of careers. Different careers include Doctor of Veterinary Medicine (D.V.M.), Animal Health Technician, Medical Lab Assistant, Nutritionist, Animal Science Teacher, Feed Manufacturer, Animal Trainer, Pack Station Operator, Zoo Animal Keeper, and Blacksmith. In considering the amount of schooling necessary for these careers, it ranges from no schooling for an Animal Training career, Medical Lab Assistant career, or a Pack Station Operator career to two years of schooling (college) or other specialized training for a Zoo Animal Keeper career, Blacksmith career, or an Animal Technician career, to four or more years of college for an Animal Science Teaching career, Doctorate of Veterinary Medicine career, or Nutritionist career.

Both people and my sources of reading strongly suggest that you get involved in the career of your choice before wholeheartedly deciding to spend four college years working towards something you may discover later is just not right for you. In order to really enjoy a career you must understand and accept the pitfalls along with the joys and inspirations because the pitfalls do exist. It is often said among veterinarians that "Loving animals is not enough to get you through veterinary school or a veterinary career, you really have to love medicine and science too!"

(continued)

DR. LYNN FAUGHT, Doctor of Veterinary Medicine

The dark, brown building loomed ominously before me. The wooden brown sign reading "Village Parkway Veterinary Hospital" seemed to reflect the afternoon sunlight almost as if it were a mirror. Gathering my wits and taking a deep breath, I entered the hospital. The smell of antiseptic greeted my nostrils as I stepped in. Finding myself in a small, brown panelled waiting room with cream colored vinyl seats and colorful animal posters, I paused to get my bearings. The waiting room was vacant and I glanced at my watch to assure myself that it was a little after 12:30 p.m. I remembered the pleasant voice on the phone and our arrangements to meet for an interview during her lunch break. But where was she now?

Then I heard a doorknob click and, turning, I saw an older woman enter through a side entrance. She flashed me a welcoming smile and her eyes gleamed at me from behind silver-rimmed glasses. She wore a white smock over a blue cotton blouse and blue jeans and I smiled at the Nike tennis shoes she wore. "Sorry to keep you waiting," she said. "I had a couple of things that had to be done." I nodded and told her I hadn't been waiting that long. "Have a seat," she added and I dropped thankfully into the soft vinyl chair opposite her.

"Tell me about yourself," I asked. "How did you become interested in a veterinary career and where did you get your education?"

"When I was a little girl, I used to have fantasies about the animals I was going to have when I grew up. My father was dead, we lived with my grandparents in the East, and although I was crazy about animals, I wasn't allowed to have many pets. I remember once they did give me a puppy. I was ecstatic—but three days later it died of distemper. And once I had a little black cat that had been injured, and we weren't able to housetrain it. Very soon, it disappeared; I found out later my grandmother had disposed of it.

"So I used to dream that when I grew up I would have a great big house with many, many dogs and cats, and they would all have their own rooms and belongings and whatever special foods they wanted, and we would all be so happy. I planned also to have a huge barn and pasture where old, worn-out, unwanted horses would live out their days in bliss. (I guess I had read *Black Beauty* a hundred times!) In my fantasy, I could take in every homeless animal I met, and it would grow fat and sleek and happy. Maybe my ideas about veterinarians formed vaguely then, all I know is that my mother and grandparents tried to discourage me at first. After all, this was in the 1950s— women veterinarians were still looked upon as freaks. 'Didn't I want to be a nurse instead?' they asked me. 'Or a teacher?'

"But I was a stubborn child, and once my mother saw how determined I was, she supported me. When I was in high school, she arranged for me to visit a local veterinarian regularly and watch him work. He also encouraged me. I was accepted at Cornell University and a year later was accepted at a veterinary college."

"Did any problems arise because you were a woman in a so-called man's career?" I continued.

"I had heard that in some of the lab courses, the male students grumbled about having a female lab partner, and there I was, the only girl in my class. I was apprehensive at first. But the boys were nice—I always had a lab partner. In fact, throughout my veterinary college years, it was like having thirty-nine brothers."

"How did you come by this job?" I asked.

(continued)

 Writers in Training © 1984 Dale Seymour Publications

"Most veterinarians take an internship or apprenticeship right after graduation and get some supervised experience, but I didn't so I was very nervous about taking in surgical cases. I didn't want to take on someone's pet and mess up. So for quite a long time I referred any surgical cases to other vets, but then we moved. I found new work here at the Village Parkway Veterinary Hospital and it was then that I began gaining experience with surgical cases."

"Is there something you wish you could change?" I continued.

"Yes, in my experience as a vet, I see a great deal of neglect of animals, and usually there's nothing you can do about it. I wish there was something I could do. Millions of animals each year suffer and even die from neglect."

"Is your career satisfying?" I questioned.

"To me, a practicing veterinarian of thirty years experience, each case pulses with excitement, truth, sincerity and the humor that is somehow always bound up with the treatment of animals. I don't think I could be happy doing anything but what I'm doing."

DR. DONALD GARDNER, Doctor of Veterinary Medicine

The white house I pulled to a stop in front of on Sunol Blvd. could have been any other home on the road except for the white sign hanging out front reading "Town and Country Veterinary Hospital." I climbed out of my car and walked up the brick walkway, through the landscaped front yard to the tall, oak door. I grabbed the golden door knocker and let if fall three times in rapid succession. I heard footsteps and then a dark haired man of about thirty, wearing brown slacks and a plaid shirt, opened the door. His brown eyes looked questioningly at me for a second, then with a reassuring smile, he opened the door wider and bade me to accompany him to his office. Following him down a short hallway, I entered his office—an ivory carpeted room, with blue sofas and chairs, complete with a desk and a wall containing some six different degrees and certificates of schooling. Sitting across from me behind the desk he said, "Fire away!" in a calm level voice, and fire I did.

"Tell me about yourself and how you became interested in becoming a veterinarian?" I asked.

"I never wanted to be anything but a veterinarian. My father was a veterinarian, my uncle, my grandfather—it never occurred to me that there was anything else worth becoming. When I was a kid, the high point of my life was helping my father in his clinic on Saturdays and holidays, sometimes all summer."

"Have you encountered any rare or dangerous cases in your veterinary practice?" I continued.

"So far, in the two and a half years I've been practicing, I haven't seen many rare, medically unusually cases, but there sure have been a lot of challenging ones. Dogs mostly—in the country they are always getting run over by mowing machines or hit by cars, and they all are brought in broken and mangled, with their bones sticking out. It makes you feel really good if you can succeed in putting them back together and make them well again."

"What have you learned that you wish you might have learned sooner?" I questioned.

"One thing I've learned is to always answer my clients' questions fully, no matter

(continued)

how difficult, or dumb, or in some cases—funny. Some weeks ago, for example, a lady brought in a six-week-old puppy for a checkup. It was the first puppy she had ever owned. I examined him, and he was a real healthy little pup. But in the course of the conversation the lady said, 'You know, Doctor, he does seem to have a problem that worries me.'

"'Well, what's that?' I asked.

"'He doesn't seem to know how to urinate,' she said hesitantly. 'As a male dog, he should lift his hind leg, but he only wants to pee squatting down like a female dog. I've been trying to teach him the right way. When I take him for walks, I tie a rope around one of his hind legs, and then lead him up to a tree and lift his leg with the rope so he's in the right position for a male dog to be peeing in. But he doesn't seem to be catching on! Do you think he's sick?'

"I'm happy to say that I was able to contain my laughter and keep a straight face. I told her that all pups urinate that way, and that when he was full grown and more mature he would lift his leg."

"What are some things you would suggest to a beginning veterinarian?" I asked.

"First-year-itis is the trouble with most young vets at the end of their first year of private veterinary practice. They come out of veterinary school wanting to lick the world and cure every disease. But those who go right into private practice find themselves swamped with heavy case loads before they are really ready. Handling emergency cases all by yourself is especially scary. The pressure builds up and then the young vets begin to give under the strain. If help is not soon given, the young vets lose their practices and lose interest in their career."

"Is your job satisfying?" I questioned.

"The people we deal with as veterinarians are usually under some degree of emotional strain. They have an involvement with their animal, or they wouldn't be seeing us in the first place. They may be farmers with a herd of milk cows they know intimately, or hog farmers with only a financial involvement with their hogs, or pet owners who think of themselves practically as parents of their pets. You have to remember their feelings at all times, even when you are having a bad day, and they are exasperating you with their unreasonable demands. In the long run, though, I find that most people who come to us with their animals are nice. And the satisfaction I get when I'm able to help the animals—well, I think I have the best job in the world for an animal lover!"

DR. MELODY ROELLKE, Doctor of Veterinary Medicine

My final interview was under surprising circumstances. I was in Oregon for a state soccer tournament when we visited Wildlife Safari Land, a wilderness preserve in which people drive through actual habitats where lions, tigers, cheetahs, elephants, rhinos, antelopes, monkeys, and birds of all kinds run free and uninhibited by cages or fences! At the end of our tour, an idea struck me and I rushed over to the Wildlife Safari Clinic and asked to see the veterinarian. I was lucky enough to find her in her office and agreeable to have me interview her. Dr. Melody Roellke sat before me in a black desk chair with framed pictures of animals surrounding her on the walls of her office. She was a woman of about twenty-five, with long, brown hair, brown eyes, and a dark complexion. Her white teeth gleamed at me from behind her smile.

(continued)

"Tell me about yourself and how you became interested in being a veterinarian?" I asked.

"I was born and raised on a Willamette Valley farm in Lebanon, Oregon. I developed an early concern and love for animals and when I was fourteen I was lucky enough to get a job at the Portland Zoo. I was fascinated by the veterinarian and his dealings with exotic animals. It was then that I realized that I wanted to be a Zoo Veterinarian! I went to school and three years later I was hired to the post of Wildlife Safari Veterinarian over fifty other hopeful applicants!"

"What was your most satisfying moment?" I questioned.

"It had to have been treating Tanga, a 700-pound baby African elephant for a fractured tibia (lower bone in the leg). Tanga fractured his leg while jumping over a fallen tree and it took two tractors and a dump truck to get him back to the clinic and seventy pounds of plaster to cast his leg. But four months later, Tanga was back on the Wildlife Safari range, running and frolicking just as well as any of the other elephants."

"What rare or dangerous cases have you encountered?" I asked.

"I once treated a boa constrictor with a toothache. It was one of the strangest cases I have ever encountered! The constrictor, whose name was Bo-Bo, wouldn't eat and a ranger noticed it knocking its head up against a tree stump. I got out there as soon as I could and, failing to locate a throat obstruction or abscess, I looked at its teeth. Sure enough, there it was, a huge, rotten tooth! Five minutes later, with Bo-Bo under anesthesia, I extracted the tooth. When Bo-Bo woke up, he was right as rain! It was the oddest thing that ever happened to me!"

"Is your career satisfying?" I questioned.

"I wouldn't live any other way. The animals and the people here are the only family I know and I wouldn't give them up for anything!"

Some veterinarians take a roundabout route to arrive at their profession. Instead of studying a pre-veterinary course in college and then going straight into veterinary school, a few people start off in a different direction. Later realizing what they really want to do is go to veterinary school, they eventually wind up happy and busy in the type of veterinary practice that's right for them. I have already decided that a veterinary career is right for me. Before me lies a rough road, but I am willing to follow it to the end. I believe that if my love for animals will not carry me through, then my love for science and medicine will.

1. What did the writer set out to find in her I-Search?

2. What did she discover?

3. What techniques did she use that you most enjoyed or found most effective?

4. Where could the writer have made improvements?

WHAT MAKES ME SPECIAL   *(ROUGH DRAFT)*

The only thing that I can think of that makes me special is, that I am a pretty good shot with a gun. I know that I am because every time I shoot at something I hit it *Show* and every time I go hunting I always come back with something. You might not think this is anything special but it's the only thing I can think of right now. If I were in any competition I might win but then again I might lose. It all depends on how I feel that day.

What would you tell the writer you like about his paper?

Notice the telling sentence that is underlined to indicate to the writer that he should *show* more.

CHANGING TELLING TO SHOWING

Every time I go hunting I always come back with something. For example, one time me and my grandfather went hunting somewhere over by Mt. Diablo. There was a huge buck about 50 to 100 yards away. My grandfather was about to shoot it and all of a sudden I shot it and it went down. We ran over to it and there was a big hole in its head where it was hit.

This is how the writer shows the telling sentence. What would you tell him?

WHAT MAKES ME SPECIAL   *(FINAL DRAFT)*

The only thing that I can think of that makes me special is that I am a pretty good shot with a gun. I know that I am because every time I shoot at something I hit it and every time I go hunting I always come back with something. For example, one time me and my grandfather went hunting somewhere over by Mt. Diablo. There was a huge buck about 50 to 100 feet away. My grandfather was about to shoot it and all of a sudden I shot it and it went down. We ran over to it and there was a big hole in its head where I had shot it. Another time me and my dad went pheasant hunting up in the Sierras for the weekend and I brought my 22 and my dad brought his shot gun. Everyone thought that my dad would shoot more of them because he had a bigger gun than me but he didn't. I brought back 5 of them and he only got 3. If I were in any competition I might win because I'm an even better shot at still targets than I am with moving targets.

Find where the writer inserted the showing paragraph in his final draft. Did he add any other details?

A MEMORABLE EXPERIENCE   *(ROUGH DRAFT)*
Topic: Describe a memorable experience with a best friend.

Well I remember an old friend I had back when I was about 4 or 5 years old. We had just moved here from Walnut Creek into a housing tract called Valley Trails. I went out to play one day and that's when I met him. We used to play over at his house most of the time because he had a lot more neat stuff to play with than there was over at my house. He had a play house out in his back yard and we used to pretend it was a fort. As we moved along in age we used to love to go fishing with his dad or mine. We'd catch these little sun fish and think it was the catch of the day, the biggest fish ever. But one day my friend's father got a letter from his business saying they would have to move back East somewhere. So they moved and I don't think I'll ever see him again, but we still keep in touch by phone and send pictures every few years.

What did he have?

show more of fishing.

What would you tell this writer you like about his paper?

Notice that two telling sentences have been underlined to indicate where the writer might show more.

(continued)

CHANGING TELLING TO SHOWING #1

My friend always seemed to have a lot more better things to play with over at his house for some reason. Maybe they were rich or something but I didn't really care. I would just go over there and have the time of my life. One of the best toys he had was this great big playhouse, painted to look like a castle. I mean that never wore out. We could pretend somthing new every day. We could have played in that little house all day every day and never gotten bored. But there were other neat things too, like he had this huge racing set that seemed at the time to stretch through the whole living room, and we would play with that for hours, too. Well there were a lot more things we did, but those were my favorites.

CHANGING TELLING TO SHOWING #2

Well as we moved along in age we used to love to go fishing with either his dad or mine. We'd go to Shadow Cliffs or Del Vale and it was great. We'd leave at about 9 or 10 in the morning and get there at about 10:30 or 11 because when we were that young we didn't know that fish bite more in the early morning hours. So my dad told us the fish bite most around lunch time because I think he liked to sleep in in the morning. So we'd get there and set up and sit there for hours looking at the dead water, thinking every little movement in the water was a giant fish waiting to be hooked. I'm sure my dad was bored to death the way he would just kind of fall asleep all day and we may have never caught anything but we loved it.

Notice the details this writer adds as he writes a paragraph showing each *telling* sentence.

(continued)

Writers in Training © 1984 Dale Seymour Publications

A MEMORABLE EXPERIENCE   (FINAL DRAFT)

Well I remember an old friend I had back when I was about 4 or 5 years old. We had just moved here from Walnut Creek into a housing tract called Valley Trails. I went out to play one day and that's when I met him. We used to play over at his house most of the time because he seemed to have a lot more neat stuff to play with. Maybe they were rich or something but I didn't really care. I would just go over there and have the time of my life.

One of the best toys he had was this great big playhouse painted to look like a castle. I mean that never wore out. We could pretend something new every day. We could have played in that little house all day every day and never gotten bored. But there were other neat things to do too like this neat racing set that at the time seemed to stretch through the whole living room and we would play with that for hours. Well there were a lot more things to do but those were my favorites.

As we moved along in age we used to love to go fishing with our dads. We'd go to either Shadow Cliffs or Del Vale. It was great. We'd leave at about 9 or 10 in the morning and get there at about 10:30 or 11. Because when we were that young we didn't know that fish bite more in the early morning hours. So my dad told us that fish bite the most around lunch time because I think he liked to sleep in the morning. So we'd get there, set up our poles, and sit there looking at the dead, still water, thinking every little ripple in the water was a giant fish waiting to be hooked. I'm sure my dad was bored to death the way he would just sort of sit there and sleep, and though we may have never caught anything we had a great time.

But one day my friend's father got a letter from his business saying they would have to move back East somewhere. And when I got the news it was terrible. It seemed like the neighborhood got so quiet after he left. But we still keep in touch by phone and send pictures every few years.

Notice how the writer inserted his showing paragraphs into his rough draft to create a longer, more detailed final draft. Did he add any new details?

TAKING OFF WITH A BEST FRIEND   *(ROUGH DRAFT)*
Topic: If you could take off with a good friend, today, where would you go? What would you do?

    If I had a choice of going somewhere with one of my friends I would go to a motorcycle park called Hollister. My friend would be Keith because we both like to ride bikes.
    I would have a lot of money for beer and food. Also for gas and oil for my bike. We would be there for about a week. They let you camp out there during the 4 WD races.
    Sometimes they let you go night riding all over the park. The first day is when they tell you all about the rules and regulations.
    They have a lot of things you can do there. They have a poker run. The mudhole contest and racing on tracks.
    As you can see you can have a lot of fun out there doing the races and the other events they have there.

show what this is like.

Good! what's This like?

What would you tell the writer you like about his paper?

Notice that two telling sentences have been underlined to indicate where the writer might show more.

Writers in Training © 1984 Dale Seymour Publications

CHANGING TELLING TO SHOWING #1

They let you camp out there during the 4WD races.

When you camp out there they let you go anywhere. There are
places to go right next to the mud hole and one of the race tracks. You
can also camp on the hill right above the mini track that has a lot of
obstacles for the trucks to race on. But for the people that like to go
near the showers there is another campground at the other end of the
park. The quiet people like it there better too because you can't hear the
trucks so bad.

CHANGING TELLING TO SHOWING #2

They have a poker run, the mud hole contest, and just racing around on
the tracks.

They have a variety of contests to go in. One is the poker run. The
poker run is when they make up a race track that has different pit stops
for every truck entered. Say the poker hand is five card stud, you would
have 5 pit stops. Every time you stop at them you get a card. When it is
over you see if you got a good hand or not. It is just like poker. If you
had a bad hand you would fold and if you have a good hand you would
stay in the game. Also they have a mud hole contest. The mud hole
contest is when the people of the park dig a big pit and fill it with water
and dirt to make mud. They start out with the smaller trucks to see who
can get across it without getting stuck. But when you get stuck you are
buried up halfway to the doors. After the small trucks they have the big
4 wheelers to try and get across. The big wheelers have a hard time in it
because they have big tires and they just get themselves buried because
they hit the hole too fast. And the other contest is the race tracks. They
have different tracks for different trucks. The small trucks and jeeps have
real sharp corners on the tracks. Also they have small obstacles too. But
the big trucks have longer tracks. The big trucks have big mud holes
and rivers to go through.

Notice the details this writer adds as he changes his *telling* sentences
to *showing* paragraphs.

(continued)

TAKING OFF WITH A BEST FRIEND   *(FINAL DRAFT)*

If I had a choice of going somewhere with one of my friends I would go to a motorcycle park called Hollister. My friend would be Keith because we both like to ride bikes.

I would have a lot of money for beer and food, also for gas and oil for my bike. We would stay there for about a week. When you camp out there they let you stay anywhere. There are places to go right next to the mud hole and one of the race tracks. You can also camp on the hill right above the mini track that has a lot of obstacles for the trucks to race on. But for the people that like to go near the showers there is another campground at the other end of the park. The quiet people like it there better too because you can't hear the trucks so bad.

Sometimes they let you go night riding all over the park. The first day is when they tell you all about the rules and regulations.

They have a variety of contests to go in. One is the poker run. The poker run is when they make up a race track that has different pit stops for every truck entered. You get a card at every stop. When it is over you see if you got a good hand. It is just like playing poker. If you have a good hand you would stay in the game and try to win.

Also they have a mud hole contest. The mud contest is when the people of the park dig a big pit and fill it with water and dirt to make it muddy. They start out with the smaller trucks to see who can get across it without getting stuck. But when you get stuck you are buried in mud halfway to the doors. After the small trucks they have the big 4 wheelers to try and get across. The big wheelers have a hard time in it because they have big tires and they just get themselves buried because they sink too fast.

And the other contest is the racing on the tracks. They have different tracks for different trucks. The small trucks and jeeps have real sharp corners on the tracks. Also they have small obstacles too. But the real big trucks have longer tracks. The big trucks have big mud holes and rivers to go through.

As you can see you can have a lot of fun out there doing the races and other events they have there.

Notice how much the writer expanded his paper by inserting his *showing* paragraphs. In fact, his second *telling* sentence became three new paragraphs because he was describing three different things.

Writers in Training © 1984 Dale Seymour Publications

HIDE-AND-SEEK

A writer describes playing hide-and-seek with her brother, focusing on the suspense around the moment of being found. She writes:

> Leonardo was approaching her. He was getting closer and closer. She thought for sure she was going to be caught.

Why do you think her response partners suggested that she show the underlined sentence?

Here is her revision, in which she changes the telling sentence to showing:

> Leonardo was approaching her. She could hear him near the barn, his footsteps crunching the gravel. Next he was on the lawn, and the sounds of the wet grass scraping against his boots made a loud, squeaky noise. Next she could hear him breathing. She thought for sure she was going to be caught.

How do the additional details improve the writing? Which details work the best?

SHE LOOKED EXHAUSTED

This writer is trying to describe a very tired-looking person. She writes:

> Sitting on the sofa, she looked exhausted.

When her response partners suggested that she show the exhaustion, she revised it this way:

> Her eyes told of her pain—deep, set back, reaching inside of herself. Dark caves formed where her cheeks were. Her mouth was a hardened straight line, down at the corners.

How do the additional details improve the writing?

THE AUDITORIUM

Another writer is trying to create the mood at a concert, to use as an introduction to a short story. He writes:

> The auditorium was dimly lit.

His response partners suggested he show the effects of "dimly lit." This is the way he revised it:

> The newcomers into the room paused for a moment at the door as their eyes adjusted to the difference in light. Each object and figure had a long, faint shadow.

How do the additional details improve the writing?

Writers in Training © 1984 Dale Seymour Publications

LEAVING HOME

This writer, in her introduction to a personal essay, explains the impact of an important decision she made in her childhood. She describes having chosen between going to a public or private school when her parents lived abroad one year. Choosing the private school meant leaving home for the first time. Here is the original opening paragraph to her essay:

Show

I was aboard the London-bound train now. In just eleven hours I would be five hundred miles away from home. Staring at my flowered overnight bag, I frantically reflected upon the decision that I had made. Inside I gasped, "Oh, God, did I make the right decision? Pull yourself together," I thought, "and just think the whole thing over logically; then you'll realize that your decision was wise." Swallowing hard and trying to keep the tears away, I remembered that first day at Brechin High School.

Why do you think her response partners suggested she show the underlined sentence?

Here is her revision, in which she changes the *telling* sentence into *showing:*

I was aboard the London-bound train now. In just eleven hours I would be five hundred miles away from home. "Home." I caught myself repeating the word; how winsome and beautiful it suddenly sounded. Home, where stark white plasterboard walls were softened with woven baskets, dried flowers, and herbs that hung upside down from exposed rafters. I could smell the cardamom from my mother's kitchen, mingled with the pungent aroma of sweet pekoe tea that floated up from the shiny copper teapot. I could see a radiant and crackling fire, dancing to the music of Scott Joplin and the New Orleans Preservation Hall jazz band. I was so overcome by the remembrance of home that I jumped when the conductor opened the door to my compartment to check the ticket which was damp and crumpled in my hand. As he left, the compartment door slammed shut, and the crash of metal against metal echoed in my head. Shivering for a moment, I pulled my woolen sweater across my chest and buttoned it up.

How do the additional details improve the writing? Underline the details that you feel work the best.